D1067512
PT. GALLINAS
L. MARACAIBO
BARBADOS
(BR.)
Caracas
TRINDAD AND TO
Port-of-Spain
GULF OF DARIEN
ORINOCO
LLANOS
VENEZUELA
Georgetow
Pa
Cayenne
Roraima
9 219
GUIANA
(BR.) (NETH.) (FR.)
Bogota
GUAVIARE
COLOMBIA
GUIANA HIGHLANDS
BRANCO
MARAJÓ I.
JAPURÁ
NEGRO
AMAZONAS
Quito
V. Cotopaxi
19344
PUTUMAYO
SOLIMÕES (AMAZONAS)
XINGU
TOCANTINS
TAPAJÓS
JURUÁ
MADEIRA
ROOSEVELT
PURUS
ARAGUAIA
PERU
MARAÑON
UCAYALI
SÃO FRANCISCO
BRAZIL
BENI
MAMORÉ
UAPORÉ
PLATEAU OF
MATO GROSSO
BRAZILIAN
HIGHLANDS
Brasília
El Misti (Vol.)
19 144
Illampu
21490
La Paz
L. TITICACA
BOLIVIA
PARAGUAI
L. POOPÓ
ATACAMA DESERT
ATACAMA TRENCH
Sucre
GRAN CHACO
PARAGUAY
PILCOMAYO
BERMEJO
PARANÁ
Picó da Bandeira
9462
Rio de Janeiro
Llullaillaco
22 146
Asuncion
CATARATAS DEL IGUAÇU
SAN AMBROSIO
(CHILE)
SALADO
URUGUAY
Aconcagua
22 834
Santiago
JUAN FERNÁNDEZ
(CHILE)
CHILE
ARGENTINA
ANDES MTS.
URUGUAY
ATLANTIC
OCEAN
PAMPAS
Buenos Aires
Montevideo
RIO DE LA PLATA
COLORADO
NEGRO
GULF OF SAN MATIAS
Earth's terrain represented
with natural summer vegetation
CHILOÉ
CHUBUT
CHONOS
GULF OF ST. GEORGE
Mt. San Valentin
13 314
WELLINGTON I.
HANOVER I.
STRAIT OF MAGELLAN
FALKLAND IS.
(BR.)
Port Stanley
DESOLACIÓN I.
TIERRA DEL FUEGO
Mt. Sarmiento
7 546
CAPE HORN
GEO-PHYSICAL SOUTH AMERICA

STRATEGY FOR MOBILITY

STRATEGY FOR MOBILITY

By WILFRED OWEN

The Brookings Institution
TRANSPORT RESEARCH PROGRAM
Washington D. C.

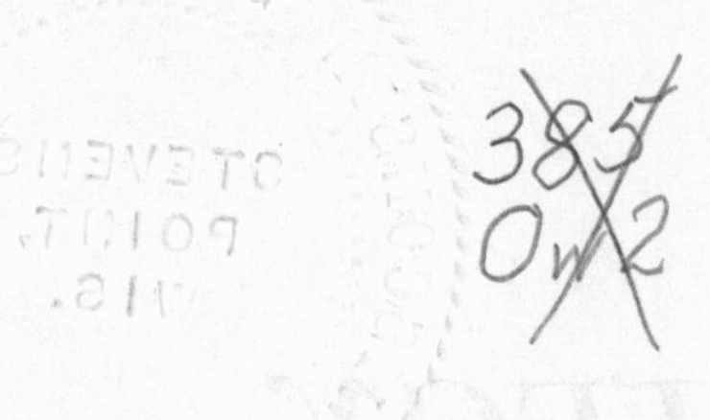

Published July 1964

Library of Congress Catalogue Card Number 64-20997

THE BROOKINGS INSTITUTION is an independent organization devoted to nonpartisan research, education, and publication in economics, government, foreign policy, and the social sciences generally. Its principal purposes are to aid in the development of sound public policies and to promote public understanding of issues of national importance.

The Institution was founded December 8, 1927, to merge the activities of the Institute for Government Research, founded in 1916, the Institute of Economics, founded in 1922, and the Robert Brookings Graduate School of Economics and Government, founded in 1924.

The general administration of the Institution is the responsibility of a self-perpetuating Board of Trustees. The Trustees are likewise charged with maintaining the independence of the staff and fostering the most favorable conditions for creative research and education. The immediate direction of the policies, program, and staff of the Institution is vested in the President, assisted by the division directors and an advisory council, chosen from the professional staff of the Institution.

In publishing a study, the Institution presents it as a competent treatment of a subject worthy of public consideration. The interpretations and conclusions in such publications are those of the author or authors and do not purport to represent the views of the other staff members, officers, or trustees of the Brookings Institution.

Foreword

THIS IS THE FIRST in a series of Brookings Institution studies undertaken as part of a major program of research on the role of transport in development. It is being carried out through a grant from the United States Agency for International Development.

The Brookings program focuses on an area that has been neglected by both the development economist and the transport specialist. It is an attempt to look at transport in relation to the total environment. Since accessibility and mobility are involved in almost everything that developing countries are striving to accomplish, transport can be a key factor in the success or failure of the entire development effort.

The work is thus designed to help guide the allocation of resources in emerging economies and in foreign assistance programs, to shed light on the possibilities that science and technology offer for the solution of transport problems, to develop criteria for judging the economic potential of transport investments, and to determine effective means of implementing transport programs.

The present study is an overall view of the problem initiated with funds from the Ford Foundation and completed as part of the AID research program. In the course of his study, Wilfred Owen, who is the Director of the Transport Research Program, has participated in transport and development studies in many countries of Asia, Africa, and Latin America. His views of the problem and approaches to its solution reflect the general framework of the

Brookings program and furnish a guide to areas in which research efforts need to be focused.

Among previously published works, Wilfred Owen is author or co-author of *Cities in the Motor Age* (1959), *The Metropolitan Transportation Problem* (1956), *National Transportation Policy* (1949), and other books.

The reading committee for the study has included Edward S. Mason, Harvard University; Robert Sadove, the International Bank for Reconstruction and Development; Lloyd Reynolds, Yale University; Edwin T. Haefele, The Brookings Institution; and Merton J. Peck, Yale University. The book was a project of the Economic Studies Division, formerly directed by Ralph J. Watkins and now under the direction of Joseph A. Pechman. A. Evelyn Breck with the assistance of Medora Richardson edited the study, and Adele Garrett prepared the index.

The opinions expressed in this study are those of the author and do not purport to represent the views of the Agency for International Development, or the views of the trustees, officers, or other staff members of the Brookings Institution, or of those who reviewed the manuscript.

Robert D. Calkins
President

April 1964
The Brookings Institution
1775 Massachusetts Avenue, N.W.
Washington 36, D. C.

Author's Acknowledgments

THE IDEAS EXPRESSED in this manuscript were developed with the help of numerous officials and friends in twenty-five countries. Their participation has made the manuscript truly a joint venture, and a clear demonstration that technical assistance is a two-way process.

In addition to members of the Reading Committee mentioned in the Foreword, appreciation for criticisms of the manuscript is also expressed to Robert E. Asher, Robert T. Brown, Robert D. Calkins, D. A. FitzGerald, Herbert C. Morton, and Joseph A. Pechman of the Brookings staff. It was the expert help of Edwin T. Haefele in getting the Transport Research Program into high gear, however, that made the luxury of book-writing possible. Special acknowledgment is also made to Inai Bradfield, who as research assistant provided much of the supporting data as well as editorial assistance and criticism, and to Joan Canzanelli, who handled the secretarial burdens.

Excerpts from the study were first published by the United Nations in the *Economic Bulletin for Asia and the Far East,* December 1960. Other materials have appeared in issues of the *American Economic Review,* in *Europe's Needs and Resources,* published by the Twentieth Century Fund, and in pamphlets published by the Government of Pakistan. Conclusions on technological aspects were presented in the United States Government publication, *Science, Technology, and Development: Transportation.*

Wilfred Owen

April 23, 1964

Contents

Introduction

THE PROCESS OF DEVELOPMENT has many components and no one of them is sufficient in itself to bring about the improvement in living conditions that people and nations everywhere are striving to achieve. Better health and education, the discovery and use of resources, greater industrialization, better organization and administration, and a willingness to accept new ideas are some of the factors that together foster development and offer the promise of a more satisfying life.

Granted this variety of elements and their obvious interrelations, the attempt in this study is to seek a better understanding of the problems and potentials of development by focusing on one area of activity—the way people and goods are moved. Not that transport alone is the key to progress. But transport has special significance because of the pervasive role of mobility in facilitating other objectives. Transport is a necessary ingredient of nearly every aspect of economic and social development. It plays a key role in getting land into production, in marketing agricultural commodities, and in making forest and mineral wealth accessible. It is a significant factor in the development of industry, in the expansion of trade, in the conduct of health and education programs, and in the exchange of ideas.

The need to assess more carefully the contribution of transport to economic growth is suggested by the size of the financial commitment. Among expenditures for national development, transport generally ranks first or second in magnitude. It is typically absorbing 20 to 40 percent of the resources being invested in economic and social progress. This emphasis is reflected in economic assistance programs. Transport has accounted for a third of all loans made by the International Bank for Reconstruction and Development and for one-fifth of American aid for development projects.

The principal questions to be considered in this study are how transport influences development, how the obstacles imposed by poor transport can be reduced, and how improved transport can further economic, social, and cultural ends. Specifically, how can a country estimate how much transport it needs and how much it can afford in the light of other requirements? What factors should be taken into account in weighing the desirability of different methods of transport? What are the financial, organizational, and administrative requirements for building and operating the facilities needed? What role can be played by foreign assistance programs, and how can such assistance be made more effective? In short, what must be done to achieve as quickly as possible the minimum standards of transport needed for rising levels of living?

The nature and complexity of transport problems differ widely from place to place, and useful solutions are not easily generalized. The most that can be hoped for in this broad view of the problem is to achieve a better understanding of the relationship between transport and the rest of the economy. Such an understanding would assist nations in various stages of development to judge how transport can contribute to their development, what factors need to be taken into account in programing transport improvement, and what means will be most effective in achieving mobility and accessibility. The focus is on the problems of the low-income countries, but the discussion will frequently draw on the experience of the more developed countries. In addition, it should be remembered that all countries have their underdeveloped areas, and that much of what is prescribed for poor nations is also relevant to those that seem to be rich.

There are optimistic signs that the twentieth century revolution in transport is spreading into Asia, Africa, and Latin America. Some dramatic results have already followed from transport development programs in these areas. Yet it is obvious that the transport revolution has failed to affect the lives of most of the world's people, and that the task of overcoming the barriers to mobility is formidable.

If the developing countries are to narrow the gap between themselves and the more mobile countries, the cost in time and resources will be heavy indeed. Both the developing countries and those participating in assistance programs will have to be guided by a total strategy if the potential impact of mobility on development is to be fully realized. All nations, in all stages of development, have a stake in the outcome. For a successful attack on immobility and isolation is essential to engaging the world's resources effectively.

CHAPTER I

Immobility and Poverty

THE TWENTIETH CENTURY revolution in transport has made us aware of the relation of immobility to poverty. Air transport has shrunk the earth to less than a tenth its previous size, and the jets have reduced this smaller world again by half. The results may be seen in the almost perpetual motion of heads of state, in the endless calendar of international conferences, in the ubiquitous technical assistance missions, in the growing ties among business and professional people of all nations, and in the global dimensions of tourism. Most of these peregrinations would have been unthinkable in the relatively immobile world of three decades ago.

This international exchange has resulted, among other things, in making it possible for millions of travelers to see for themselves the discrepancies in material well-being between the rich countries and the poor. Visitors from developing countries have returned home determined to see their people participate to a greater degree in the fruits of economic progress, and travelers from more opulent societies have become aware of the poverty of distant lands that have suddenly become their neighbors. In most respects the transport revolution has by-passed two-thirds of the world's people.

What one finds is that time and energy are being dissipated in vast areas of the underdeveloped world in an effort to get things moved. The observer who arrives in a poor country for the first time gets the impression that nearly everyone is working in transport. The human being serves as a beast of burden along with the donkey, the camel, and the bullock. It is only on the principal arteries and in the major cities that mechanical transport has replaced the most primitive methods. But even in these cases, mechanical solutions often yield unsatisfactory results because of ancient and obsolete equipment, faulty operation, and lack of maintenance.

The Effects of Poor Transport

Poor transport is a major factor in world hunger. The high cost of moving farm products and the long delays and consequent damage and loss to perishables have been powerful deterrents to increasing food supplies. Produce rots on the ground because transport is not available. Oranges and other valuable foods are used for fertilizer because transport capacity is unavailable. Commercial fertilizers may arrive after the growing season is half over.

As a result of these conditions, much of the world's resources lie untouched because there is no way to reach them. A major proportion of the earth that is suitable for cultivation remains idle. Much of the acreage that has been put under cultivation is overworked and the soil depleted. A tremendous wealth of forest and mineral resources that could help in the struggle against poverty makes no contribution because no one can get to it or move it to where it is needed.

The agricultural sector does not suffer simply from the inaccessibility of land, or from the failure to move what is produced. Farmers have no incentive to grow surpluses when they know from experience that what they grow cannot be moved. Isolated communities remain ignorant of market opportunities or of new ideas and new techniques, for information, like everything else, travels slowly on mud roads and primitive trails. Communication with the outside world may come to a complete halt during the wet season, and even in dry weather, when roads are dusty but passable, the time and cost of travel preclude regular contacts.

Industrial activity is also severely hampered by lack of transport. The factory depends on continuing supplies of fuel, raw materials, and spare parts, and on a reliable means of marketing what is made. Poor transport makes it necessary to maintain excessive inventories at high cost to compensate for uncertain deliveries. Often it is necessary to shut down operations or to produce at a fraction of plant capacity because of fuel or material shortages. Inadequate investment in transport reduces the effectiveness of investments elsewhere.

The ability to sell in world markets is often limited by the difficulties of overland transport. Moving fifty miles to port may be costlier than moving thousands of miles by sea. And nearer home, there may be no land transport connections with neighboring countries, hence no way to benefit from specialization and trade. The problem is not always the complete absence of transport, but its unreliability, high cost, slow schedules, and high rates of damage and pilferage. These obstacles to movement restrict the market, increase the cost of production, and raise prices beyond the reach of consumers.

Goods often wait for months to be shipped by rail, but a considerable volume of traffic is not even offered because of the known shortage of capacity. As for the goods that are actually offered, often only those with highest priority can be expected to move promptly. In some instances space must be reserved months ahead of a proposed shipment.

In Afghanistan, half of all trade still moves on the backs of men, camels, and donkeys. Poor transport has increased the price of goods to as much as five times their original cost. The movement of freight from coastal areas to interior points of Brazil may take six months by river, and a month to a month and a half by truck. Paraguay's trade involves journeys of a thousand miles by river to the Atlantic Ocean. Ninety percent of farm to market transportation is confined to oxcarts on primitive trails.

Transport difficulties have their political and social as well as their economic impacts. Poor transport makes it exceedingly difficult to achieve national unity. The growth process is retarded by limited opportunity for public officials to travel through their country, and by the difficulties of conducting business. Poor transport can be a major obstacle to maintaining internal security. It also limits the effectiveness of technical assistance programs.

The Spreading Revolution

An indication of what transport modernization can do for development can be observed in nearly all the large cities of the world and along many of the major intercity routes. In Asia the ricksha and pedicycle are giving way to the truck, the bus, the motor scooter, and the taxi. The bullock cart is disappearing from Delhi and the camel from Karachi. On the Chao Phya in Thailand, ancient sampans are being pulled by diesel tows, and along the klongs of Bangkok fresh vegetables are propelled to market by outboard motor. Beef in Bolivia moves to consuming centers by air, pipelines distribute Sui gas over hundreds of miles of West Pakistan, and in Lagos a 1401 computer keeps track of railway freight cars. During the first election in Nigeria at least one tribal chief was campaigning by helicopter.

These changes have been remarkably sudden. In much of the world only a few years ago, it was considered good transportation when a man carried sixty pounds fifteen miles a day on his back. Now one man driving a diesel truck transports sixteen tons two hundred miles in a day. Transport by animal was until recently the most economical method of overland movement. The cost ranged from 40 to 50 cents per ton per mile. Mechanization can reduce these costs to 5 cents or less.

In a world where one out of every three people is inadequately fed, the ability of modern transport to make available more food is perhaps its most significant contribution. In Costa Rica, before the Inter-American Highway was constructed, driving beef cattle on the hoof from grazing lands to San José often resulted in a 40 percent loss of weight, and imports were necessary to supply local needs. Now, with an all-weather highway, it is possible to deliver truck-trailer units of cattle overnight, and Costa Rica is self-supporting in meat.[1]

In Thailand, the Friendship Highway, completed only five years ago, has transformed partially used jungle land along its hundred-mile route into highly productive and prosperous farms. Travel is now possible in all weather between Saraburi and Korat, and travel time has been reduced from eleven hours on the old dirt road to three hours on the new. Within three years the production of sugar cane, vegetables, bananas, and other fruits more than tripled in tonnage. A substantial surplus of corn is exported to Japan. Expansion of swine and poultry production has far exceeded livestock trends in nearby areas not served by the new highway.[2]

In Bolivia, the highway from Cochabamba to Santa Cruz reduced travel time in the rainy season from several weeks to fifteen hours and provided a link between the country's food supplies and its people. Until then the price of home-grown rice was 50 percent higher than imported rice because of the high cost of transport. The highway has now largely eliminated costly imports. And in the Philippines, the cost of moving a bale of abaca 35 miles to port by native bearers, river barge, and finally by truck was reduced from three dollars to fifty cents by a road link that made truck movement possible for the entire distance.

Transport has also played a major role in supplying raw materials to industry and in moving finished products to market. In India,

[1] U. S. Department of Commerce, "Motor Transport in Middle America," World Trade Information Service, 4, No. 55-13.

[2] Wisit Kasiraksa, "Economic Effects of the Friendship Highway," SEATO Graduate School of Engineering, Bangkok, 1963.

about 87 percent of the additional demand for rail transport to be met during the Third Five Year Plan represents requirements for iron and steel, mineral ores, coal, and cement. To keep pace with its industrial growth, India has invested a fifth of its development funds in railways, and has doubled its port and shipping capacity as well as the number of its trucks. Expenditures for transport during the current plan period are second only to the industrialization program itself.

The greater mobility provided by transport investments has also played an important part in extending the benefits of education, in communicating new ideas, and in overcoming the isolation that has been a principal factor retarding economic progress. The cost of education is being reduced by good roads that make possible consolidated schools, and all-weather transport is causing a marked improvement in school attendance. Greater mobility also facilitates the travel of technical personnel and enables them to cover more territory in less time.

Even modest improvements in transport change the life and attitudes of the people affected. Primitive roads built in Bolivia to connect densely populated regions with hitherto inaccessible land have altered the outlook of whole communities. The work, done almost entirely by manual labor, has had the effect of persuading thousands of families to move from impoverished soil to untouched land along the new roads. Ethnic groups that previously lived apart have been encouraged to join in cooperative efforts to build a better future.

Transport is also helping to combat sickness and disease. In India, mobile hospital units move over the road to villages that have no local doctor. In Liberia, health services have been established over a wide area by flying materials, equipment, and personnel to remote airstrips for the establishment of field dispensaries. Along the Nile River, an Egyptian hospital ship brings medical care to patients along its route who would otherwise have no access to modern methods of treatment. Egyptian physicians maintain that improving transport has been a principal means of

TABLE 1.1. *World Population and Rail and Road Transport Trends by Continent, 1950–60*

(Freight in billions of ton-kms., others in millions)

Continent	Population			Rail Freight			Motor Vehicles[a]		
	Total 1960	Total Increase 1950–60	*Percentage Increase 1950–60*	Total 1960	Total Increase 1950–60	*Percentage Increase 1950–60*	Total 1960	Total Increase 1951–60	*Percentage Increase 1951–60*
Africa	254	45	*22*	57	22	*62*	2.6	1.3	*100*
North America	199	31	*19*	930	−14	*−2*	79.2	24.5	*45*
Latin America[b]	206	43	*26*	48	10	*26*	4.4	2.1	*91*
Asia	1,679	290	*21*	379	264	*230*	4.0	2.8	*233*
Eastern Europe[c]	641	65	*11*	1,535	916	*148*	—	—	—
Western Europe				220	48	*28*	28.1	17.5	*165*
Oceania	16	3	*27*	15	3	*25*	3.4	1.5	*79*
World	2,995	477	*19*	3,184	1,249	*65*	121.7	49.7	*69*

Sources: 1951 Motor vehicle data from United Nations, *Statistical Yearbook, 1957;* others from United Nations, *Statistical Yearbook, 1961*, and *Statistical Yearbook, 1962*.

[a] 1951 was chosen as a base year since complete motor vehicle data for 1950 are not available.

[b] Includes Mexico and Central America.

[c] Comprised of Bulgaria, Czechoslovakia, East Germany, Hungary, Poland, Romania, and USSR including traffic in Asian USSR.

improving health.

These achievements, when looked at in the aggregate, provide impressive statistical evidence of progress. In recent years, the growth of transport capacity in the poor countries has been much more rapid than in the rest of the world. In the decade of the fifties, for example, rail freight traffic increased 230 percent in Asia, compared to 28 percent in Western Europe, as shown in Table 1.1. During the same period the number of motor vehicles in Asia, Africa, and Latin America more than doubled. The increase was over six million units.

The Mobile and the Immobile

Despite substantial accomplishment, there is a tremendous gap between the transport capabilities of rich countries and poor. For development to take place, it will be necessary to narrow this gap, and to do so will be a formidable task. Asia, Africa, and Latin America contain 71 percent of all the world's people, but account for only 15 percent of the world's rail freight and 17 percent of the world's trucks and buses. Africa accounts for 22 percent of the land area of the globe, but only 4 percent of its surfaced roads. Only 2 percent of the world's merchant shipping is owned by Latin America. (See Table 1.2.)

The situation in India illustrates the enormity of the transport gap. Despite extensive efforts to improve Indian transport, 60

TABLE 1.2. *World Population, Area, and Transport, 1960*[a]
(Percentage distribution)

Continent	Population	Area	Ton-Miles of Rail Freight	Number of Trucks and Buses[b]	Miles of Surfaced Roads[b]	Gross Tons Merchant Shipping
Africa	8.5	22.5	1.8	3.1	4.2	9.1
North America	6.6	15.9	29.7	54.7	48.0	24.2
Latin America[c]	6.9	15.2	1.0	4.9	2.8	2.2
Asia	56.1	19.9	11.9	9.3	15.9	8.3
Europe—total	21.4	20.2	55.1	24.0	24.9	55.5
Eastern Europe[d]	(10.4)	(17.3)	(48.2)	—	—	—
Western Europe	(11.0)	(2.9)	(6.9)	—	—	—
Oceania	0.6	6.3	0.5	4.0	4.2	4.0
	100.0	100.0	100.0	100.0	100.0	100.0

Sources: United Nations, *Statistical Yearbook, 1961;* highway data from the International Road Federation, "World Highway Statistics—1960," *Staff Report* (1960).
[a] Figures do not always add to 100 because of rounding.
[b] Excludes Albania, Bulgaria, Mainland China, Czechoslovakia, East Germany, Hungary, North Korea, North Vietnam, Romania, and USSR.
[c] Includes Mexico and Central America.
[d] Comprised of Bulgaria, Czechoslovakia, East Germany, Hungary, Poland, Romania, and USSR including Asian USSR.

percent of existing roads are unimproved dirt surfaces that are impassable during the rainy season. Even on the principal arteries of the national highway system, five-sixths of the mileage is one-lane. India's modest objective is that by 1980 no village in a developed area will be more than four miles from some kind of paved road. The achievement of this goal will still spell partial isolation for tens of millions.

Other transport difficulties demand attention. Coastwise shipping that might relieve the railways is dormant, and Indian ships can carry very little of India's overseas trade. The railways continue to operate under heavy strains, and there is severe congestion in the principal industrial regions. Even at present levels of economic activity, the long haul from northwestern coal fields to the large coal-consuming urban centers has resulted in severe congestion.

The cost of providing adequate transport in large cities has also become a heavy economic burden on developing countries, and even heroic efforts to cope with the problem have not permitted an escape from the consequences of congestion. Many people must walk long distances to work, railways are overwhelmed by commuters, motor vehicle traffic is being strangled by inadequate street systems, and the entire urban environment suffers from planless growth and lack of amenities.

Roadbuilding efforts illustrate how the gap may be widening. Of the $19 billion spend for highways in all countries during 1960, approximately $16 billion was being spent in the developed countries of Europe and North America. Road expenditures in the European Economic Community were $4,500 per square mile, compared to only $33 per square mile in Africa and $102 in Latin America.[3] As shown in Table 1.3, Europe and North America already accounted for more than 4 million of the world's 5.7 million miles of surfaced highways in 1960.

If Latin America, Africa, and Asia (excluding the Soviet Union) were to have half as many miles of surfaced roads per square mile as the European Economic Community, twenty million miles of good roads would have to be built. This compares with about one million miles of roads now available, most of which are inadequate. To equip the less developed continents with trucks and buses in sufficient numbers to achieve the EEC ratio of these vehicles to

[3] See Table A.1. for world highway expenditures.

TABLE 1.3. *World Commercial Vehicles and Highways, 1960*

(Vehicles in millions, miles of road in thousands)

Continent	Trucks and Buses			Miles of Road[a]	
	Total	Per 1000 People	Per 100 Sq. Mile	Total	Per 1000 Sq. Miles
Africa	0.7	2.8	5.9	241	20
North America	13.3	67.2	177.3	2,737	367
Latin America[b]	1.7	8.3	21.3	160	20
Asia	2.3	2.4	40.4	905	159
Europe	5.8	15.0	305.2	1,420	742
(EEC Countries)	(3.2)	(18.5)	(711.1)	(709)	(1,573)
Oceania	1.0	76.9	32.3	240	77
World Total	24.8	12.4	65.4	5,703	150

Sources: Commercial Vehicle data from United Nations, *Statistical Yearbook, 1962*. Highway data from International Road Federation, "World Highway Statistics—1960," *Staff Report* (1960).
[a] Paved roads include miles of road with gravel or crushed stone or stabilized soil surface.
[b] Includes Mexico and Central America.

population would require 26 million motorized units compared to the 4.7 million operating in 1960. In that year there were only 2.4 trucks and buses for every thousand Asians, while in the European Economic Community there were 18.5. (See Tables 1.3 and A.2.) The question to be answered is what increase in transport services will be needed for development goals to be achieved. Will the developing countries have to attain the transport levels of the rich countries? Or will new methods introduced by science and technology hold the cost within bearable limits?

An Index of Mobility

The nations of the world may be classified into two groups—the mobile and the immobile. The present degrees of mobility and immobility in specific countries are indicated in Table 1.4. The freight mobility index for France is expressed as 100. Countries with a mobility index above 30 have been arbitrarily placed in the

TABLE 1.4. *Index of Per Capita GNP and the Mobility of Nations, 1961*[a]
(France=100)

Country	GNP	Freight Mobility	Passenger Mobility
IMMOBILE NATIONS			
Ethiopia	3.2	1.7	1.7
Nigeria	6.0	4.0	3.5
Indonesia	6.1	4.5	5.5
Iran	15.5	4.7	4.3
Burma	4.3	5.3	5.5
Philippines	8.6	5.8	5.2
Pakistan	5.5	6.7	8.3
Syria	11.2	6.8	5.7
Thailand	7.1	7.2	8.0
Egypt	8.8	7.5	9.3
Sudan	6.9	8.8	—
India	5.9	10.0	11.5
Ghana	14.6	10.1	9.5
Ecuador	13.4	10.2	8.7
Colombia	20.8	11.3	9.2
Guatemala	12.9	12.5	—
Peru	13.3	12.7	10.8
Turkey	14.2	13.7	—
Paraguay	9.6	15.7	14.7
Malaya	20.6	15.8	17.0
Algeria	20.6	17.3	16.0
Greece	31.7	17.8	18.7
Ceylon	10.1	18.2	21.5
Taiwan	10.7	18.8	—
Brazil	13.7	19.7	19.8
Bolivia	8.3	20.0	18.2
Portugal	20.8	24.5	27.7
Israel	59.8	25.2	21.7
Mexico	23.0	27.8	22.8
MOBILE NATIONS			
Japan	37.2	30.5	46.3
Spain	27.5	33.2	34.8
Chile	33.3	38.2	36.2
Lebanon	30.2	39.2	40.3
Yugoslavia	24.2	39.5	38.8
Italy	51.8	45.3	53.2
Netherlands	77.3	58.2	69.3
Argentina	27.8	63.8	68.0
Norway	98.1	64.0	61.8
Finland	81.4	65.2	61.7
Austria	64.5	66.8	71.8
South Africa, Republic of	31.3	70.5	—
United Kingdom	104.0	86.0	94.5
Sweden	130.8	93.0	104.5
Ireland	50.9	93.8	—
West Germany	105.4	99.3	91.0
France	100.0	100.0	100.0
Belgium	101.1	103.2	116.7
New Zealand	114.3	106.5	—
Denmark	102.6	110.0	119.0
Luxembourg	109.5	136.5	—
United States	207.3	189.0	147.2
Australia	112.3	216.7	—
Canada	147.9	223.1	148.9

Sources: United Nations, *Statistical Yearbook, 1958*, and *Statistical Yearbook, 1959;* highway data from the International Road Federation, "World Highway Statistics," *Staff Report* (1957 and 1958); per capita GNP computed from *Amendment to the Constitution of the International Labor Organization*, S. Rep. No. 179, 88 Cong. 1 sess. (1962), tables, pp. 24–25.

[a] Freight Index=Average index for rail lines per 100 sq. miles, rail lines per 10,000 population, surfaced highways per 100 sq. miles, ton-miles per capita; and commercial vehicles per capita. Transport data based on 1957–58 figures. Passenger Index=Average index of the following: passenger miles per capita, passenger cars per capita, and rail lines per 100 sq. miles, rail lines per 10,000 population, surfaced highways per 100 sq. miles, and surfaced highways per 10,000 population.

category of mobile nations. All these countries have relatively high per capita incomes. Spain, Japan, and Chile are on the margin, with mobility indexes of 30 to 38, while Canada, Australia, and the United States have the world's highest indexes, from 189 to 223. At the other end of the scale, with a freight mobility index of 10 or less, are Iran, Thailand, Sudan, India, Nigeria, Ethiopia, Burma, Indonesia, and Pakistan. Most of these countries have per capita incomes below $100.

Passenger mobility index numbers are roughly comparable. Nations with a rating under 10 include such countries as Nigeria, Indonesia, Burma, Pakistan, Syria, Ghana, and Ecuador. Countries with passenger mobility exceeding 30 include Japan, Spain, Chile, and Yugoslavia at the bottom of the scale and such countries as Belgium, Denmark, Canada, and the United States at the top. These indexes provide a rough indication of the gaps between the rich and the poor, the tasks that lie ahead, and the areas in which the greatest volume of work remains.[4]

The Growing Transport Burden

When current transport deficiencies are viewed in the light of anticipated population growth and projected economic development, however, the task of narrowing the gaps becomes even greater. Population trends indicate that by far the largest gains will take place in areas that are least prepared to accommodate expanding numbers of people. For example, in 1950 there were about 1.6 billion people in the less developed countries. By 1975, the total will be more than a billion higher, and between 1975 and 2000 this larger number will probably double. It is expected that 5.5 billion people will be living in Asia, Africa, and Latin America, 4.1 billion of them in Asia alone. In this period a heavy concen-

[4] Note that the index fails to reflect mobility by air or water, which are especially important in such countries as Colombia, the Philippines, Ethiopia, Indonesia, and Pakistan.

tration of population growth will occur in four already crowded countries. Totals for China, India, Pakistan, and Indonesia will increase 40 to 50 percent.[5] These increased burdens on the less developed countries will continue for many decades regardless of the effectiveness of measures to control population.

In addition to increased population, economic development programs will lead to a rise in living standards and therefore to more materials produced and consumed per capita. The size of the transport task will as a result be even greater. For example, if the assumption is made that the volume of energy resources consumed by Asia, Africa, and Latin America four decades hence will achieve anything like the West European levels of the 1960's, this would require a fifteen-fold increase for the developing areas. The amount of food consumed by the year 2000 would have to be greatly increased to approach present European standards. These food goals would require among other things that extensive areas of land be tapped that are now inaccessible and unused, that much greater amounts of commercial fertilizers be produced and applied, and that marketing capabilities be greatly improved over the current situation. There is also expected to be a six-fold increase in the global demand for iron ore and ferroalloys, and a quadrupling of lumber output. Such demands would magnify transport problems that are already intractable.[6]

Obstacles to Improving Transport

A variety of natural and man-made obstacles will have to be overcome to narrow the transport gap between the immobile and the mobile nations to meet growing requirements. The most ob-

[5] Irene B. Taeuber, "Population Growth in Underdeveloped Areas," *The Population Dilemma*, edited by Philip Hauser (The American Assembly, Columbia University, 1963), p. 37.

[6] Projections from Joseph L. Fisher and Neal Potter, "Resources in the United States and the World," *The Population Dilemma*, p. 114.

vious natural obstacle is the combination of unfavorable topography and bad weather. Poor countries generally have to cope with a formidable combination of mountains, excessive heat, vast deserts, untamed rivers, and either too much rain or too little. Some areas cannot supply enough to feed, clothe, or shelter more than a sparse and poor population, and here the difficulty of transport is to supply adequate service over great areas for scattered settlements. In other areas a hot climate and heavy rains, or heat and irrigation, make it possible to grow the food to sustain life in large numbers, but the task of providing all-weather transport to assure accessibility and trade for the attainment of more than mere subsistence is extremely burdensome.

Countries that are broken up by mountain ranges have to cope with difficult engineering, high-cost construction, and circuitous routes. The immense barriers thrown up by the Andes, for example, have played a prominent role in the heavy commitment to transport in Colombia. A large proportion of the nation's resources had to be devoted to the task of penetrating the three tiers of mountains that for so long kept the capital weeks away from the coast. In other countries, such as Brazil, it is enormous land masses that defy efforts to provide adequate transport.

To these natural obstacles man has added his own creations. In many parts of the world, the transport system was deliberately designed by colonial powers to meet military requirements and to foster exports. Railways were built with different gauges and without connections. The resulting patterns of transport ignored internal growth requirements, promoted overconcentrated growth and congestion in port cities, and left a vast inaccessible hinterland in its original state of immobility.

Failure to maintain or renew transport facilities is another traditional problem in low-income countries. Mechanized transport services are typically old, of limited capacity, and rundown. Rail systems operate with ancient locomotives, rail cars are over-age, and track is in poor condition. One country reports sixty varieties of locomotives that pose unmanageable maintenance problems.

Roads are often built in isolated short pieces rather than in an interconnected system, and maintenance is apt to be completely neglected after the facilities have been built. Motor vehicle performance is frequently poor due to the condition of the roads, the lack of parts and servicing, and regulations that make economical use impossible.

Water transport provides important avenues of commerce in some countries, but often the potential is limited because of silting, the absence of navigation aids, and seasonal interruptions due to lack of water or to storms. Ocean shipping, too, is often obstructed as much by unnecessary paper work and dilatory customs procedures as by the lack of berths and cargo handling equipment, or the absence of adequate land transport connections.

In addition to these conditions, many countries lack organization and personnel, both in government and in the private sector, to build and operate transport facilities. In many areas, there is no one responsible for accomplishing what needs to be done. And everywhere there is the problem of obtaining the capital and foreign exchange to get things built, and to keep them going.

The Transport Function

It would be plausible to conclude from the transport successes enumerated earlier that the task of accelerating development is essentially one of overcoming the obstacles to good transport. But the evidence is conflicting. For every case in which transport has produced notable social and economic impacts, there seems to be another in which the effect of transport on levels of living has been limited. Sometimes high standards of mobility have been achieved at the expense of higher standards of living. For transport affords unparalleled opportunity to make mistakes, including errors of location, technology, design, timing, or the mistake of investing in transport at all.

A good case can be made, however, that appropriate transport facilities are the key to development. For without transport, supply and demand are restricted by the high cost of moving, and by ignorance of whether goods can be sold and for how much. Improvement in living conditions is dependent on the ability of people to communicate and on their capacity to trade. But the case is seldom made. Most studies emphasize some other factor as the primary element in economic development, including improved agriculture, industrialization, the supply of capital, standards of education, and the availability of managerial talent. The silence of development literature on the role of transport can be explained in part by the failure to recognize that whether agriculture, industry, power, capital, or human resources are stressed, the development of each is partly dependent for its success on mobility and accessibility.

Transport, then, is a necessary but not a sufficient condition for economic development. Whoever first coined the axiom summed up the reality that can hardly escape the traveler in developing areas. What one sees very clearly is that no country where there is a critical lack of transport facilities is moving ahead very fast, but that some countries that have fairly impressive transport facilities also seem to be going nowhere.

It is apparent from figures of traffic carried and levels of national income, however, that the volume of transport operations is closely related to economic progress. Where a nation's economy is undeveloped, there will be a low volume of movement; and conversely, where transport is minimal, the economic system is retarded. But cannot the same be said for the relation between per capita consumption of food, electric power, or cement? These, too, are essential ingredients of economic growth. Thus the question to be answered is not whether transport is important, or more important than something else, but rather in what circumstances and on what basis the supply of this ingredient of economic progress is critical.

In some cases, transport provides the increment of investment needed to get results. In other cases, additional things have to be done as well. If one part of a country has large food surpluses, but another part has most of the people and industry, the need for transport to connect the two is clear, and providing transport produces the desired results. Often, however, an area may be only potentially capable of producing food, and production is dependent not only on transport but on the availability of such additional facilities as power, irrigation, fertilizer, education, or health services. Transport will not produce the desired result by itself, although it may still be a prerequisite to realizing these other necessary conditions.

A variety of causes can make transport ineffective. Lack of anything to transport is one. A road across the North Pole will not generate much traffic. This may also be true of a road across North Borneo, but for different reasons. A road may fail to stimulate development because its design is inadequate to guarantee all-weather travel. As a consequence, subsistence farmers are reluctant to shift to cash crops that they might not be able to market. Another road, built along a ridge rather than in the valley, may result in no new economic activities because the strip of adjacent hillside land is narrow and unfertile, and the task of manhandling crops from the valley to the road is too great a burden. Still another road may not promote development because there is no desire or use for money, or because tribal custom places greater importance on raising buffalo and taking it easy.

If there is to be a set of clearer guides to the transport aspects of development policy, the start will have to be an understanding that transport is quite different from most other economic activity. Its importance is derived from other goals it is designed to serve. Transport is not a separate sector of the economy, but a web of communications that joins other sectors together. The nearest analogy is power, but it is not a good one because the needs for power derive from a much more limited set of activities. Transport is unique because it contributes to the success or failure of nearly everything else. The need is to be able to identify the conditions under which this catalytic process will pay off, and other situations in which investments in mobility will lead to disappointments.

In the light of the many demands on scarce resources, then, how is it possible to assure that investment in transport is necessary and that providing it will be more effective for development than alternative resource use? Are emerging nations putting too little or too much of their effort into transport in current development programs? To what extent should transport investments follow from decisions in other sectors, and to what extent should transport be built ahead of other projects as a means of promoting development? How can priorities be established to assure that what is undertaken will contribute most to economic growth?

These are some of the issues that will be considered as the transport function is viewed in the perspective of development as a whole. The basic question is how to reach the two-thirds of the world that remains relatively untouched by the transport revolution, in order to help achieve economic revolution.

CHAPTER II

Breaking the Transport Barrier

It is sometimes difficult to realize that transport in the more developed parts of the world was once no better and frequently much worse than it is in most low-income countries today. Yet it was little more than a century ago that the railways introduced cheap overland transport, and only in the past thirty to forty years that mud roads gave way to all-weather pavements for motorized transport. How did the developed countries set about the task of breaking the transport barrier to achieve the mobility they now enjoy? How can countries in early stages of development benefit from this experience? What unique factors are at work that make much of the past inapplicable?

Transport in the United States

The early stages of transport in the United States sound familiar to those beginning the arduous task of overcoming shortages of transport. Inland commerce was at first limited almost entirely to bulky farm products that could be moved on natural waterways. Overland trade consisted of a few high-value imports that could absorb the high costs of transport by animal over difficult roads and trails. In the early nineteenth century, it took two yoke of oxen three days to make a round trip of thirty-five miles. The cost of transportation was so high that even if corn had cost nothing to produce, it could not have been marketed twenty miles from where it was grown. It was cheaper to move a ton of iron across the Atlantic than to carry it ten miles through Pennsylvania.[1]

Many early American towns were so completely isolated that they operated on a virtually self-supporting basis. The typical New England farmer wore clothes made from the wool of his own sheep, woven and dyed in the home. Many farmers made shoes and other articles in their spare time, to be sold or bartered for other goods they needed—the counterpart of cottage industries in the less developed countries today. Rural roads were generally no more than a clearing to permit the passage of horses. Neither the use of stone nor proper drainage had yet been introduced, and winter rain and snow made it impossible to travel at all during four months of the year.

In the late eighteenth century, a limited number of communication lines were established through the postal service. The beginning of mail delivery provided monthly service from New York 400 miles south to Virginia, with an elapsed time of four weeks when the weather was good and eight when it was bad. Horses provided the transport. The postage rate was sixty cents a page, and due to the uncertainty of the journey the payment was made on delivery. Often the mail would not depart until it was clear that the trip would pay its way, and cancellations often resulted from what today would be called a benefit-cost ratio of less than one.

State and local governments undertook programs of highway improvement without benefit of plans or engineering services. Further attack on the problem was made by financing highways with tolls. The heavier loads and higher speeds made possible by hard-surfaced highways reduced transport costs and provided a demon-

[1] Percy W. Bidwell and John I. Falconer, *History of Agriculture in the Northern United States, 1620–1860* (Carnegie Institution of Washington, May 1925), p. 181; and Howard R. Smith, *Economic History of the United States* (1955).

stration that led private investors to put their capital into turnpike developments throughout the East. A century and a half ago toll roads blanketed the seaboard states, with four hundred of them in New York State alone. The fact that users were willing to pay the toll reflected the savings in time and money made possible by using them. A system of modern toll highways in the United States in the mid-twentieth century, moving large volumes of traffic, reflects the same opportunity for trading road costs for vehicle operating costs.

It was the canal, however, that brought the most spectacular reductions in transport costs. When the Erie Canal opened in 1825, freight rates from the Great Lakes to New York City fell from $100 to $15 a ton.[2] And the combination of canals and roads, including turnpikes, reduced transport costs and permitted increased range and carrying capacity for barge and wagon. The West could now supply food to the cities of the East, while eastern manufacturers in turn could pay their food bill by selling cloth, shoes, and other goods to the West. Manufacturing came to be centered in New England and the East, sugar in the South, and wheat in the West. This territorial division of labor and the greater productivity that resulted was made possible because of soil and climate conditions, together with the distribution of population and human skills. But improvements in transport acted as the catalyst to bring together these ingredients of a prosperous regional economic integration.[3]

Agricultural experts observed more than a hundred years ago what is often overlooked today about the relation between transport and the supply of food. It was recognized then that ability to market one's produce was the essential condition for the improvement of agriculture. Only a ready demand at remunerative costs could induce farmers to increase their production. Conversely, no one in those times would be willing to raise more than was needed

[2] Harold Underwood Faulkner, *American Economic History* (Harper and Brothers, 1925), p. 312.

[3] Guy Stevens Callander (ed.), *Selections from the Economic History of the United States, 1765–1860* (1909), pp. 271–75 and 345–48.

by his own family if there was no expectation that the surplus could be moved.[4] It was also recognized that the cost of providing the necessary transport improvements could be offset by the increase in farm income generated from expanding markets, and this economic philosophy was written into the preambles of many local laws appropriating money for transport improvements. Improved methods of transport and marketing were considered as important as better seeds, fertilizers, and improved agricultural techniques.[5]

To a large extent the promise of economic gains from improving transport was the underlying cause of local enthusiasm for financing canal and turnpike developments. But public works were also supported by the practice of local governments to require men to work on the roads and waterways for a specified number of days a year, and this provided the essential manpower. The national government, on the other hand, did little either to help plan or pay for internal improvements. When Congress passed legislation in 1817 designed to facilitate road improvement on a national scale, the bill was vetoed on the grounds that the Constitution gave no such authority to the federal government. A more liberal interpretation of the Constitution made possible limited financial assistance for roads and waterways a decade later, but even as late as mid-century, federal aid was limited by presidential opposition. In the late eighteenth and early nineteenth centuries the improvement of transport was thus left principally to private investors aided in part by state and local governments.

From Men and Animals to Machines

With the introduction of the steam engine and its use in rail and water transport, America was provided with the major thrust that broke the transport barrier. For the first time men and animals were relieved of the major responsibility for motive power. Mechanization brought with it great advances in the economy,

[4] Statement written in 1826. Bidwell and Falconer, *op. cit.*, pp. 202–03.

[5] Frederick A. Cleveland and Fred W. Powell, *Railroad Promotion and Capitalization* (Longmans, Green & Co., 1909), p. 86.

speed, and capacity of transport, and it created many supporting economic activities that added to the impact of this new transport era.

Railways lowered the costs of internal transport and brought new areas and products into the stream of commerce. They made possible an increase in exports, and attracted private foreign capital for internal development. Between 1850 and 1890, construction of railroads absorbed more capital than any other sector of the American economy. In the years prior to 1850, a total of $533 million had been invested in all types of manufacturing enterprises, compared to $318 million in railroads. By 1889 the investment in manufacturing had multiplied twelve times to $6.5 billion, while rail investment had multiplied thirty times to $9.7 billion. Railway investments were nearly half again as great as the investment in all manufacturing activities combined.[6] The railways accounted for 20 percent of United States gross capital formation in the 1870's, then declined to 15 percent in the 1880's and 7.5 percent in subsequent decades up to 1920.[7]

The task of providing mobility for America, then, was a slow and costly undertaking. As recently as 1850, there were only nine thousand miles of rail routes in the United States. Most of them were short lines, independently operated. Transfers and transshipments caused considerable delay, inconvenience, and cost. A 500-mile trip from Maine to western New York State, for example, took four days and a dozen railroads. Passengers on trips westward to the Mississippi changed trains seven times, and there were no rail facilities across the country. To get from one coast of the United States to the other it was necessary to move overland by covered wagon or sail around the southern tip of South America.[8]

[6] Thomas C. Cochran, "The Entrepreneur in American Capital Formation," *Capital Formation and Economic Growth*, A Conference of the Universities—National Bureau Committee for Economic Research (Princeton University Press, 1955), p. 354.

[7] Ross M. Robertson, *History of the American Economy* (Harcourt, Brace, and Co., 1955).

[8] Final Report of the Industrial Commission (Washington, 1920), Vol. XIX, pp. 304–06, in Ernest L. Bogart and Charles M. Thompson, *Readings in the Economic History of the United States* (Longmans, Green & Co., 1916), p. 659; Bidwell and Falconer, *op. cit.*, p. 306.

To create the extensive nationwide railway system now in operation required a tremendous construction program backed by the full cooperation of the national government. The disinterest in transport that had prevailed in the Congress during the era of canal and turnpike building changed to active participation in the railway program. The War Department made elaborate surveys of four proposed rail routes from the Mississippi to the Pacific, and in 1863 President Lincoln signed the bill authorizing construction of two transcontinental routes. Grants of public land were provided for each mile of track that was laid, creating a powerful incentive for the two private companies, the Union Pacific and the Central Pacific, to build as quickly as possible.

State and local governments, eager to improve their competitive position, also offered inducements that would put them on the railway map. These included direct grants to private investors, purchases of railway stocks and bonds, tax abatement, gifts of public land, and a variety of other privileges and incentives. The result was a combination of private capital and public financial support. By 1860, public funds were 40 percent of the total railway investment in the North and 60 percent of the total in the South.[9]

Capital assistance from wealthier nations was a primary factor in the development of rail transport in the United States. Much of the financial backing came from private sources in Europe. In the 1890's approximately 65 percent of the stock of the Illinois Central Railroad was owned by foreign investors, 73 percent of the Louisville and Nashville, 52 percent of the Pennsylvania, and 33 percent of the Great Western.[10] By the end of the century, foreign holdings of American rail securities exceeded $3 billion. Technical assistance from abroad was also a key factor, but instead of today's whirlwind missions, it was immigrants from the more advanced economies of Europe that made possible a transfer of knowledge and experience.

[9] William Z. Ripley, *Railroads: Finance and Organization* (Longmans, Green & Co., 1923).

[10] *Ibid.*, p. 5.

The railway boom increased the demand for a wide variety of products and the manufacture of railway supplies and equipment became major industries. These activities in turn supported developments in other sectors, including coal, iron, and steel. Transport mechanization was thus both the cause and effect of the overall rate of industrial growth. In 1899, there were 10,113 establishments in the country manufacturing vehicles for land transport, with a total value of half a billion dollars. The output included railway cars, carriages, wagons, streetcars, bicycles, and sleds. These activities closely paralleled the development of the American economy. The average rate of growth for transport from 1860 to 1914 was 5.8 percent per year, compared to a 5.4 percent increase in industrial production.[11]

From Roads to Riches

Preoccupation with railway construction left the United States at the end of the nineteenth century with a completely inadequate road system that brought road transport virtually to a halt in bad weather. The early turnpikes had fallen into disuse as a result of railway competition, and public roads were not maintained because there were no administrative or financial provisions for doing so.

A partial response to public pressure for a network of highways was the decision by the Congress in 1893 to establish an Office of Road Inquiry in Washington. This office was to begin research in an area that has since become one of the major civilian programs of the federal government. The $10,000 voted was modest even by contemporary standards, and little could be accomplished. The absence of state administrative agencies to carry out a road program was a principal obstacle. In 1900, only seven states had established highway departments. Four years later, there were only 104

[11] Based on an index of rail mileage, rail freight and passenger traffic, canal and coastal shipping, street railways, motor vehicles, and port traffic. Edwin Frickley, *Production in the United States, 1860–1915* (Harvard University Press, 1947), p. 57.

miles of high-type rural roads in the United States, most of them brick. In thirteen states, less than 1 percent of rural road mileage was paved.

The basic federal-aid law of 1916 that initiated the good roads movement is still in effect after nearly half a century. This and subsequent legislation contained a variety of terms on which the states would be eligible for federal assistance. The federal law required the states to establish appropriate highway departments, to designate a limited system of federal-aid routes on which federal funds would be spent, and to adhere to federal standards of design and maintenance. Most federal-aid projects had to be matched by the recipient states, but there were important exceptions where matching would not have been possible.

The great transformation in highway transport since the initial action of the federal government is still within the memory of many persons living today. The first transcontinental motor trip was not completed until 1911. One part of the journey, from Denver to Los Angeles, took 66 days.[12] The problem at that time was not only poor roads but poor vehicles. It was not until 1914 that the United States was producing more motor cars than horse-drawn carts and carriages, and it was even later before the argument subsided over whether horses or internal combustion provided the more economical transport.

Then, in the short space of twenty years, from 1920 to 1940, nearly a million miles of roads were surfaced and over $40 billion were spent for construction and maintenance. Annual road expenditures throughout the period were equivalent to 1.5 percent of the gross national product. Public and private investment in all forms of transport during the period 1920–40 ranged from 13 to 23 percent of total investment in the United States. (See Table 2.1.)

Better roads were the product of a strong federal-aid program carried out through technically competent state highway depart-

[12] U. S. Bureau of Public Roads, *History of Highways* (Government Printing Office, 1957).

TABLE 2.1. *Transport Investment in the United States, 1920–40*
(Dollar items in millions)

Year	Total Investment[a]	Transport Investment	Transport as Percent of Total
1920	$13,042	$1,670	12.8
1921	9,637	1,593	16.5
1922	11,364	1,555	13.7
1923	14,718	2,212	15.0
1924	15,327	2,199	14.4
1925	16,712	2,096	12.5
1926	17,898	2,237	12.5
1927	17,396	2,331	13.4
1928	17,395	2,291	13.2
1929	17,748	2,510	14.1
1930	14,096	2,649	18.8
1931	9,886	1,990	20.1
1932	5,588	1,284	23.0
1933	4,895	1,048	21.4
1934	6,479	1,384	21.4
1935	7,960	1,277	16.0
1936	11,445	1,968	17.2
1937	13,048	2,067	15.8
1938	11,415	1,917	16.8
1939	13,182	2,159	16.4
1940	15,009	2,357	15.7

Source: Data compiled from J. Frederic Dewhurst and Associates, *America's Needs and Resources: A New Survey* (Twentieth Century Fund, 1955), pp. 1009–21.
[a] Includes all expenditures for publicly and privately owned capital goods.

ments and financed in part by the gradual imposition of charges on road users. Registration fees paid by motor vehicle owners were collected in most states at an early date, and the gasoline tax, first introduced in Oregon in 1919, spread rapidly to other states. As late as 1921, motor vehicle owners were paying only 12 percent of the more than $1 billion of revenues raised for highway purposes, but by 1941 special taxes on motor vehicles amounted to half the total road budget. Recently the figure has been augmented by the collection of federal road taxes that have brought the user contribution close to the total amount spent for roads.

The expenditure of these revenues was first concentrated on main highways connecting principal cities and centers of local government, comprising up to 10 percent of total road mileage. The most important one percent of these roads, forming a nationwide system of some 40,000 miles, is now 90 percent paid for through special federal taxes. Secondary farm-to-market roads share state-collected user revenues through state-aid to local units of government, and many of these roads receive help from the national government as well. The routes designated as federal-aid secondary roads include the most important 20 percent of total road mileage after the 10 percent primary system. Outside these systems there remains a large mileage of lightly traveled roads under local jurisdiction.

The most urgent needs were not always given priority attention in the United States roadbuilding program, but the insistence of pressure groups of bicycle riders and later automobile owners helped to guide the program. In the developing countries there are few pressures of this kind, and road transport development follows a course that is the reverse of the American experience. The emphasis is on building roads first, in the hope that vehicles will follow.

The "prestige project" was a problem in the early days as it is now, and a proposal to connect the Atlantic and Pacific coasts by road threatened at one time to divert resources from other needed projects. This one was never built as originally planned but was ultimately completed by connecting numerous individual state and federal projects. Other roads that were not needed were built, however, and often those that were needed were built to excessive standards. Overemphasis on roadbuilding is indicated by a 1950 inventory which reported that 148,000 miles of roads in the United States were providing no essential traffic function and should be discontinued as a public service.[13]

[13] U. S. Bureau of Public Roads, *The Local Rural Road Problem* (Government Printing Office, January 1950), p. 49.

Transport in Other Countries

Other developed nations that overcame poor transport did so with some variations in the organizational, administrative, and financial means used in America. But all experienced one thing in common: a big push was required in the transport sector, and the effort took large amounts of time and money. It was necessary in earlier periods for all countries to pass through a series of evolutionary stages in transport development as new transport technology gradually came into use.

Transport in Japan was part of a combined plan of the national government aimed at simultaneous advances on many fronts, including education. In the Meiji era (1868–1912) the construction of a unified national rail system was conceived from the start. This period also saw the simultaneous development of a merchant marine and the modernization of communications by telephone, telegraph, and the carriage of mail. The combination of these developments played a crucial role in linking the various parts of the empire domestically as well as in providing communication with the outside world.

Japan's transport absorbed more than half of the total capital invested in all private companies and government-owned enterprises. In 1896, approximately 56 percent of capital investments was in transport and petroleum. In 1913, the figure was 49 percent, and by 1929, the transport share of total investment was still as high as 36 percent. It was not until after 1925 that the growth of manufacturing proceeded at a more rapid rate than transport.[14] During this period the Japanese government emphasized the training of civil servants, sent numerous missions abroad, and lured western experts to aid in the introduction of technical skills.

[14] See William W. Lockwood, "The Scale of Economic Growth in Japan, 1868–1939," in *Economic Growth: Brazil, India, Japan*, edited by Simon Kuznets, Wilbert E. Moore, and Joseph J. Spengler (Duke University Press, 1954), p. 148.

Today the rapid advances being made in transport methods, together with the wealth of advice that many countries can offer, indicate that the exchange of knowledge is as important to the emerging nations as it was to Japan and the United States. It is also clear that financial assistance from abroad continues to be vital to the success of transport programs, for the developing countries in all periods typically lack adequate local sources of investment funds or export volumes sufficient to finance transport equipment imports.

British efforts to break the transport barrier were primarily in the private sector. The role of government was more that of a regulator than an initiator. Legislation limited the toll road and canal rates that private operators could charge, set limits on profits, and authorized the formation of turnpike and canal companies. Private rail lines were chartered and built in relatively short links that were subsequently combined for purposes of operation. The development of the railway network in Great Britain was controlled only by the action of the special parliamentary committees whose primary concern was the protection of investors.[15]

The national government of France, on the other hand, took the leadership in transport and developed a different kind of public-private partnership. Government engineers laid out the general pattern of the rail system and the state contributed a substantial subsidy per mile as an aid to construction by private firms. The road bed was publicly owned, but private companies chartered by the government carried out the planned development. These companies matched government contributions with nearly an equal amount of money per mile for construction, equipment, and operation.[16]

Transport in Germany was also the primary concern of govern-

[15] See Witt Bowden, Michael Parpovich, and Abbott Payson Usher, *An Economic History of Europe Since 1750* (American Book Co., 1937), pp. 393–405.

[16] Frederick Austin Ogg, *Economic Development of Modern Europe* (Macmillan Co., 1925), pp. 244–45.

ment, but, unlike France's nationally planned rail construction, each individual state was allowed to handle its own railway development. Prussia provided state subsidies to private companies in the form of guaranteed interest on railway bonds. Public purchase of these private rail lines was later made possible through the proceeds of a special railway tax. And Belgium, which led all of Europe in the construction of railways, decided from the outset that railways would be national undertakings built according to a systematic plan, and aimed at exploiting the nation's geographic position as a transit corridor.[17]

The fact that solutions and methods of arriving at them have been different in the United States than in Europe and Japan is understandable because the latter were already well settled when improvement of their transport facilities was undertaken. Industrialization had already created the demand for cheaper inland transport in Europe, and in Japan the transport program was linked with simultaneous public efforts to force industrialization. In the United States, it was more the expectations that underscored the need for improved transport, and there was no certainty that new transport facilities could support themselves. In this respect, the situation in the United States resembles that of many of the less developed countries today, but many of the methods used in Europe and Japan seem more appropriate to the solution.

Continental European and Japanese experience indicates a much greater dependence on national planning, public financing, and public management. But whatever the level of government participation, in all countries the result was a mixed effort of government and private enterprise, and the mixture was to an important degree a matter of geography, government institutions, current technology, and financial capacity.

[17] Dionysius Lardner, *Railway Economy: A Treatise on the New Acts of Transport*, p. 416, as quoted in J. H. Clapham, *The Economic Development of France and Germany, 1815–1914* (Cambridge University Press, 1921), p. 142.

The appropriate mix of public and private activity for today's conditions, however, will differ with circumstances. It would hardly be fitting now to suggest that private enterprises vie with each other in the emerging nations to determine who could build the greatest mileage of railways or turnpikes in the shortest length of time for the greatest private gain. Nor would it be feasible to suggest that a large number of railway companies should engage independently in the process of constructing and operating uncoordinated networks of rail routes. The days of the "robber barons" have passed, and in their place are transport ministries, planning commissions, and the International Bank.

Today the chances are better that facilities can be built where needs are greatest, that financial distress will be lessened, and that needless duplication and waste of resources can be avoided. Whether public enterprise can compensate for the disappearance of the pot of gold that rallied the pioneering spirit in earlier history is difficult to say. Certainly, more experimentation with joint public-private ventures is in order, granting that overall plans and large-scale investments will continue to be principally the province of government, while transport operations will often be more effectively carried out in the private sector.

From Evolution to Revolution

Past efforts to overcome poor transport were limited by the rate of innovation. Progress had to wait for invention, and it took the developed countries a century and a half to get things moving the way they move today. Five stages can be distinguished in the long struggle toward higher standards of transport. These stages are overlapping, and their time and duration are by no means definitive. However, they represent a general sequence of events in which advances in transportation and progress toward higher levels of living are clearly related. The question facing development planners today is whether—and how—these stages can be telescoped into a shorter time span.

First was the period of immobility and the traditional society. In this period, it was difficult and costly to develop trade and cultural relations on any large scale except where channels of communications were provided by the rivers and oceans. The pattern of living emerging from these conditions was predominantly one of localized agriculture and handicraft industries with a minimum of economic integration and social intercourse. Most people of the world still live in this initial stage of primitive transport, and their efforts to break out of a subsistence environment and to achieve a better life are being thwarted by the same barriers to movement that plagued all generations before them.

A second stage of transport development was the period of internal improvements and the growth of trade. Human and animal power was made much more effective by the development of turnpikes and canals which reduced the cost of transport by traditional methods of moving on land and water. This period of declining transport costs saw both an expansion of capacity and a lengthening of the radius of trade and travel.

A third stage in the evolutionary process toward greater mobility and higher standards of living was the period of transport mechanization and industrialization. This was the period of steam power, which introduced both the steamship and the first railways. It was a period marked by heavy investments in transportation, as well as the establishment of a wide assortment of manufacturing industries.

A fourth period in the evolution of transport has been the development of motorization and the new mobility. This has been an era marked by growing dependence on trucks, buses, and automobiles, and by extensive efforts to provide all-weather roads. This is the period when people and economic activity were freed from the limited mileage of fixed routes provided by railways and waterways.

A fifth stage still in the process of development is the air age and the conquest of distance, a period in which the world is being united by transport speeds that are obliterating political boundaries and adding a third dimension to the solution of transport problems. This stage, however, has not yet affected local and short-haul transport that comprises a major part of the transport problem.

Looking beyond these stages in transport innovation, we may now be moving toward a sixth stage, far removed from the era of immobility and poverty—the stage of immobility and affluence. For many of the great cities of the world are bogging down from too much traffic with much the same results as other areas that are totally lacking in transport. Arterial highways, city streets, railway yards, public transit, and major airports are key points in the growing congestion. They account for a large part of the time and resources consumed in transport. Even the less developed nations need to be on guard to avoid stage six. In some countries, rapid economic development combined with population increases and urbanization are creating traffic loads that far exceed the capacity available to handle them.

Although generally the underdeveloped areas are regarded as being predominantly in the initial stage of primitive transport, many of them are operating in a mixture of all stages at once. Rural areas may be completely isolated, while major cities in the same country are served by modern diesel railways, jet airliners, modern highways, and motor trucks and buses. Where inland waterways are available, too, they are likely to represent both primitive and advanced transport techniques simultaneously.

The situation in underdeveloped areas, therefore, is not comparable to the period of primitive transport in which the developed economies previously found themselves. Transport in Asia, Africa, and Latin America reflects at once a continuation of the immobility that constrained societies of earlier times, a projection into the most advanced transport technologies, and an exposure to the same frustrations of overcongestion that beset the most affluent societies.

From this mixture of the old and the new, it is obvious that two dissimilar types of transport problems must be dealt with in underdeveloped countries. Where the latest in technology serves the principal arteries of commerce, the problem may be little different from that which is encountered in the economically advanced countries. The same is true of the largest cities. In many rural areas, however, where immobility and subsistence go hand in hand, the transport problem may require more elementary solutions. Social and cultural factors may weigh more heavily than economic factors in programing transport improvements, and the approach to financial and organizational solutions may differ considerably from practices governing major intercity transport facilities.

In the more developed countries, breaking the transport barrier took a long time and a large proportion of available resources. Most of the countries now attempting to overcome the obstacles of poor transport cannot pay the costs, and, under pressure for economic emancipation, cannot spare the time required in an earlier period to achieve mobility essential to development. Newly independent states are unable to exact the initial sacrifices that development demands, and there are no large volumes of private capital seeking investment in basic facilities such as transport.

Although the underdeveloped areas of the world lack some of the key assets enjoyed by Western nations, and in addition have pressing problems of hunger and disease,[18] the advent of modern technology offers many compensating advantages. In earlier times there was no machinery available to accomplish the clearing, grading, and other earth work preparatory to construction. Rails had to be made of wood, and explosives needed to cut through bedrock were improvised on the job. There had been little or no progress in the study of soils and their stabilization, materials were of inferior quality, and equipment was untested and unreliable. Numerous errors and accidents occurred because there was no background of previous experience on which to build.

[18] See Gunnar Myrdal, *Rich Lands and Poor: The Road to World Prosperity* (Harper and Brothers, 1957).

Those earlier obstacles are in sharp contrast to the wealth of materials, equipment, and experience available to the underdeveloped countries today. The time element can be overcome. The current setting is one in which it is possible to leapfrog parts of the evolutionary process and to avoid the traditional sequence of transport development.

Recent Examples of the Big Push

If the time obstacle to providing mobility no longer holds, what about the dedication of resources? A high proportion of resources has always been allocated to transport in the past. Does this indicate the course of events for the future? Two factors in the modern world influence the answer. One is that people today are conscious of so many needs that it no longer is feasible to allocate a major share of a nation's resources to transport. These needs include education, health, more food, and better housing. The second factor is the emergence of national planning, which provides a mechanism by which a greater balance and consistency among these various wants can be achieved. As development proceeds, a planned approach increases the chance that a greater variety of needs can be met and counteracts the tendency to overemphasize one sector at the expense of all the others.

There are two examples of a "big push" in transport from more recent history that shed light on what happens when a country makes an extraordinary commitment of resources for transport improvement. In both Colombia and Turkey an attempt was made to concentrate development efforts in the transport sector, to the neglect of other needs. There is room for debate over the merits of the courses that were taken. But the cases are cited as evidence of the problems that can be expected when a nation puts so much into transport that it puts too little into other things that are also vital to its development.

The task of overcoming the transport barrier in mountainous Colombia has absorbed a heavy share of that country's public investment program over a period of several decades. The initial development was on railways in the 1920's, and the focus in the next decade was chiefly on roads. These investments played a vital part in the effort to achieve greater political and economic integration, and in creating markets of sufficient size to permit large-scale production.

The contribution to national development that resulted from improved mobility and ease of access is demonstrated by transport advances in Colombia. Between 1938 and 1960, total freight movement increased more than seven-fold. Rail and water transport more than doubled. Truck transport expanded to thirteen times the 1938 volume, and air cargo multiplied nineteen times. Petroleum pipelines coming into use in the early 1950's soon accounted for 40 percent of the total ton-kilometers moved in Colombia. Personal mobility registered equally spectacular gains. Air travel multiplied nearly thirty-five times to become the primary passenger carrier, and the number of passenger cars and buses registered a six-fold increase. During this period of expanded transport in the 1950's, Colombia's gross national product rose 48 percent.

The results of dedicating a major proportion of investment to transportation can be seen in every aspect of Colombia's development today. Many rural areas that were once completely isolated are producing food and agricultural products for consumption in distant cities. New industries in the growing urbanized areas have benefited by reduced costs and by the growth of national and international markets. Resources that once lay idle for lack of transport have been made available to support the economy. During this period, however, Colombia was unable to provide for adequate schools and hospitals, or to meet the extraordinary demands for low-cost housing, water, sewerage, and other public services. As a result, education and training lagged, urban slums persisted, and the development program became lopsided.

Of the total public investment in 1959 by all units of government in Colombia, 41 percent was allocated to transportation and communications and only 3 percent to education. Of the national government's total investments, 63 percent went to transportation and communications and only 5 percent to health, education, and industry. (See Table 2.2.) Retrenchments in the transport sector might have made possible the emphasis on social needs so lacking in the sixties. Recently a transport mission to Colombia concluded that transport should receive less relative attention than before. Common sense suggested a halt to the emphasis on transport in order to help strengthen other development programs.[19]

TABLE 2.2. *Transport Investment in Colombia, 1959 and 1960–70*
(In percent)

Sectors	Investment by All Government Units	Investment by National Government	Ten Year Plan 1960–70
Transport and Communications	41	63	21
Electric Power	14	5	7
Housing	12	10	16
Agriculture and Livestock	10	4	12
Industry	2	1	19
Health	1	2	
Education	3	2	25
All others	17	13	
Total	100	100	100

Source: Colombia Plan Organization, Bogota, for the 1959 figures, Projection for 1960–70, *International Financial News Survey*, Vol. XIV (March 23, 1962), International Monetary Fund, p. 85. (Data based on Revista Banco de la Republica, Bogota, Colombia, December 1961.)

This is the dilemma, then, that is posed by a big push in transport. Construction and maintenance of transport facilities have to be sufficient to assure the capacity to meet growing traffic requirements. At the same time, transport developments are so costly that their claim on a country's limited resources should be weighed with an awareness of other vital requirements that might yield a greater return in better living.

Turkey provides another example of a nationwide effort to im-

[19] Planning operations in Colombia are discussed more fully in Chap. III.

prove transport quickly without relating the effort to a comprehensive development plan. The program was largely military in character, and the emphasis was on building a system of modern roads. During the ten-year period 1948–57, half of all investment by the central government was in transport and communication, with 28 percent in agriculture, 13 percent in public works other than transport, and 7 percent in industry, mining, and power. As a result of this concentration of effort, rapid strides were made in the improvement of ports, airports, roads, and railways. In five years the mileage of all-weather roads in Turkey nearly doubled. Average speeds on state highways rose 50 percent, average capacity of trucks increased 35 percent, and the number of vehicles using the roads nearly tripled. From 1948 to 1959, rail freight traffic increased 87 percent and motor freight increased six-fold.[20]

The social impact of one road is illustrated by events in Balgat, which in 1950 was a forgotten village two hours from Ankara with almost no road.[21] Four years after a new highway had been completed connecting with the capital, the village experienced a complete metamorphosis. Trip time from Ankara was reduced to twenty minutes, regular bus service was established, water and electricity were provided, ten times as many houses had been built, there were a hundred radios instead of one, there were fewer farmers but more food, and attractive wages in the city had made Balgat a relatively prosperous commuter town.

But the fact that the road program in general proved less efficacious in promoting higher living standards is indicated by aggregate data for the Turkish economy. For while gross national product increased substantially from 1950 to 1956, the country encountered severe financial difficulties. Only large credits and grants made available through the United States aid program plus extensive shipments of spare parts, raw materials, and operating

[20] U. S. Department of Commerce, *Basic Data on the Economy of Turkey*, World-Trade Information Service, Part I, No. 55–81. Also James Morris, "Recent Problems of Economic Development in Turkey," *The Middle East Journal*, Vol. 14 (Winter 1960), pp. 1–14.

[21] Daniel Lerner, "The Grocer and the Chief," reprinted from *Harper's* (September 1955). Distributed by Turkish Information Office, New York.

supplies helped to offset foreign exchange deficits and to restrain inflationary pressures. The evidence indicates that the transport program had been too ambitious in relation to other aspects of the development effort.

The period has been passed when single-minded attention to transport is an acceptable prescription for overcoming economic troubles. The developing countries can learn much from what has been evolutionary, but the application must fit into a strategy that is essentially revolutionary. The growing capacity to establish transport requirements in relation to development goals will keep the transport program within bounds, and the potentials of science and technology will reveal the best tactics to hold cost and time to a minimum. The two efforts combined will help to lighten the burden on those who now prepare to break the transport barrier.

CHAPTER III

Transport Requirements for Development

IF TRANSPORT PROBLEMS are to be prevented from frustrating economic growth, developing countries will have to determine how much of their resources should be dedicated to transport compared to industry, education, health, and other urgent requirements. But charting a course to higher standards of mobility is not easy. Determining what is really needed includes the identification of immediate and urgent priorities, the demands for transport imposed by further growth and development, and the growth potentials likely to result from transport improvements. Everywhere the process of making these judgments is frustrated by lack of data, of trained personnel, and of understanding. These obstacles increase the chance that plans will be poorly conceived, and that even desirable plans will be poorly implemented. But the move toward more carefully conceived transport programs is underway.

Current Transport Plans

Most countries have some type of transport plan. Many of these plans are merely a compilation of individual projects. Others are based on a detailed survey of transport needs as a whole. Both approaches have been taken with or without the guidance of an overall development plan. Whatever the approach, the allocations to transport have proved to be substantial. The percentage of public investment devoted to transport (including a small proportion for communications) is often as high as 25 to 30 percent or more of total public investment. In Nigeria approximately 47 percent of all public investment was at one time allocated to transport. (See Table 3.1.)

TABLE 3.1. *Planned Transport and Communication Investment*[a]

Selected Countries	Plan Period	Percent of Total Public Expenditures
Afghanistan	1956–60[b]	16.1
Burma	1956–59[b]	23.8
China		
Mainland	1953–57	11.8
Taiwan	1957–60	18.4
Malaya	1956–60	22.3
India	1956–60[b]	28.8
Indonesia	1956–60	25.0
Iran	1949–55	26.7
Nepal	1956–60[b]	33.8
Nigeria	1955–59	46.5
Pakistan	1955–59[b]	17.8
Philippines	1957–61	25.0
Senegal	1961–64	18.7
Thailand	1952–56	42.1
Vietnam, S.	1957–61	31.4

Sources: For the Colombian figure see Table 2.2; Thailand, International Bank for Reconstruction and Development, *A Public Development Program for Thailand* (Johns Hopkins Press, 1959), Tables on pp. 18 and 25; Nigerian data from Stanford Research Institute, *The Economic Coordination of Transport Development in Nigeria* (1961), Table I; Senegal, *Le Plan Quadriennal de Developpement*, 1961–64 (1961); and the remaining Asian countries, the United Nations, *Economic Survey of Asia and the Far East* (1958), p. 85.
[a] Note that these percentages are influenced by the relative importance of the public and private sectors.
[b] Fiscal years.

The decisions behind these allocations are based on a mixture of past trends, current experience, and future goals. And since needs always exceed available resources, the task is to compress a long list of transport projects into a shorter list that will be defensible economically and acceptable politically.

In this process, there are a number of pressures in the direction of allocating more money for mobility. In early stages of development, transport is an obvious need, and improvements are politically desirable because they can be readily observed over a wide geographic area. In official quarters other factors favor a substantial transport program. Port improvements are attractive because they are localized investments with a specific earning power, and national railway systems, which often have a disproportionate share of the nation's administrative and planning personnel, submit plans and projects that are generally well prepared and ready to go. Air transport has a special appeal as a means of enhancing international prestige.

At the same time, there are offsetting factors that tend to reduce allocations to transport. Upper limits may be imposed by technical considerations, such as the capacity of the domestic construction industry, or by limitations on the supply of foreign exchange. Transport needs may also be neglected in the desire to emphasize "productive" sectors such as agriculture and industry, or the development of "human resources" through education and better health. The fact that transport is generally an integral part of these efforts can easily be overlooked.

Transport Needs and National Product

In the effort to arrive at a more considered judgment of transport needs, some general statistical guides can be useful where data are available. A first approach to making overall estimates of national transport requirements may be based on the relationship between a nation's output and the total volume of goods movement that various levels of economic activity involve. If the gross national product of a country is known and transport statistics are available, projections of gross national product make it possible to arrive at a broad view of probable transport demands. The estimate of transport requirements can be made by first establishing past ratios between the volume of freight traffic and the level of GNP and then projecting what is likely for the future.

As nations grow, there is a continuing increase in the need for transport. Modernization of agriculture requires supplying tools, machinery, and fertilizer to rural farms, and moving food and other products to consuming centers. Increasing industrial production means bringing together greater volumes of materials for processing, and distributing larger quantities of finished goods to consumers. Expanding output may be accompanied by an extension of the area from which materials are assembled, as well as the area over which the increased production is marketed. The number of goods exchanged will multiply with increasing specialization and rising incomes. Thus the increase in freight movement is faster than the increase in GNP.

In more developed countries, the relationship between freight movement and economic activity is likely to be relatively stable. In the United States, over an extended period of time, about 3.5 ton-miles of intercity freight have moved for every dollar of gross national product, expressed in 1954 dollars. Canadian experience also shows a close relation between transport and economic activity. During the past two decades the number of ton-miles per dollar of gross national product (in 1949 Canadian dollars) has averaged approximately 5.4. (See Table 3.2.)

In less developed countries, ratios between transport and economic activity not only vary among countries but are likely to be moving up or down, depending on the characteristics of the economy and its stage of development. In the earlier stages, industrialization may be expected to increase the volume of heavy materials moved. In these circumstances, transport requirements may be expected to rise at a considerably higher rate than the rise in economic activity. Later, as development proceeds, the further processing of raw materials will result in greater values in product for given volumes of transport. In addition, it is likely that more services will be included in gross national product rela-

TABLE 3.2. *Relation of Freight Traffic to GNP in the United States and Canada, 1940–60*

	United States		Canada	
Year	Ton-Miles of Intercity Freight (In billions)	Ton-Miles per Dollar of GNP[a]	Ton-Miles of Intercity Freight (In billions)	Ton-Miles per Dollar of GNP[b]
1940	618.6	3.0	58.9	5.4
1941	772.1	3.2	71.9	5.8
1942	929.0	3.5	76.1	5.1
1943	1,031.3	3.5	84.4	5.5
1944	1,088.4	3.4	85.9	5.4
1945	1,027.1	3.3	85.1	5.5
1946	903.9	3.2	74.5	4.9
1947	1,018.7	3.6	82.5	5.3
1948	1,045.1	3.6	84.1	5.3
1949	915.8	3.1	82.7	5.1
1950	1,062.6	3.3	87.7	5.0
1951	1,178.1	3.5	100.7	5.4
1952	1,144.3	3.2	108.5	5.4
1953	1,204.1	3.3	110.1	5.3
1954	1,123.1	3.1	102.1	5.1
1955	1,274.9	3.3	118.7	5.4
1956	1,355.4	3.4	141.2	5.9
1957	1,335.5	3.3	132.2	5.5
1958	1,215.1	3.0	126.6	5.2
1959	1,295.3	3.0	133.7	5.3
1960	1,330.9	3.0	128.7	5.0

Sources: U.S. ton-miles of intercity freight from Interstate Commerce Commission, Bureau of Transport Economics and Statistics, "Intercity Ton-Miles 1939–1959," Statement 6103 (April 1961), pp. 4–5 (for 1940–58); Interstate Commerce Commission, *Annual Report, 1961*, p. 15 (for 1959–60). Canadian ton-miles of intercity freight from George A. Wagdin, "The Role of a Central Statistical Organization in the Field of Transportation," presented at the IV World Meeting of International Road Federation, Madrid, Oct. 14–20, 1962, Appendix V. U.S. GNP figures from *Economic Report of the President, 1961*, and *1963;* Canadian GNP figures from *National Accounts Income and Expenditure, 1950–61*, Research and Development Division, Dominion Bureau of Statistics, Ottawa.

[a] Calculated from U.S. GNP in 1954 prices.

[b] Calculated from Canadian GNP in 1949 prices.

tive to goods. Thus the rate of traffic growth will eventually be closer to the growth rate for the economy.

In most countries of Asia, the combined volume of rail and road freight shows a much higher rate of increase than the gross domestic product. Recent increases in domestic product have commonly ranged from 2 to 5 percent per year, while rail and road traffic increases per year have ranged from about 6 percent in the Philippines to nearly 20 percent in Thailand. (See Table 3.3.)

TABLE 3.3. *Relation of Freight Traffic to GNP in Asia, 1948–57*
(In percent)

Country[a]	Increase in GNP	Increase in Rail and Road Traffic (Ton-kms.)	Increase in Rail and Road Traffic (Pass.-kms.)
Thailand	4.4	20	24
Vietnam, S.	—	13	13
Taiwan	6.3[b]	12	11
Cambodia	3.7[b]	12	20
Indonesia	—	11	10
Korea, S.	3.6[c]	9	9
Federation of Malaya	1.8[d]	9	13
Japan	8.6	9	5
India	2.5[e]	8	5
Ceylon	3.2[f]	7	3
Pakistan	2.2[e,g]	7	4
Philippines	5.2[g]	6	11
Burma	3.5	0.25	10

Sources: *Economic Development and Planning in Asia and the Far East, VI. Transport Development,* U.N. Economic Bulletin for Asia and the Far East, Vol. XI, No. 3 (December 1960), p. 4. Data on gross domestic product in constant prices are based on Asian Economic Statistics published in ECAFE, *Annual Economic Survey* (1955 and 1959).
[a] Countries are arranged in descending order of the rate of rail and road traffic in ton-kms.
[b] 1951–57.
[c] 1953–57.
[d] 1949–53.
[e] Net national product.
[f] 1950–57.
[g] 1949–57.

Past trends in the Soviet Union also demonstrate the rapid growth of transport compared to increasing national product. During the period 1928 to 1937, most estimates of the annual growth in net national product averaged about 7 percent. Annual rates of traffic growth, during the same period, averaged 15.5 percent. Over the entire period from 1928 to 1950, there is evidence that a 10 percent increase in total Soviet output has resulted in a 16 percent increase in freight transported, while increases in industrial production appear to have caused a roughly comparable rate of increase in freight.[1]

In many newly developing countries, of course, a reliable statistical basis to provide an estimate of total transport needs is

[1] James H. Blackman, "Transportation," in Abram Bergson, ed., *Soviet Economic Growth: Conditions and Perspectives* (Row, Peterson, & Co., 1953), pp. 128, 154, 158.

often lacking. Neither national production statistics nor data on past and present freight movements are complete and reliable, and they seldom cover a sufficient period of time. Moreover, adequate transport statistics are generally limited to rail traffic. Data for motor and water transport are often unavailable, and for non-mechanized methods no statistics are compiled.

Dealing with the Obvious

In these circumstances, it is fortunate that consultants to developing countries who arrive with high hopes of applying the latest statistical methods find themselves confronted by a large backlog of needs that are obvious. The first problem is to assure that what is already in being is kept in operation or made operative. This means doing whatever will yield the greatest impact for a given amount of resources in the shortest period of time. If seventeen ships are in port awaiting their turn to unload, the key projects needed to break the jam may be the purchase of another tug, the improvement of communications, the construction of a new port, or the expansion of road and rail facilities serving the port.

The immediate task is to identify all the needs that are urgent, and then to establish the order in which these improvements should be accomplished to produce the most significant results. Here concern is only with investment, but obviously the greatest immediate needs may involve no capital outlays, but rather the establishment of an organization, the reduction of excessive paper work, the reorganization of a port's administration, or the supervision of freight-handling operations.

In India and Pakistan, the transport programs that were part of the first five-year development plans were little more than a listing of obvious requirements. In these countries, most of the basic transport plant and equipment had been left in a state of disrepair by economic depression and world war, and afterwards by the disruption following partition of the subcontinent. All the things that had to be done were apparent, but what should be done first was open to question.

In most of Asia, Africa, and Latin America, there is no lack of obvious projects required to restore or improve existing transport networks. Where locomotives are more than a half century old, they are generally ready for retirement. Port facilities may be crowded with waiting ships due to lack of adequate piers or cargo handling equipment, and ocean vessels or inland water craft may be ancient and uneconomical to operate. Defective bridges or no bridges at all may be interrupting the flow of rail or road traffic, and many miles of main road may need improvement to make them passable during the rainy season.

Ideally, the identification of needs and the establishment of sensible priorities have to be based on an understanding of the ultimate objectives to be served. But many transport tasks are too urgent to wait for this. A nation must resort to interim means of getting the job under way. This may require identifying projects that seem to make sense before a total transport plan can be developed and before transport plans can be integrated with a comprehensive development plan. Risks can be reduced by estimating physical requirements and costs, assessing probable results, and establishing priorities based on getting maximum results in the shortest time. High priority should also be given to preserving useful investments previously made. The main point is that waiting for programs that embody a high degree of perfection is likely to result in no program at all.

Planning from the Ground Up

Estimates of total traffic demand from aggregate growth data provide a rough measure of future transport requirements, and easily identified urgent needs provide a way to get started. But what is needed to supplement these guides are detailed analyses of individual projects, studies of the transport system as a whole, and a continuing process of transport programing geared to overall development plans.

To arrive at specific physical requirements for transport and to determine financial needs, it is essential to depart from national aggregates and build estimates of traffic, physical needs, and financial requirements from the ground up. The basis of such a build-up is, first, a knowledge of the existing transport plant and its current use, and second an estimate of the additional transport demands deriving from the economic and social goals envisioned for the economy. These data establish the dimensions of the transport task and the extent to which additional transport capacity or improved quality will be required. Where such needs are indicated, the added question is whether existing facilities can be made to perform more efficiently, whether additional capacity is needed, or whether the burden of estimated transport demands can be reduced by regulating traffic flows or otherwise reducing their impact.

To judge the need for a proposed transport investment in terms of development, the essential consideration is how it will be used to raise levels of living. Goals for agriculture may call for making additional land accessible, for encouraging farmers to shift from subsistence agriculture to cash crops, or for raising per capita rural incomes. The goal of the cities may be to provide a cheaper source of raw materials for industry, or better food supplies. There may also be a need for transport improvements to serve as a means of communication, enabling the residents of remote villages to travel and exchange views with other people. Improvement in schools and in school attendance also results when more reliable transport permits the establishment of better educational facilities serving a wider area and larger numbers of pupils. The contribution of transport will be measured in the movement of traffic related to these activities.

Certain other needs are in the nature of standby benefits, such as the knowledge that medical attention is within reach, or food supplies available from other areas if famine conditions should arise. These considerations do not invalidate the conclusion, however, that most of the need for transport is satisfied through the movement of people and things, and that the task of estimating need is in the last analysis one of estimating traffic. It is true that volumes of traffic are not a precise measure of development impact. A bus carrying children to school may fulfill development objectives to a greater extent than a bullock cart carrying corn husks, and an automobile carrying an industry advisor may have special implications compared to other traffic. The significance of various units of traffic will differ, but volume of use provides a rough measure.

When a proposed transport project is being assessed, it is important to determine whether improved transport alone will meet the traffic requirement, or whether other investments will also have to be made. The construction of a road may result in the movement of more food grains, for example, only if the port is also improved, if farmers apply fertilizer, and if there is a concurrent effort to provide irrigation, storage, and marketing. In other words, there should be assurance that other measures will be taken to guarantee that the transport provided will be used.

Traffic projections are too often based on what may be expected to happen rather than on what can be made to happen. The first approach is guessing the future, while the second is planning it. The second approach reflects the realization that improved transport of itself may not lead to any results—that what is called the effects of a transport facility are the combined effects of many factors. The absence of these other factors explains why the development potentials of a transport facility are often not realized.

When a manufacturing plant is constructed, provision is made for delivering to the site the raw materials that will permit the plant to be used. A factory is not built in the hope that sources of materials will later be found to permit production. But often a road is constructed merely on the chance that materials will find their way to it as a result of economic activities created by the new route. To produce the ton-miles for which the road was designed, however, it may be necessary to expand agriculture and establish new industries. Otherwise, these activities may be slow to appear or never develop. In this case, the result is the same as if a factory were built with no materials to feed it—the road, like the manufacturing plant, will stand idle.

Evaluating the need for a transport project, therefore, has meaning only as it is looked upon as one element in a combination of measures aimed at development. Some of these may be taken care of by private investments induced by better transport, but some will have to be carried out in the public sector as an integral part of a comprehensive development scheme. The instances in which transport can go it alone are limited to those in which existing traffic pressures already establish the need.

For facilities already in use, the need for improvement has to be expressed in two ways: by an estimate of the savings in transport costs that can be expected to result for existing traffic, and by estimates of new traffic that such improvements will generate.

Estimating need introduces many imponderables that can influence traffic projections to an important degree. The mystique of what happens when a road is built is illustrated by a project in Uganda. At first there were no visible results following completion of an all-weather highway. The people served by these facilities were not interested in growing market crops because they had no need for cash. Later, however, as the desire for education spread to this area, money became necessary to finance school attendance. The result was a shift to cash crops and a substantially greater use of the road to get produce to market.

Other road projects have turned out not to be needed because people would not settle on the new lands to better their economic position if such a move would disrupt family ties. Even when the government provided buildings, tools, and food to help new settlers get started, they were reluctant to leave familiar surroundings. However, when roads open up fertile land and maintain connections with former places of residence, the desired migration can be expected to follow.

Tribal attitudes can produce opposite effects from similar roads built in areas adjacent to each other. One such road led to rapid development of a market economy because the tribal group took advantage of the ability to move cash crops over the new facility. Another road was not used because people refused to alter a satisfying way of life based on cattle-raising and subsistence farming. Marketing of livestock was not undertaken because the number of cattle owned was an index of social standing.[2]

It is clear, then, that the need for transport is influenced by many social, cultural, and political factors, and not merely by economic considerations. These non-economic factors have to be taken into account in arriving at an estimate of physical requirements. Fortunately most of them will be reflected in actual movement. The extent to which improvements in transport will be justified, therefore, can be determined essentially by the relation between traffic volumes and the investment required to accommodate them.

Looking at the Cost Side

The need for a transport facility has to be determined on the basis of its cost as well as its use if meeting the need is to be justified as part of a country's development program. If the need is expected to be met by the movement of a hundred tons of traffic over a route per day, the satisfaction of that need will not warrant building a railway or a four-lane highway. It may suggest only a

[2] R. S. P. Bonney, "The Place of Transport, Particularly Road Transport, in the Economic and Social Development in North Borneo," United Nations Conference on the Application of Science and Technology for the Benefit of the Less Developed Areas, Geneva, 1963.

low-type road. Determination of how the facility should be designed physically will be based on the carrying capacity of alternative means of transport. Need will be justified by comparing the cost of the facility and related investment with the net addition to the national product that building the facility is expected to create.

Adequate records of experience with projects in developing countries are needed to help remove some of the uncertainty about the cost of building a project, what will be required to maintain it, and how long it is likely to last. Soil surveys can help to dispel some of the unknowns by identifying subsoil conditions; and laboratory testing can evaluate the quality of road-building materials. Human factors also affect costs and have to be taken into account, including workmanship, adherence to specifications, adequacy of maintenance, and the effect of undesirable operating practices, such as overloading of trucks.

The cost of transport is only partly the cost of building the facility over which equipment is to be operated, however. The total cost incurred is a combination of both basic facility and equipment. A road adequately designed to carry the traffic volume projected will be one that minimizes total transport costs. If a facility is underdesigned, the savings will be offset by the high cost of operating the equipment under conditions of congestion or other below-standard conditions. If the facility is overdesigned, operating costs will be low but the unit costs of providing the basic facility will be high. The objective, then, is to so adjust facilities to traffic as to produce a satisfactory standard of service for the lowest total commitment of resources.

The effect of transport improvements on the cost of vehicle operation is illustrated by studies of the performance of transport equipment on different types of roads. Records of truck operation in Peru, for example, indicate that it costs 50 percent more to operate a truck on rough gravel than on asphalt surfaces. Good roads, by permitting the use of larger vehicles capable of heavier loads, and by extending vehicle life, were found to reduce the cost of moving freight per ton-mile to half what it was on poor roads.

In Nigeria, products transported over dirt roads are priced from 40 to 60 percent higher than goods moving on tarred roads.[3]

There is nonetheless a considerable area of uncertainty about the net cost savings attributed to improved transport facilities. Better roads make possible higher speeds, but tire wear and fuel consumption may increase at high speeds rather than be reduced. Or improved facilities may encourage overloading, with consequent savings to truck operators but rapid deterioration of the highway surface. The private sector saves at the expense of the public sector, and returns from vehicle taxes are not likely to recoup the loss to the highway system. More needs to be known, therefore, about the net savings that transport investments can achieve under specific operating conditions, and how new technology can help to achieve net reductions in cost along with improved service.

The situation may be somewhat different for railways and other transport systems where unified management is responsible for total transport costs. When new railway tracks are laid, the cost can be offset by the ability to move longer and heavier trains, and the net benefit accrues to the railway system. The situation for aviation, however, is comparable to that for road transport. Improvement in airports and other ground facilities contribute to the economy of aircraft operation, but may increase the total cost of air transport.[4]

As noted earlier, transport project costs may also need to include certain nontransport investments. Without them, the anticipated traffic on the transport facility would not be realized. These may include investment in irrigation, flood control, water supply, or other facilities. In addition, cost calculations must take into account the effects of individual project decisions on the rest of the transport system. For example, the required outlay for rail mod-

[3] International Bank for Reconstruction and Development, *Economic Development of Nigeria* (Johns Hopkins Press, 1955), p. 493.

[4] As noted in Chapter 4, new aircraft designs that are less dependent on long runways or sophisticated navigational aids are an important aspect of air transport planning strategy.

ernization may be considered unjustified because of the light traffic expected to use the facility. But if the railway is allowed to deteriorate to the point of discontinuing service, existing traffic will have to be accommodated another way. The decision not to modernize the railroad, therefore, assumes the decision to provide the necessary capacity somewhere else.

By way of contrast, critical congestion on the railway system may make it seem desirable to concentrate investment almost exclusively on the task of increasing rail capacity. Looking at the railway alone, the proposal might make sense. But looking at transport as a whole often provides another diagnosis. Part of the solution may be in accelerating the development of road transport so that short haul traffic and small shipments clogging rail terminals can be diverted to trucks, thus freeing the railways to perform their appropriate role.

The importance of relating project costs to system costs was revealed in another respect by plans for providing diesel locomotives in Colombia. The benefits from such a changeover were estimated to be considerably in excess of the costs, but it later became apparent that not all the costs were being counted. For along with investment in diesel power, it would also be necessary to buy new freight cars capable of withstanding the strain of the more powerful traction. Heavier locomotives would also require stronger bridges and structures. Moreover, effective use of diesel traction would be possible only by hauling more cars, which would require longer sidings and improved signal equipment. What was initially a proposal for buying new locomotives turned out to be a proposal to rebuild the railways.

Facility costs are affected by a number of additional factors. Transport projects that have high capital requirements and long lives require a sacrifice of present consumption for future benefits, and entail commitment of capital assets for varying periods of time. The interest on capital so committed (plus maintenance outlays) should reflect what might have been earned if capital had been applied in other uses. Costs will depend not only on the interest rate, but on when the capital will be needed (all at once or in stages), and for how long. It is also necessary to take into account how quickly the costs incurred are likely to bring a return. Some projects may have a quick pay-off; others may involve an excess of costs over returns for a considerable period.[5]

A true picture of the cost of a project relative to other possible investments may also suggest measuring real scarcity or abundance by assigning to wages and foreign exchange the costs that reflect real values to the economy rather than market prices. This can be done through so-called accounting prices, which in developing countries may increase the cost attributed to scarce foreign exchange, and lower the cost of plentiful labor. Wages paid may be substantial, but the real cost to the economy of putting idle or underemployed people to work on useful projects may be low.[6]

Assessing the need for transport and the cost of providing it offers considerable latitude for judgment, therefore. Meticulous traffic and engineering studies can turn out to be of doubtful value when some aspect of the calculation is forgotten or is wide of the mark. Conceptually, the goal is to assure that the contemplated investment will permit a net contribution to national product, and that this contribution compares favorably with what might be achieved if the same resources were applied in some other way. When all transport projects are added together, their total development role is reflected in the number of ton-miles carried per unit of gross national product. For the nation as a whole, the transport input required to yield a given output of goods and services will depend on the wise selection of individual projects and their effective use.

Such a computation involves many complexities, but essentially the problem is to estimate traffic and to relate it to the cost of the needed facility. A unit of traffic represents a certain value added

[5] For a detailed discussion of project evaluation techniques, see Tillo E. Kuhn, *Public Enterprise Economics and Transport Problems* (University of California Press, 1962), Chap. VI.

[6] See Jan Tinbergen, *The Design of Development* (The Economic Development Institute, International Bank for Reconstruction and Development, 1958), pp. 39–41.

to the economy, and if this contribution can be estimated, the traffic necessary to warrant a given outlay for transport can also be determined. Field studies of the impact of transport on development are beginning to provide some indications of the net contribution that can be expected in various circumstances from specific volumes of movement. Thus it may eventually be possible to conclude how much transport outlay is economically warranted for a specified volume of traffic.

Scrutiny of individual projects will always be necessary in programing transport development, but looking at projects alone rather than as part of a larger system can be misleading. For often an individual project by itself makes no significant contribution, but when viewed in relation to the whole it may be of vital importance. The determination of priorities hinges on regional or national needs rather than the circumstances surrounding one isolated project.

Transport projects should also be related to a coordinated transport system for highways, rail, water, and air transport. The effort almost invariably falls short of the goal. Typically, each method of transport is studied separately for the reason that most transport experts are specialists in one aspect of transport and not in transport as a whole. The focus is on what needs to be done to improve specific types of facilities rather than on the economics of alternative transport methods. In some cases a restricted approach is adequate, since for many transport problems there are no alternative solutions. But in other cases alternative methods or alternative solutions outside the transport field may offer the most satisfactory answer.

Planning Approach to Transport

A survey of transport needs, whether for a single route or a system, creates the temptation to view transport for its own sake and to forget that the goal is development. Since transport's role is to serve other sectors of the economy, the transport survey should be based on what traffic can be expected to flow if production trends and targets are to be served, or if other goals for development are to be attained. Conversely, those responsible for activities in other sectors have to take into account the transport implications of development plans and potentials. A transport study, then, has to derive from studies of resources, agriculture, and industrialization.

Many of the attempts to estimate transport needs have suffered from the absence of any development goals that could provide a picture of what the transport system will be called on to do. Some countries are not yet in a position to establish the goals to provide this guidance. In other countries, goals have been established, but techniques for translating development objectives and potentials into transport requirements have been inadequate.

The problem calls for a national and regional planning process that can provide the framework for transport plans, their execution, and their adjustment to changing conditions. Surveys and reports, however helpful, are not a substitute for operations. Ideally, the necessary institutional arrangements and staff should be available on a continuing basis to develop and analyze meaningful data on the nation's resources, the trends in its growth, plans and prospects for development, and the condition of the transport system. These provide a basis for estimating transport needs.

Such a process is important because it makes possible the two-way relationship between transport and production targets in various sectors, and it introduces consideration of a wide variety of factors that have important development implications, such as balance of payments effects and employment aspects. Also of importance are the opportunities for trade-offs between transport and other investments to get the maximum development impact. Further possibilities lie in relating transport programs to policies governing communications, energy, and other nontransport investments.

The experiences of India and Pakistan illustrate the problems and potentials of the planning process. It would be an error to imply that every developing country needs to follow the same procedures, or that it would be equipped to do so. Nor is it suggested that the procedures themselves have been wholly successful. But they indicate an approach from which all countries can learn something useful.

Translating Indian Targets into Transport

India has been making a pioneer effort to establish transport requirements on the basis of projected economic activity. Transport needs are being estimated not through isolated surveys but as part of a continuing planning process. The objective has been to allocate funds to the transport sector on the basis of the existing condition of facilities, their use, and the probable increases in traffic anticipated as a result of planned expansion in agriculture, power, industry, and other sectors. The task is not an easy one, and India has not been able to avoid some serious transport problems. But the Indian experiment can provide important guides for other countries.

It has already been noted that during the First Five-Year Plan the problem of rehabilitating the transport system was so critical that plans for transport investment were no more than listings of urgent needs for obvious repairs and replacements. It was hardly necessary to relate these needs to development objectives, and it was not until the Second and Third Plans that relations between transport and activities outside the transport sector played a significant part in determining what the transport program should be.

In preparing the Second Five-Year Plan, however, after the initial rehabilitation had been completed, the concentration on industrialization posed the major problem for transport. Steel, coal, chemicals, textile machinery, electrical equipment, cement, and many other items placed new and heavy burdens on available transport capacity. The production of coal was to be increased by twenty million tons, two-thirds more than the pre-plan level. Iron ore production was to be increased by eight million tons to nearly triple the pre-plan total, and cement production was to be doubled.

The increasing demands of agriculture also had to be taken into account. More food has to be produced for a rapidly growing population. Production targets for food grains were increased by ten million tons, and the added output involved extensive public works to irrigate and provide access to an additional twenty-one million acres of land. The production of another two million tons of fertilizer was also called for each year, which meant that four times as much output would have to be moved, together with the raw material components.[7]

The increase in freight traffic on Indian roads and railways during the decade of the fifties was considerably more rapid than the rise in economic activity. While national income increased 42 percent from 1951 to 1961, freight traffic increased 111 percent. Rail traffic nearly doubled and road traffic tripled. (See Table 3.4.)

TABLE 3.4. *Trends in Indian Transport, National Income, and Production, 1951–61*

(Index, 1950–51 = 100)

Fiscal Year	Freight Traffic			National Income[a]	Industrial Production	Mining and Quarry Production[b]	Agricultural Production[c]
	Rail	Road	Total				
1951	100.0	100.0	100.0	100.0	100.0	100.0	95.6
1956	135.0	162.9	138.1	118.4	138.6	115.0	116.9
1961	198.9	315.7	211.2	141.6	194.3	171.8	135.0

Source: K. L. Luthra, "Transport in a Growing Economy: Indian Experience During the First Two Five-Year Plans," United Nations Conference on the Application of Science and Technology for the Benefit of the Less Developed Areas, Geneva, 1963, p. 4.

[a] At 1948–49 prices.

[b] The figures are for calendar years: the base year 1951 = 100.

[c] The figures are for crop year ending June; the base year 1949–50 = 100.

This rapid growth in transport demand is continuing through the Third Plan period. From 1961 to 1966, national income is expected to increase by 30 to 34 percent, with agricultural output

[7] Government of India, Planning Commission, *The Second Five-Year Plan, Summary* (1956), p. 23.

rising 30 percent and industrial production 70 percent. But freight traffic on the railways is expected to expand 80 percent, and commercial motor transport 120 percent. Thus the projected overall increase in freight traffic is three times the rate of growth of national income.[8]

To meet requirements for transport during the First Five-Year Plan, India allocated 24 percent of total public capital to transport and communications projects compared to 10 percent for agriculture, 7 percent for power, and 8 percent for industry and mining.

TABLE 3.5. *Public Investment in India*

(In percent)

Sector	First Plan	Second Plan	Third Plan
Agriculture	10	7	14
Community development	5	4	14
Irrigation and multipurpose projects	20	9	9
Power	7	9	13
Industry and mining	8	21	24
Transport and communications	24	30	20
Health, education, housing	22	18	17
Miscellaneous	4	2	3
Total[a]	100	100	100

Source: Government of India, Planning Commission, Statistics and Surveys Division, *Selected Plan Statistics* (February 1963), Table 10.

[a] Figures may not add to 100 because of rounding.

During the Second Plan, however, it was considered necessary to increase the allocation of public capital for transport and communications to 30 percent of the total in order to overcome deficiencies. This larger allocation reflected the fact that the transport system was badly congested in the last year of the First Plan, with the traffic backlog spilling over into the Second Plan period. In the Third Plan, the proportion of public investment going to transport and communications was reduced to 20 percent. (See Table 3.5.)

[8] K. L. Luthra, "Transport in a Growing Economy: Indian Experience During the First Two Five-Year Plans," United Nations Conference on the Application of Science and Technology for the Benefit of the Less Developed Areas, Geneva, 1963, p. 5.

A major part of the investment funds directed to transport was allocated to the railways. Estimates of railway needs were based on projections of the total volume of four commodities accounting for a major share of rail traffic. These included food grains, steel production, coal, and cement. Together they accounted for three-fourths of all rail traffic. Estimates of other freight traffic and of passenger travel were based on a combination of past trends plus projections of population and national product. (See Table 3.6.)

TABLE 3.6. *Public Investment for Indian Transport and Communications*

(In percent)

Type of Transport Expenditure	First Plan	Second Plan	Third Plan
Railways	47	67	60
Roads	24	16	20
Road transport	2	1	—
Ports and harbors	6	4	—
Shipping	4	4	10
Inland water transport	6	—	—
Civil air transport	6	3	4
Other transport	6	0.3	0.1
Tourism	—	0.3	0.5
Posts and telegraphs	9	4	4
Other communications	2	0.7	0.5
Total[a]	100	100	100

Source: Government of India, Planning Commission, *Selected Plan Statistics*, Statistics and Surveys Division (February 1963), Table 52.
[a] Figures may not add to 100 because of rounding.

The Indian experiment demonstrated the necessity of examining production targets in order to measure their effect on the volume of materials to be moved. In the planning stage, it was found necessary to make adjustments in production goals in order to match them with available transport capacity. A balanced program was sought by submitting production targets to the railway to obtain estimates of the transport capacity and additional investment that would be needed. Targets were brought into line with what was judged to be feasible in the transport sector.

The assumptions that freight on the railways would increase about twice as fast as national income, and that passenger travel would increase less than half as fast were very close to what happened during the Second Plan. The increase in national income during the period was 20 percent, the rise in railway freight traffic 42 percent, and the increase in passenger travel 11 percent.[9] But shortages developed because of the uneven distribution of the traffic burden. Overall figures conceal actual conditions of transport supply and demand on particular routes. Failure to establish plant locations and to estimate other geographic factors in advance meant that traffic flows could not be anticipated. As a result, serious congestion developed in certain parts of the system. For example, traffic in limestone and coal rose abruptly in areas where steel capacity was concentrated, and ultimately the inability to move coal became a major deterrent to increased steel production.

Difficulties of the Indian railways can be traced to other factors as well. Efforts have been made to retain marginal lines and marginal traffic when both might advantageously have been converted to truck and bus operations. The resistance of railways to new technology is a global occupational disease, and as a result India has been slow to realize important benefits that other forms of transport could bring to the economy and to the railways themselves. As long as the railways attempt to carry everything, they will continue to be overburdened with traffic they are not equipped to carry. This condition will persist regardless of how much investment is allocated to ease the congestion.[10]

Indian planning has not regarded road transport with anything like the concern it has shown for the railways. The reason is partly that road transport is a powerful competitor of government-owned railways and therefore viewed more as a threat than an opportunity. Another reason is that the railways make a better case for

[9] Government of India, Planning Commission, *The Third Five-Year Plan, A Draft Outline* (1960), pp. 17, 243.

[10] The next chapter will discuss what railways and other methods of transport are best suited to carry.

their needs, with their good statistical records, capable staff, and planning operations. Road transport, by way of contrast, is relatively disorganized and lacks both the political power and the personnel to make a persuasive case for its needs. The dispersal and individual ownership of road transport and the historic neglect of roads prior to the introduction of motor vehicles add to the difficulties. The road system of the subcontinent received little attention in the colonial period. Some road projects were undertaken, but they were generally short and confined to the boundaries of local jurisdictions. The result was a patchwork, and most of the mileage was no more than earth tracks for bullock carts, passable only in the dry season.

The first major step to estimate road transport needs in India on an orderly basis was not taken until 1943. The approach was quite different from the effort to translate planning targets into railway traffic. A national highway survey was made and an improvement plan was adopted that would bring every village in any developed area within five miles of a main road. This goal, established by the Nagpur Report for postwar road development, aimed at surfacing 123,000 miles of main roads and improving another one-third of a million miles of district and village roads. Two-thirds of this objective had been accomplished by the end of the Second Plan.

Since the partition of India and Pakistan, another blueprint to cover India's road needs was drawn up, with the goal of increasing national highway mileage by 60 percent in twenty years. The new plan provides for every village in a developed area to be no more than four miles from a surfaced road, and not more than 1.5 miles from some type of road, regardless of condition. This program would give India 52 miles of road for every 100 square miles of area, or double the objective of the Nagpur Plan.[11]

The approach to road transport, then, has been entirely separate from the approach to the railways. Rail needs were based largely on existing traffic, plus traffic resulting from further de-

[11] See Government of India, Planning Commission, *The Second Five-Year Plan, Draft Outline* (1956), p. 145.

velopment, which it was assumed would move by rail. Road improvements were planned on the basis of geographical considerations and physical inadequacies, and goals were not related to specific estimates of traffic to be moved. Mechanized road traffic was new and played only a limited role. And in contrast to the rail program, which involved some 10,000 miles of line, road needs were spread over a system of nearly half a million miles. Work on them was justified on the probability that new traffic would be generated if roads were built, and not on the grounds that building specific roads would help accommodate the transport demands of the development program.

Estimating Pakistan Transport Needs

The Pakistan Planning Board, as it was called in the early years of the nation's life, provides another example of how the planning process gets underway and of the obstacles to its realization. As in India, an accumulation of urgent needs had to be met at the outset, and for several years this left little opportunity for long-range planning. During these years, the Planning Board was an advisory body only, without power to follow up, evaluate, or enforce its program. In addition to these disadvantages, the absence of qualified personnel made it extremely difficult to launch immediately into a complex planning operation that required a high degree of professional competence. The Ford Foundation and the Harvard Advisory Service helped provide staff to get the First Five Year Plan on paper, but it was in many respects only a paper plan.

With the creation of Pakistan, ancient avenues of trade and communications had been severed, and vast new needs for transport investment had been created. New ports were required, the rail system had to be rebuilt, and the country faced an almost complete lack of road transport. Many essential commodities once supplied domestically shifted overnight to international trade, and long-established markets and sources of supply were suddenly lost.

Division of the country into two parts separated by a thousand miles compounded the problem of communications, which was resolved only by air travel and the long sea route around India and Ceylon.

Because of the nature of these conditions, many of the proposals for transport investment to be undertaken in the period of the First Plan were so pressing that the resulting program could hardly be called a plan. The process of determining what was to be done was one of paring down the long lists of what various transport agencies of the government, and especially the railways, claimed to be necessary. When these claims were weighed against those of all the other sectors of the economy, the First Plan allocated 24 percent of public capital to transport and communications. Sixty percent of this was for the rehabilitation of the railways and the construction of new port facilities.[12] (See Table 3.7.)

It is not clear whether this proportion of the Pakistan investment plan for transport was too much or too little. But due to the

TABLE 3.7. *Allocation of Public Investment in Pakistan*[a]

(In percent)

Sector	First Plan[b]	Second Plan
Agriculture	14.3 (Agriculture and Village aid combined)	14.4
Village aid		4.2
Water and power	29.7	27.3
Industry	13.6 (Industry and Fuels and minerals combined)	10.2
Fuels and minerals		2.6
Transportation and communications	24.4	18.3
Housing and settlements	12.4	11.5
Education and training	4.0	7.7
Health	1.4	3.0
Manpower and social service	0.2	0.8
Total	100.0	100.0

Source: Government of Pakistan, Planning Commission, *The Second Five-Year Plan* (1960), p. 408.
[a] Includes amount contributed by the government to the semi-public sector under the Second Plan.
[b] First Plan implementation figures were adjusted to Second Plan definition of development expenditures.

[12] Government of Pakistan, National Planning Board, *The First Five-Year Plan* (1957), p. 491.

backlog of transport demands, strict priorities had to be imposed on rail transport, and the growth of road transport was unequal to the tasks imposed. These facts indicate the extent of the needs that were unmet, but they do not necessarily measure the adequacy or inadequacy of planning objectives. For the use of funds within the transport field was often poorly conceived and ineffectively carried out.

Not all the money allocated to the transport rehabilitation program during the First Plan was spent. In East Pakistan, for example, no part of the inland water transport plan was carried out, due to organizational difficulties. This added to the burden on the railways. In addition, other investments that might have alleviated transport difficulties were not completed. The plan called for an adequate storage system for food grains, but this was not provided. These omissions added to the gap between the capacity of the rail system and the mounting volume of traffic that accompanied the expansion of such products as textiles, paper, chemicals, and cement, and the heavy importation of food grains.

Other factors helped to avert more serious congestion on the railways. Most important, only half the originally projected increase in national output was realized, with a consequent depressing effect on traffic volume. Secondly, the discovery of natural gas and the introduction of pipeline transport relieved the railways of a heavy burden of oil and coal traffic. Two sixteen-inch pipes from the Sui fields in Baluchistan south to Karachi and north to Multan were in 1957 delivering the equivalent of a quarter of a million tons of fuel oil.

As events unfolded, the Pakistan transport program was not well tailored to the problems the development plan was creating. As in India, part of the problem was the failure to locate and measure probable increases in traffic that would be likely to result from developments programed in various sectors. The tendency was to seek the improvement of everything that was antiquated or in a state of disrepair, on the grounds that this in itself was evidence of the need for rehabilitation.

The railways received the major share of investment allocated to transport partly because they were already the principal transport medium, and often the only one, but also, perhaps, because the railways were in the best position to establish their claims. As in India, the railways had the staff, the organization, and the data. Conversely, the disorganization of other transport agencies made it difficult to make the necessary presentation and to support estimates of need with facts. In any event, individual and separate estimates of need by each transport agency made it impossible to arrive at a logical overall transport plan. Whether the emphasis on transport was too much or too little may have been less important than whether the total allocation was spent for the kinds of transport that were needed in the places where the need was greatest. (See Table 3.8 for public investment in transport.)

TABLE 3.8. *Public Investment for Pakistan Transport*

(In percent)

Transport Sector	First Plan[a]	Second Plan[b]
Ports	9.1	0.9
Shipping	4.4	0.1
Inland water transport	5.9	—
Railways	48.0	59.2
Roads	25.3	33.6
Road transport	1.8	—
Civil aviation	5.5	6.2
Total	100.0	100.0

Source: Government of Pakistan, National Planning Board, *The First Five-Year Plan (1955–60)*, Draft, Vol. II (May 1956), p. 357; *The Second Five-Year Plan (1960–65)* (Revised estimates, November 1961), p. 279.

[a] Allocation of public resources before implementation.

[b] Does not include amount contributed by the government to semi-public sector.

The first real effort to relate the transport function to the development program was made after the First Five-Year Plan began, and was accomplished by the railways rather than the Planning Board. This study was undertaken to determine the probable increase in rail traffic that could be expected in West Pakistan if the programed expansion of economic activity under the First

Five-Year Plan were achieved. Each of the commodity targets included in the national plan was analyzed to determine how much would move and what would be the probable origins and destinations of the materials transported. The resulting traffic flows were then added to existing traffic in both directions along 1,800 miles of railway routes. The study assumed that transport would be entirely by rail, and did not include the possibilities of alternative transport media.[13]

The results showed that under the assumed 20 percent increase in national income, the railway system of West Pakistan would be called on to carry a 28 percent increase in railway traffic. The analysis also provided traffic data for individual routes, thus identifying probable bottlenecks and establishing priorities for investment. This route-by-route analysis revealed that traffic increases on some routes would be as high as 100 to 200 percent.

The railway report was a step in the right direction, for it built traffic estimates from the ground up on the basis of the specific production goals of the proposed plan. It should have been possible to limit the products studied since 57 percent of what moved on the railways of West Pakistan was coal and coke, cement, food grains, and firewood. Potential bottlenecks and priorities for improvement could have been identified by projecting these items of traffic in detail and using past relationships between traffic and national income for the balance. A further weakness of the study was the assumption that all increases in traffic would be accommodated by rail.

The transport program continued to be distorted by the fact that each method of transport was submitting its own separate estimates of need. It was impossible out of these estimates to arrive at a total program that reflected a considered choice of alternatives. In East Pakistan the reliance to be placed on road, rail, and inland water transport required that the problem be looked at as a whole, but there was no agency in the government in a position

[13] Abdul Qadir, "An Assessment of the Traffic Development on the North Western Railway 1955–60," *Northwest Railway* (April 6, 1960).

to take such a look. In addition, there were many engineering questions left unanswered concerning the feasibility of construction in areas of extensive flooding, the problems of bridging untamed rivers, the possibilities of inland and coastal water transport, the role that might be played by air transport, and the relative advantages of rail and road.

There was also an absence of communications between those planning the development programs in agriculture and industry and those responsible for transport development. In addition, the Planning Commission (formerly called the Planning Board) was in a weak position, even if it were adequately staffed, to pass judgment on the experts in other agencies who submitted separate estimates for rail, water, and road transport. By the time these needs had been submitted to the commission, much of the opportunity to weigh alternatives had already passed.

The magnitude of the transport problem facing the Planning Commission led to the conclusion that government efforts to deal with these matters required the assistance of outside consultants. With the financial assistance of the United States, surveys were undertaken to determine in greater detail the transport deficiencies and requirements of Pakistan within the framework of its long-range development plans.[14] The resulting reports on both East and West Pakistan provided a large mass of statistical information that filled several volumes. The field work was accomplished in great detail, and proposed transport improvements were enumerated for a twenty-year master plan that extended to 1980.

Despite the thoroughness of these undertakings, it is difficult to avoid the uneasy feeling that this may not really be the most helpful approach. The effort to cover every topic seems to have been carried out at the expense of detailed and readily usable analyses of high-priority projects. Despite the discussion of production targets, a convincing translation of these economic trends

[14] See U. S. Department of the Army, Corps of Engineers, *Transport Survey of East Pakistan* (1961); U.S. Department of the Army, Office of the Chief of Engineers, *Transportation Survey of West Pakistan* (1962).

into transport requirements was not accomplished, and the relationships between transport and other development goals were not given the attention they deserved. Even key questions of the relative merits of road, rail, air, and highway transport were bypassed, and separate estimates of need for each method of transport were presented instead.

Pakistan has thus had the advantage of an official national plan, an active planning commission, and the assistance of an engineering survey of transport needs. Yet it cannot be said that there is a blueprint for the country's transport program that really answers the difficult questions that are involved. Transport surveys have established some of the physical dimensions of the problem, and overall plans have provided a guiding framework, but neither has shed real light on what transport is needed, nor on the appropriate roles to be played by alternative transport technologies.

Relating Transport to Other Programs

It is apparent from efforts to date that there are many weaknesses in efforts to judge the need for transport. One of these is the failure to consider the possibility of decisions outside the transport field that can significantly affect the nature of the transport problem and its solution. Transport needs are created by what takes place outside the transport field, and ways to meet these needs may also be found in other sectors. The selection of economic activities, the location of industries, the processing and storage of perishables, the generation and transmission of power, and the establishment of communications—all these and many other aspects of development have a vital role in determining the nature and level of transport investment. To look at the transport system alone is to approach the problem with blinders.

Alternative courses of action in agriculture, industry, or other sectors can result in different requirements for transportation. The transport burden may be substantially greater under one set of goals than under another. In planning transport requirements, therefore, an effort should be made to weigh the transport aspects of activities in other sectors. Developing nations are in a position to influence the demand for transport facilities as well as their supply. The opportunity that is offered is particularly important when scientific innovations are rapidly introducing new materials, new energy sources, new industries, and new approaches to getting things done.

Energy Resources Policy

The movement of mineral fuels absorbs a substantial proportion of total transport capacity in most countries. Coal for the railways and for industrial users and utilities often accounts for as much as 25 to 40 percent of total railway traffic. For this reason, a nation's energy policies will be a major factor in determining transport requirements. And the economic advantages and disadvantages of alternative energy policies will have to take into account the different transport burdens involved.

The railways of India, for example, are heavily congested with coal movements, and an estimated $2 billion in railway investment will be required to meet the anticipated growth in coal transport during the next decade. One-third of the coal tonnage is for use by the railways themselves, so that electrification or conversion to diesel power would greatly reduce the volume of coal to be transported. Further reductions might be accomplished through the development of natural gas and nuclear power. Even at present high costs, nuclear energy might permit substantial savings in equipment requirements, reduce railway congestion, and help to avoid the obsolescence of expanded rail facilities that would eventually result with the later introduction of nuclear power.

In Pakistan, the lack of rail equipment has restricted coal production, and it has frequently been necessary to deliver coal in box cars. Oil is sometimes moved in drums because of the lack of tank cars. Part of the problem is being solved by the construction of hydroelectric plants and part by the exploitation of natural gas. Hydroelectric installations have substituted investment in electric transmission lines for investment in coal-carrying equipment, which for large power supply is more economical than hauling solid fuels. The use of pipelines for moving natural gas has also greatly reduced surface transport of coal and oil. The economic trade-offs in the fields of energy resources and transport are, in any event, formidable, and the pay-offs promised by combined planning are obvious.

Food Preservation and Processing

Other investments that can alter the demand for transport include facilities for the storage, processing, and preservation of agricultural products. Because of the predominant role of agriculture in underdeveloped countries, the demand for transport is highly seasonal, and peak tonnages at harvest time create extraordinary pressures on transport facilities. It may be possible to reduce these peaks by investing in adequate storage. This solution may be relatively inexpensive, yet as effective in stretching transport capabilities as investment in transport itself.

The point is illustrated by the arrival of grain shipments at Karachi, which often disrupts transport on the North Western Railway as cars are rushed to the port and other demands for transport left unfilled. One solution is to buy more cars and increase rail capacity. Another less costly remedy may be found in providing a place to store grain, which can then be moved onto the system gradually as rail capacity becomes available. Warehouses located in consuming areas may also be desirable to reduce transport demands at times when the railway system is over-burdened.[15]

The rapid movement of perishables of all kinds poses a difficult

[15] See Abdul Aziz Hussein and Omar Foda, "Progress in the Conservation of Surplus Agriculture and Fishery Products in the U.A.R.," United Nations Conference on Science and Technology, Geneva, 1963, p. 3.

problem for the transport system. Refrigerated transport and speedy delivery cannot be expected in underdeveloped countries without substantial investment. An effective alternative, however, may be supplied by establishing plants close to sources of supply where food can be processed. The movement of livestock provides a similar problem. Long journeys and slow transport cause substantial weight losses on the way to market, reducing the availability of meat and the price obtained by farmers. The journey from Quetta to Karachi results in an average loss of eight pounds per head of sheep, but the cost of speeding up transport to cut these losses is prohibitive. The ultimate solution appears to be the location of slaughtering establishments close to producing areas.

A number of devices are available for preserving food and thus reducing the need for investing in refrigerated transport and high-speed transit. They include age-old techniques of sun-drying, pickling, salting, or par-boiling as well as new techniques of radiation, dehydration, and antibiotics. Preserving perishables through dehydration has a special advantage in tropical climates where high temperatures make it difficult to preserve fresh foodstuffs by refrigeration. Various techniques for prompt dehydration include application of heat directly or through the medium of air or gas and spraying dry air directly over foodstuffs. Such methods reduce the volume of goods to be moved as well as level the seasonal variations in traffic.[16]

Substituting Communications for Mobility

Another important possibility in policy planning is that communications may serve as a substitute for transport. As shown earlier, a century ago transport and communications were closely allied activities because communications were possible only through the transportation of messages. The Post Office in the United States has always had a keen interest in all forms of trans-

[16] M. B. Rouge, "Dehydration of Foodstuffs in Countries of the Tropical Zone," United Nations Conference on Science and Technology, Geneva, 1963.

port, from the early development of roads for rural mail routes to the payment of subsidies to airlines. With the development of telegraph and telephone services, however, the link between transportation and communications was broken. The gap was widened by radio and television.

The importance of these developments lies in the fact that whereas communication networks were extremely limited when they depended entirely on transport, now through electro-magnetic means they can provide infinitely greater coverage. Thus the limited communications capacity of the transport system can be supplemented by new methods of transmission with far greater capacity for overcoming space and time.

Classroom radio has already demonstrated the ability to multiply the effectiveness of scarce teaching personnel. Television will have increasing application in the future. These and other developments have implications for investment in transport. In the United States, for example, it was once necessary to maintain thousands of one-room schools in order to provide education for a relatively immobile population. The consolidated school with adequate teaching staff and physical plant was made possible only after an extensive roadbuilding program that permitted the transportation of pupils in school buses. Today, construction of schools alone will require a great deal of equipment and material. It has been calculated that for Ethiopia to achieve universal primary education by conventional methods it would be necessary to invest triple the present national budget.[17] Radio and television may reduce these costs substantially.

In Chile, a radio school system is being operated by the Institute of Rural Education. To date, more than 1,300 rural schools, both public and private, are receiving lessons distributed by the radio school, involving 100,000 children.[18] Similar radio systems in Colombia and Egypt provide national networks of instruction in public health, agriculture, and in reading and writing.

[17] R. Greenough, *Africa Calls,* UNESCO (Paris, 1961).

[18] Hernán Poblete Varas, "Communications and Audio-Visual Systems in Rural Education," Summary from UNCAST (1963), pp. 1–2.

It is apparent that the transistor television will introduce further improvement over the transistor radio, and that the communications function of the transport system can be supplied through the air to hasten the benefits of education and to disseminate ideas. But the attempt to provide educational television in the less developed countries involves heavy cost. A ground-based TV system involves hundreds of broadcasting stations and interconnecting microwave communications. Each station serves only about 6,000 square miles.

Now it appears that the use of an earth satellite repeater system may prove more economical than the conventional ground system with limited coverage. Programs could be transmitted to the satellite and rebroadcast directly to community sets. The total ground area over which the satellite signals could be seen would range from one to three million square miles. This would be equivalent to the size of India or Brazil, or could encompass a group of countries that might conduct television education programs jointly. The programs themselves could be nationally controlled or operated by groups of countries in the region.[19]

As communications continue to substitute in important respects for the transporting of people and ideas, some of the effects of improved personal mobility that once took years to accomplish can be achieved almost overnight.

Industrial Location and Urban Planning

The importance of considering the implications of investments outside the transport field are also apparent in industrial location and urban planning policies. In newly industrializing countries development policy makers have an opportunity to locate factories and other industrial establishments where unnecessary transport burdens can be avoided. Heavy industry should have access to water transport, and industrial sites should be selected to balance

[19] N. I. Korman and A. Katz, "Television Broadcasting from Satellites," American Rocket Society, 17th Annual Meeting, Los Angeles, California, Nov. 13–18, 1962.

the flow of railway traffic. Site planning on a national basis could make it possible, in conjunction with the development of modern transport, to avoid the overconcentration and congestion typical of countries that industrialized in the railway age.

Rapid industrialization and urbanization have already introduced critical problems of mobility in the large cities of developing countries. Congestion in major urban centers is not only reducing the efficiency of economic activities but is requiring heavy capital investments in highways, buses, and rail facilities. Asia has more large cities and more people living in them than either North America or Europe. Out of 866 cities in the world with 100,000 or more persons, 289 are Asian. Much of Asian urbanization is not the product of industrialization, but has occurred without it and has created slums that have posed a threat to development.[20]

Further growth of population and industrialization will add to the potential concentration of economic activity in urban areas. In many underdeveloped countries, the rate of urban growth is far greater than in the more developed areas of Europe and North America. Between 1900 and 1950, for example, while the large city population of North America and Europe was increasing by 160 percent, the urban population of Asia grew 444 percent. Despite this rapid growth rate, however, the underdeveloped areas still have the lowest ratio of urban to total population. Asia has only 8 percent of its population in cities of 100,000 or more, compared with 21 percent in Europe and 29 percent in North America. And some countries in Asia are only in the early stages of urbanization.[21]

There is still time, then, to avoid the transport burdens of unrestrained and planless urban growth. There is good evidence that the attempt to provide adequate mobility in urban areas simply by providing better transport is doomed to costly failure. Congestion

[20] Philip H. Hauser, "Implications of Population Trends for Regional and Urban Planning in Asia," *ECAFE Working Paper No. 2*, Seminar on Regional Planning, Tokyo, July–August 1958, p. 9.

[21] *Ibid.*

plagues all big cities, whether they are products of the motor age or are well supplied with subway and rail transport. Congestion is created by putting too many people and too much economic activity in one place, and basic solutions will be found only in avoiding densities and arrangements of land use that create these conditions. The attempt to supply transport services to meet whatever demands arise in an unplanned metropolis has cost a great deal and has failed to solve the problem.

Newly developing countries are in a position to profit by the mistakes that western industrialized countries have made in permitting uncontrolled growth of cities. This can be done in part by national plans designed to establish the location and size of cities, by land-use plans that avoid unnecessary transport and undesirable congestion, by public land acquisition policies that maintain open spaces, and by zoning and industrial location policies that take freight and passenger problems into account.

Within the city itself, there is the further need for development plans that will enhance living conditions and minimize the amount of necessary movement. Planning can be aimed at land use patterns that reduce excessive and costly street mileage, that separate motor traffic from other transport, and that accommodate the pedestrian and cyclist. In new and expanding urban areas, land can be reserved in advance for parks and recreation areas, for industrial sites, for transport rights of way, and for a variety of other public purposes. Rail yards and terminals can be located outside the city to avoid traffic congestion and to release space for more advantageous uses. But major importance should be attached to industrial location as the key to decentralization and limitation of the size of the metropolis. Only by dispersal of employment opportunities will it be possible to achieve a closer relation among home, work, and community facilities, and to reduce the time-consuming journey to work.[22]

[22] The land-use planning approach to urban transport problems is discussed in Wilfred Owen, *The Metropolitan Transportation Problem* (Brookings Institution, 1956), pp. 218–48.

In underdeveloped areas, it is still possible through central government planning of transport, industry, and employment opportunities to minimize the growth of unmanageable cities. Removal of the capital of Brazil from congested Rio de Janeiro to the new city of Brasilia illustrates the extreme steps being taken to avoid the older congested urban centers and to seek a balanced regional development. The shift of Pakistan's capital from Karachi 700 miles north to Islamabad is another move to avoid over-concentration. The transport impacts and other effects of these policies will have to be analyzed as the new cities become established, to provide guides for future urbanization policy.

Regional Economic Integration

The approach to economic cooperation and regional trade, as exemplified by the European Common Market, has important implications for the projection of transport requirements in developing areas. At present the domestic markets of less developed countries are not large enough to support industries depending on economies of scale for efficient operation. Some industries such as food processing and textiles may exist even though domestic markets are not large, but others that require a highly advanced technology and large amounts of capital cannot survive profitably without access to mass markets.

Regional cooperation through mobilization of capital and creation of integrated markets can lead to the manufacture of goods that would otherwise have to be imported. For example, a country's market may be large enough to absorb the output of a motor vehicle assembly plant, but it may be too small to establish efficient production of parts and components within its territory. These subsidiary industries must be able to take advantage of economies of scale if they are to supply equipment at low cost. In these circumstances, there is need for a program of integrated industrial development through cooperation among neighboring countries.

The high cost of distributing agricultural produce and differences in the cost of producing wheat, sugar, and cotton in various parts of South and Central America also illustrate the importance of charting the transport future on a regional basis. In some areas where production of these commodities is more efficient, output has to be curtailed for lack of markets. Elsewhere inefficient production is carried on at high cost on land that could be used to better purpose if the availability of transport made trading possible.[23]

The potentials of Latin American regional development and trade are measured by the fact that only 10 percent of international commerce is now accounted for within the area itself, while the other 90 percent is with Europe and the United States.[24] Actually, trade between adjacent countries is often more difficult than between continents. Yet for many Latin American countries, the success of development lies in the possibility of markets larger than domestic economies can support.

Part of the communications network essential to closer economic ties has already been provided by the identity of language and culture. But a united Latin America will not be realized without an extraordinary effort to plan, organize, and finance the principal surface and air connections on which closer regional ties depend. The task is no longer one of looking at the transport needs of each country separately, but of all countries regionally. The preparation of long-term development plans being fostered through the Alliance for Progress sets the stage for a broader concept of Latin America's future.

Regional organizations have been established or are in the process of formation in many parts of the world. The countries of Central America have already taken significant steps to lower interregional trade barriers and to stimulate internal development and

[23] *Latin American Development Difficulties,* Commercio Exterior de Mexico (October 1960), p. 6.

[24] Jan Tinbergen, *Shaping the World Economy* (Twentieth Century Fund, 1962), p. 250.

export through the Central American Free Trade Area. The motivation for the trade area was to meet the urgent need to develop resources, to alleviate unemployment, and to increase consumption of goods produced within the region. Trade barriers have been eliminated for more than half the commerce among the member countries, with more to come down by 1965; external tariffs have been standardized on more than 80 percent of all imported commodities.

The establishment of the Central American Bank for Economic Integration has been one of the most important steps taken by the Central American republics. Guatemala, El Salvador, Honduras, and Nicaragua have each contributed part of the original capital, together with support from the United States. The bank has also received a loan from the Inter-American Development Bank. Industrial developments financed through the bank include rubber tire and tube manufacture in Guatemala, copper wire and cable production in El Salvador, and facilities to produce insecticides in Nicaragua. The output of such items will be sold throughout the Central American region, a market of approximately 11 million people. The Central American Common Market grants to selected companies the exclusive concessions for certain essential industries, with the objective of discouraging more than one company from producing the same items, and of encouraging new industries by granting them a preferred position.

The Latin American Free Trade Association (LAFTA) came into being in 1960 with the Treaty of Montevideo and now includes the countries of Argentina, Brazil, Chile, Mexico, Paraguay, Peru, Uruguay, Colombia, and Ecuador. This nine-nation grouping embraces about 82 percent of the total Latin American population. Members of LAFTA have agreed to establish free trade among them within twelve years. Tariff reductions are to be achieved through multilateral yearly negotiations. Two such conferences have already been held, resulting in a tariff reduction of over 30 percent on 7,000 items moving in intraregional trade.

Although the reduced tariff schedules have been in effect only a short time, regional commerce has already increased substantially.

The negotiation of broad economic links has also begun for twenty sub-Sahara African countries through the Lagos Charter setting up the Organization of Africa and Malagasy State.[25] Common market schemes are also under consideration by the Casablanca group of African countries, consisting of Ghana, Guinea, Morocco, Mali, the United Arab Republic, and Algeria, and by the three Asian countries, the Philippines, Malaya, and Indonesia.

Further moves toward integrated economic development are being suggested by national planning efforts, which reveal the possibilities of cooperative development projects, and through potential improvements in transport and communications, which make economic development on a regional basis feasible. From a development standpoint, this means that the country survey is often too narrow in concept. International studies covering a much wider geographic area will have to supplement and revise efforts to determine transport requirements on a national basis.

[25] Nigeria, Liberia, Sierra Leone, Mauritania, Senegal, Ivory Coast, Niger, Dahomey, Volta Republic, Cameroon, Togo, Central African Republic, Somalia, Chad, the former French Congo, Gabon, Congo, Tanganyika, Ethiopia, and the Malagasy Republic.

CHAPTER IV

Choice of Transport Technology

DEVELOPING COUNTRIES have access to new technology that may enable them to break away from the slow evolutionary process of transport improvement and to reduce the time and resources needed to overcome the time-space barrier. In choosing the appropriate transport technology, countries should be guided by consideration of five sets of factors: the trends in transport methods today; comparative transport costs and capabilities; the broader influences of transport costs on production and distribution costs; the net effects on development of the several methods of transport; and the further potentials of transport innovation that may alter the cost and quality of the several methods of transport in the foreseeable future. All of these factors need to be weighed in arriving at choices of transport methods to promote maximum economic progress.

How the World Moves

Similar trends in transport prevail throughout the world. In nearly all countries goods movement by truck for short hauls and small shipments has become a major element in the transport system. For low-value bulk commodities that move in large volumes, water transport and railways still provide the principal method of getting things moved. Other trends that are becoming general throughout the world include the long-distance movement of passengers by airplane and reliance on pipeline transport for the movement of gas and oil. Both of these relatively new developments have added important new elements to traditional transport methods.

Three types of transport patterns have emerged from these trends. One is characteristic of the economically advanced countries—the United States, Canada, and Western Europe; another is found in densely populated countries such as Japan, India, and Pakistan, as well as in the Soviet Union and other Communist countries; a third is typical of the less populated undeveloped countries. In some respects, these patterns reflect different stages in an evolutionary process; in others, geography, population, and income levels provide the basis for the particular approach to meeting transport needs.

Trends in the United States illustrate the transport matrix emerging in an affluent society. Freight traffic in 1960 was double that in 1940. Every method of transport shared in this growth, but some grew more than others. Rail transport increased by 53 percent and water transport by 89 percent. But pipeline traffic increased 286 percent, while truck transport expanded 383 percent. As a result of different rates of growth, the railways' share of total freight movement dropped from 61 percent in 1940 to 44 percent twenty years later. Pipelines and trucks, which accounted for 20 percent of total ton-miles in 1940, were handling 40 percent in 1960. Water carriers showed a steady growth, but at the end of the two decades accounted for nearly the same share of traffic as at the beginning. (See Table A.3.)

Technological changes in passenger travel resulted in even greater shifts in American transport methods. The automobile greatly expanded total travel volume, and in 1963 accounted for nearly nine out of every ten passenger-miles. The volume of travel in public carriers also continued to rise, with a doubling of traffic between 1940 and 1960. The railways did not share in the expansion, however. Train travel declined steadily, and the railway share of the passenger business dropped from 64 percent to 28 percent. Bus travel in 1960 was above the 1940 level but below 1950 and still declining. Air transport was the major factor in the expansion of passenger transport. The volume of air travel was 34 times higher in 1960 than it had been two decades before. (See Table A.3.)

Canadian and West European experience has been quite similar. In Western Europe, however, some variations from North American experience have resulted from lower income levels, a higher density of population, shorter distances between major urban areas, and geographically smaller national units. European trends similar to those in North America include the general increase in passenger and freight traffic by all methods, the rapid growth of motor truck transport relative to rail, the stable position of water transport in the total picture, and the rapid shift of energy resources to pipelines. The outstanding differences are a continuing rise in rail passenger travel where population densities are high, and limited dependence on air travel where good rail service over intermediate distances eliminates the time advantage of air travel between city centers.

There are some industrialized countries, however, with a very different transport pattern. The Soviet Union and Japan place much greater reliance on railways for both passenger and freight traffic, and they began the shift to road, air, and pipeline transport much later than the West. The Soviet rail system carries 77 percent of intercity freight, and Japan's system is largely railway-oriented.[1]

In the less developed countries that have dense population and extensive area, too, transport is rail-oriented, as shown in Table 4.1. Other developing countries with lower population densities have placed more reliance on roads. These transport trends are

[1] For Soviet experience, see Table A.4. For Japan's intercity freight traffic, see Table 4.1.

TABLE 4.1. *Freight Traffic, Selected Asian Countries, 1957*

(Freight traffic in thousands of ton-kms.)

Country	Total Freight Traffic			*Percent Distribution*		
	Rail[a]	Road	Water[b]	*Rail*	*Road*	*Water*
India	73,415	4,550	5,950	*88*	*5*	*7*
Japan	48,991	13,724	41,000	*47*	*13*	*40*
Pakistan	6,684	438	4,960	*55*	*4*	*41*
Thailand	1,025	780	500	*44*	*34*	*22*
Burma	621	388	1,400	*26*	*16*	*58*
Indonesia	1,044	1,568	3,491	*17*	*26*	*57*
Philippines	190	1,558	300	*9*	*76*	*15*
Vietnam (South)	82	350	1,210	*5*	*21*	*74*
Cambodia	62	126	400	*11*	*21*	*68*

Source: *Economic Development and Planning in Asia and the Far East, VI. Transport Development*, U.N. Economic Bulletin for Asia and the Far East, Vol. XI, No. 3 (December 1960), pp. 6–7.

[a] Road traffic is estimated by multiplying the following assumed annual performance by the number of registered vehicles by type:

Year	Type of Vehicle	Capacity	Rate of Performance	Average Distance Traveled	Annual Performance
1957	Bus	30 pass.	0.80	40,000 km.	960,000 pass. km.
	Passenger cars	5 pass.	0.40	12,500 km.	24,000 pass. km.
	Truck	2½ tons	0.50	20,000 km.	35,000 ton-km.

[b] Except in the case of Japan, Indonesia, and the Philippines, water transport refers to inland waterway traffic only, figures of which are worked out largely on the basis of the estimates of the number of vessels, inland country-boats, the average load factor and informed opinion regarding the average length and number of journeys performed annually. For Japan, Indonesia, and the Philippines figures refer to interinsular freight traffic. In the case of Indonesia and the Philippines, estimates are made by multiplying actual tonnage carried by an average haul of 500 kms. for Indonesia and 200 kms. for the Philippines.

reflected in present or proposed investment decisions of developing countries. In most countries road construction dominates the picture. Over the next decade, Colombia expects the road program to absorb 74 percent of public investment funds allocated to transport, Senegal 72 percent, and Iran 68 percent. In a lesser number of countries, the principal focus will be on rail transport. Argentina, for example, expects to allocate 55 percent of transport investment for this purpose in the sixties.

In all developing countries the combination of road and railway investments absorbs most of the resources allocated to transport. In Argentina the two together comprise 93 percent of the transport program and in Colombia 87 percent. Ports, airports, and waterways call for relatively minor outlays. When private capital expenditures are added, the picture remains much the same. These investments may include aircraft, ships, motor vehicles, and pipelines, with the motor vehicle representing the major item privately financed. (See Table A.5.)

These are the ways the world is moving today. But the transport trends of the future will not be simply a continuation of the past. The nature of transport methods and the patterns of transport investment will depend on costs and performance resulting from technological change, and on the changing character of the transport tasks to be performed.

The Economy of Water Transport

In early stages of development, low-income countries are predominantly producers of staple commodities with a low market value. The difference between this value and the cost of production is small, which means that the amount of transport cost that can be covered is also small. Economical methods of transport are important, therefore, if a nation is to produce and move such products as wheat, rice, jute, palm kernels, groundnuts, coffee, or bananas. Unprocessed minerals and forest products will likewise be able to bear only relatively small transport charges.

Waterways can provide cheap transport for many purposes on both long and short hauls with a minimum investment and without importing equipment. Home-made country boats often provide a place to live as well as a means of transport. In Southeast Asia boats of every description ply the rivers and canals, propelled by oars, poles, sails, or by men pulling from the shore. Recently the klongs of Bangkok and the network of rivers emptying into the Indian Ocean have seen the outboard motor take over to speed home-made craft. Mechanization has drastically cut the transit time for farmers, who once took many days to paddle their produce to market. On the main streams, too, motorized launches and barges are providing high-capacity movements over substantial distances at a third of the cost of land transport.

Most of the long-haul carriers on inland rivers haul bulk materials such as fuels, building materials, and agricultural commodities. Half of the traffic moving by common carrier on the waterways of East Pakistan in 1960 was jute, 27 percent fuels and building materials, and 13 percent rice and food grains. These commodities together accounted for 90 percent of the tonnage moved. In Nigeria, the picture is much the same, with 70 percent of the downstream Niger River traffic comprising groundnuts and palm kernels, and most of the balance consisting of other agricultural commodities. On the return voyage upstream, 51 percent of the traffic is cement and 19 percent salt.[2]

The attraction of water transport lies in the fact that waterways are provided by nature, and they furnish a ready-made artery of commerce that needs only to be protected from silting and properly marked for safe navigation. Where adequate channel maintenance and navigational aids are not provided, however, capacity is often greatly reduced by inability to move at night or during the dry season. High costs may also result from equipment that is old and inefficient, from inadequate port facilities, and from inefficient methods of loading and unloading. Where river transport has to be combined with rail and road transport to serve points off the waterway, the time and cost of transshipment are often excessive, and the economy of water movement may be canceled.

Public investment in waterways is generally not charged to waterway users, so that their costs do not represent total costs. But even if such charges were included, it has been found that water carriers operating under the most adverse conditions in the United States have a substantial cost advantage over railroads operating under the most favorable cost conditions. The fully distributed costs of river barge transport have been estimated at

[2] See U. S. Department of the Army, Corps of Engineers, *Transportation Survey of East Pakistan* (1961), Table p. 54; and Stanford Research Institute, *The Economic Coordination of Transport Development in Nigeria* (1961), p. 216.

about one-fifth of a cent per ton-mile, in 1952–55 prices. Equivalent rail costs, assuming no empty return movement, were twice as much per ton-mile. Thus the economy of water transport for bulk movement of commodities that do not require prompt delivery is sufficient to absorb all terminal and transshipment costs and still remain below rail costs.[3]

Changing technology is revolutionizing the efficiency of waterborne commerce. The barge and towing vessel have introduced greater power and capacity to serve the growing number of industries that involve mass consumption of raw materials and mass output. Diesel-powered air-conditioned tow boats more than two hundred feet long can push twenty barges at a time in tows a quarter of a mile long. A single barge can carry as much as a million gallons of petroleum products, and many tows deliver eight million gallons at a time. This compares with a capacity of 1.2 million gallons for a railway train of a hundred of the largest tank cars. The economy of barge transport is indicated by the fact that a gallon of crude oil can move 1,700 miles by water from ocean port to inland refinery for less than the cost of moving a gallon of gasoline ten miles from the refinery by truck.

The turn-around time for a towboat arriving in port to deliver a tow and pick up another has now been reduced from one or two days to one hour. The modern towboat has radar to give the pilot a constant map of the river, depth finders, and long and short-wave radio for communication with other boats and with the home office. Great increases in efficiency have resulted from the shift from steam power to diesel, and from side wheels to propellers.

Newly developing countries will find modern water transport increasingly important as industrialization introduces steel mills, chemicals, cement, power plants, aluminum production, paper mills, petroleum refining, and other economic activities to which water transport is particularly well adapted. New types of vehicles, further mechanization, and the use of electronics for

[3] John R. Meyer and Associates, *The Economics of Competition in the Transportation Industries* (Harvard University Press, 1959), pp. 147–48.

navigation can thus expand the role of water transport in many parts of the world.

Railways and Industrialization

In the absence of water transport, the railway provides the most economical way of carrying heavy bulk materials long distances, and in many countries, the railway system is the principal method of mechanized movement. Indeed, railways and industrialization have gone hand in hand in the United States, Europe, the Soviet Union, Canada, and Japan. Many of the less developed countries, too, for example Argentina, India, and Pakistan, have extensive railway networks inherited from former colonial periods.

Yet the railways of the world are concentrated to a surprising degree in a few countries. Two-thirds of all rail mileage is in Europe and North America. Thirteen countries account for nearly 99 percent of the world's total rail freight, and two countries, the United States and the Soviet Union, handle 73 percent of it. If the rail systems of China and India are omitted from the inventory of rail traffic in less developed countries, the rest of the developing areas account for only 1 percent of the world total. (See Table 4.2.)

Freight movement by railway throughout the world in the decade of the fifties increased 64 percent. The relative increase for Asia was an impressive 223 percent, accounted for largely by the growing industrialization of China, Japan, and India. But three-quarters of the world increase in railway activity occurred not in the developing countries but in Eastern Europe, where expanding traffic reflected a delayed postwar rehabilitation plus the official discouragement of road transport in areas of Soviet influence. Elsewhere, rail traffic in South America was up 12 percent, in Africa the increase was 64 percent, and in North America traffic registered a 1 percent decline. (See Table 4.3.)

TABLE 4.2. *Concentration of Rail Lines and Rail Freight, 1960*

(Selected countries)

Country	Miles of Rail Lines (In thousands)	Billions of Ton-Miles	*Percent of World Rail Freight*
Union of Soviet Socialist Republics	76.8	934.8	*47.2*
United States	218.1	519.1	*26.2*
China (mainland)	19.5	164.8	*8.3*
Canada	43.9	59.4	*3.0*
India	35.2	43.0[a]	*2.2*
Poland	16.7	41.4	*2.1*
France	24.2	35.4	*1.8*
West Germany	22.7	35.1	*1.8*
Japan	12.7	33.5	*1.7*
Czechoslovakia	8.2	29.5	*1.5*
East Germany	10.0	20.4	*1.0*
Union of South Africa	13.6	19.2	*1.0*
United Kingdom	19.1	19.0	*1.0*
Total		1,954.6	*98.8*
World Total		1,979.0	*100.0*

Source: See Table A.6 for the length of rail lines. Rail ton-miles were converted from ton-kilometers shown in Table A.7.
[a] 1959.

TABLE 4.3. *Geographic Distribution of Rail Freight, 1950 and 1960*

(In billions of ton-miles)

Continent	1950	1960	*Percentage Change*
Africa	22	36	*63.6*
North America	593	588	*−0.9*
South America	17	19	*11.8*
Asia[a]	73	236	*223.3*
Eastern Europe[b]	385	954	*147.8*
Western Europe	108	137	*26.9*
Oceania	8	9	*12.5*
World Total	1,206	1,979	*64.1*

Source: United Nations, *Statistical Yearbook, 1957*, p. 333; and *Statistical Yearbook, 1961*, p. 332.
[a] Excludes Asian USSR.
[b] Includes Asian USSR, Bulgaria, Czechoslovakia, East Germany, Hungary, Poland, Romania, and Eastern USSR.

What do these trends imply for the future of the developing countries? Will industrialization result in a new railway age for Africa, Latin America, and the smaller countries of Asia? Is the focus on railways once evident in the West and more recently in the Soviet Union, Eastern Europe, Japan, and India the trend of the future? The answers will be found partly in what the railways do, and partly in what the technological future holds in store.

The characteristics of rail transport are illustrated by the traffic moving on the railways of East Pakistan and Nigeria. Minerals and fuels and agricultural products, mainly jute and wheat, comprise 65 percent of the total freight shipped by rail in East Pakistan. And in Nigeria, one-fourth of rail freight is groundnuts. Such movements are to be expected, of course, since these are the principal commodities that countries in early stages of development produce and need. But this is also the pattern of rail freight in the more developed countries.

At one time, the railways carried practically everything that moved overland for any distance. But in recent years, with a choice of transport methods, traffic patterns have adjusted to what the railroads are best fitted to carry. In the process, railways have become engaged predominantly in the movement of minerals, building materials, and unprocessed agricultural products. In the United States, 55 percent of rail traffic is minerals. In Eastern Europe, between 60 and 70 percent of rail freight is composed of fuel, ores, and metals. In the mid-1950's, more than half of the traffic moving on the railways of the Soviet Union was in these categories, and the addition of timber brought the total of these four items to 71 percent.[4] Other bulk commodities that can be moved cheaply and easily by rail include cement, stone, chemicals, and vegetable oils.

Conversely, there have been substantial reductions in certain types of traffic that formerly moved by rail. One of these is perishables, where alternative services were available by truck

[4] United Nations, *Economic Survey of Europe, 1956*, Chap. V, p. 6; and Chap. VI, p. 7.

and highway, another is crude petroleum and petroleum products, which have shifted from rail to pipeline, and a third is coal, where sources of energy have shifted to petroleum and natural gas. A decline in rail movement of forest products has also occurred, reflecting the economy of logging trucks, which provide complete transportation from forest site to mill without costly transshipment.[5]

Small shipments have also shifted from rail to other forms of transport in the more developed countries due to excessive handling costs. Rail movement, to be economical, requires sufficient traffic moving over a given route to permit the economy of large-scale operations. It has been estimated that under average European conditions about 350,000 tons of traffic have to be moved on a section of rail line annually to justify the facility. In the United States, it has been concluded that 500,000 tons are needed to justify building a new rail line. When traffic falls to 250,000 units per year and there is no indication of further traffic growth, it has generally been found desirable to abandon a rail facility.

These figures vary with circumstances, including topography, climate, and the availability of alternatives. But a rule of thumb is that a railway needs 1,000 tons per mile per day, and, in most newly developing countries, there are only a limited number of routes that can be expected to carry this much traffic. Mineral extraction or heavy industry may make rail facilities essential in some locations from the start. On some main routes, long-term plans for industrialization or mineral exploitation may suggest building a railway now on the assumption that such a facility will be economically justified later. Where heavy traffic volume has not yet been realized, however, it is generally preferable to rely on other forms of transport at the beginning, and to introduce railway facilities later if demand materializes.

The objective should be to avoid committing large sums of capital for railways merely in the hope that traffic will eventually require them. The point is illustrated by the fact that even in such

[5] James C. Nelson, *Railroad Transportation and Public Policy* (Brookings Institution, 1959), p. 41.

a highly industrialized country as the United States much of the railway system is uneconomical for the volume of traffic offered. Approximately 37 percent of rail mileage in the United States cannot be justified on economic grounds. Half the nation's traffic is carried on only 10 percent of the total system. On this busiest 10 percent, traffic averages 39,000 freight ton-miles per day per mile of line. The middle 60 percent has only 6,000 freight ton-miles per day per mile of line. The remaining 30 percent of the mileage, with only 555 freight ton-miles per day per mile of line is unjustified economically. A line with this volume of traffic can support only one train a week with about 4,000 tons of revenue freight.[6]

Traffic density is not the only factor to be taken into account, however. Distance to be covered is also significant, for railways become increasingly efficient with length of haul. In general, the unit cost of rail transport declines with distance because the high cost of terminal operations is spread over a greater number of ton-miles. Where carload shipments are handled at private sidings, however, the cost of terminal operations is reduced. The advantage enjoyed by the railways over the longer hauls is illustrated by the experience of the Nigerian railway. Rail operating costs for a five-ton shipment moving 10 miles is about 32 cents per mile, while a haul of 50 miles reduces this figure to about 8 cents. Hauls of 500 miles or more reduce average ton-mile costs to about 3 cents, and when larger shipments are moved, the cost is much lower for both long and short hauls.[7]

For heavy volumes of industrial raw material, the unit cost of movement by pipeline and waterway is often a fifth to a third of the cost of moving comparable volumes by rail.[8] To move such

[6] John W. Barriger, *Super-railroads for a Dynamic American Economy* (Simmons-Boardman, 1956).

[7] See Stanford Research Institute, "The Economic Coordination of Transport Development in Nigeria" (1961), p. 91. Based on the Nigerian Railway Corporation's "Memorandum" of November 1, 1960, p. 9.

[8] Where traffic exceeds 500,000 tons per year. W. M. Keller, "Phase Building of Railroads and Equipment for Less Developed Countries," in *Transportation, Science, Technology and Development*, Vol. V, U. S. papers prepared for the United Nations Conference on the Application of Science and Technology for the Benefit of the Less Developed Areas (U. S. Government Printing Office, 1963), p. 53. Cited hereinafter as *Transportation*.

traffic by truck would be four to five times more costly, and air cargo costs would be sixteen times greater, as shown in the table below.

METHOD	UNIT COST PER TON-MILE
Railway	1.0
Highway truck	4.5
Airplane	16.3
Waterway barge	0.29
Pipeline	0.21

An important question is whether these cost characteristics of rail transport are likely to hold for the future. Many technological methods already in use indicate that substantial economies in railway operations can and will be made. Among the most significant are the shift from steam locomotives to diesel-electric and the use of central traffic control systems to make one set of tracks do the work of two. Another significant development that has only begun to make its influence felt is the use of containers, which make it possible to transfer cargo quickly and cheaply from one method of transport to another. A container can be moved on a railway flat car over long distances, and then transferred to truck for the shorter haul at destination. Container traffic is also protected from pilferage and damage from handling or bad weather during transshipment. The economy of this type of operation, which permits interchange with water and air transport as well, suggests that for suitable types of commodities the railway may retain traffic in the future that might otherwise have shifted to other methods.

Motor Transport and Distribution Costs

How does it happen that a marked and nearly universal trend has developed toward road transport? The answer lies in three principal facts. First, the economy and reliability of road transport have increased very rapidly in recent years as better roads and improved vehicle performance have revolutionized overland transport. Second, on many routes with light traffic this is the only feasible method of mechanized transport. Third, as the pace of economic development quickens, the importance of transport costs declines, and there is greater concern for improved service. This in turn will have significant effects on total costs of production and distribution.

Thus far the discussion has concerned the cost of movement itself. But the concern of shippers and consumers is not with transport costs alone, but with the total costs of production and distribution. Methods of transport can have significant effects on these costs. The nature of such impacts is noted here for road and rail transport, but the service characteristics involved relate to air and water as well.

When total costs of production are considered, the economy of rail transport is often canceled by slow deliveries and other service deficiencies. For a wide range of shipments, including both perishables and high-valued manufactures, time is important. The need for larger inventories when deliveries are unreliable ties up working capital at considerable cost. Failure to obtain prompt delivery of fuel, materials, or spare parts can reduce output, shut down plants, and lose markets. Delays in delivery can cause high rates of spoilage.

Slow service is inherent in rail operations. The assembly of cars to make up a train takes time, as does the breaking down process at destination. Loading and unloading for local transfer to and from the railway add to the slowness of service. Only large shippers with sidings at their plants avoid this source of delay. But for all shippers the scheduling of trains is a source of time loss, since the railway must schedule departures at intervals long enough to permit the accumulation of an economical load.

Another limitation of the rail system is the relatively small mileage of routes that can be served economically. Industries are restricted in their choice of location, or shipments have their origin and destination at points off the rail system and cannot go all the way by rail. Even where it is possible to use the railway for some part of the journey, it may be inconvenient or uneconomical to do so because of circuitous routing or the high costs and delays of transshipment.

An advantage of motor transport is the wide geographical coverage afforded by the highway system. The length of the road network is usually far greater than that of the railways. The United States, for example, has ten times more miles of improved roads than railways. This reflects the fact that a system of roads can include low-cost facilities built for very light traffic as well as main highways designed to serve heavy traffic. Most motor vehicles can use all parts of the system, and the various parts can be improved as traffic warrants. It is good engineering practice to start with a simple design adequate for the traffic and to develop the facility through stage construction methods as demand increases. Stage construction makes sense for roads, but a railway has to be designed for substantial capacity at the outset.

The fact that trucks are able to provide a complete transport service from origin to destination is another asset that favors movement by road. The cost, delay, and inconvenience of transferring goods to another mode of transport en route or at either end of the journey are avoided. Flexibility in scheduling departures and arrivals is possible because it takes much less to fill a truck than a train. The truck moves a shipment when it is ready, or delivers the freight when it is wanted. When businesses operate their own trucks or contract for truck service they are freed from fixed schedules. Truck transport can thus be integrated into the production process through the scheduling of deliveries as needed, with consequent reduction of inventories and elimination of storage. The widespread use of trucks on construction projects illustrates the advantage of being able to get materials directly to the site in an ordered sequence.

The truck also permits a minimum of packaging and crating for the protection of shipments against breakage. In Japan, for example, trucks have become the preferred method of carrying electronic equipment from Tokyo to Nagoya and Kobe. This method has been adopted despite the fact that until recent years roads were poor and the cost of trucking high. The reason is that shunting of rail cars and rough stops and starts had resulted in heavy damage to fragile goods, and railway users were paying more for protective packaging than for transport.

Diversions to truck, then, often occur even when the railways are the low-cost carrier. The assumption that the cheaper method of transport is always to be preferred is incorrect. Although in many cases transport costs will be minimized by rail transport, often the cost of distribution will be minimized by truck.

The benefits of road transport differ with length of haul. The effect of distance on the type of carrier selected is demonstrated by a survey of the movement of fresh fruits and vegetables in the United States in the mid-fifties. Of all shipments destined for points less than 100 miles away, 88 percent moved over the highway, and only 6 percent went by rail. On trips of 1,000 miles or more, however, the railroads carried 66 percent of the total tonnage. When the length of haul extended to 2,000 miles or more, 93 percent went by rail.[9]

The motor vehicle has its disadvantages, then, as well as its merits. Some of its drawbacks are inherent, such as inadequate capacity for moving heavy volumes of bulk materials and the high costs of long hauls. Another difficulty, which may be overcome in time, is that inadequate roads cause high vehicle operating costs and excessive trip time. Service may also be interrupted by vehicle breakdowns or weather conditions that make some routes impassable part of the year. In most countries, too, the need to import vehicles and parts as well as petroleum creates a drain on the supply of foreign exchange. Finally, difficult financial problems may be created when traffic is diverted from existing railways, resulting in underutilization of investments already made and demands for new investments in roads.

[9] Donald E. Church, "Measuring Transportation Market Potentials," Transportation Research Forum, March 11, 1959, p. 9.

On balance, however, the changing composition of the demand for transport in underdeveloped areas will favor road carriers over rail for an increasing volume of traffic as economic development proceeds. In many countries, the shift will be from a predominance of coal, cement, wheat, and other bulk commodity movements in large consignments to heavier volumes of such items as agricultural implements, paints, glass, building hardware, textiles, machinery, and consumer goods of all kinds. Transport services have to be geared to a new mix of products as development creates new types of needs. Often the solution will be to substitute road services for rail.

The Potentials of Air Transport

The importance of total production and distribution costs has led to reliance on air transport in many developing countries. Although moving cargo by air is relatively high cost, it has proved economical because the airplane has been able to effect greater savings elsewhere. The availability of air services may make it possible to move perishables to market that would otherwise spoil. Livestock may be moved by air to eliminate the loss of weight that occurs on long journeys by hoof. The delivery of machinery and spare parts by air may be economical where the delay in waiting for slower transport would mean shutdowns or costly inventories. Air transport has introduced the most effective method of overcoming the barriers imposed by long distances and difficult topography. Despite its promise in a variety of other uses, however, aviation continues to be used mainly for long-distance passenger travel. Its use for short hauls and cargo movements still lags.

The principal aircraft that developing countries have at their disposal for low-cost air cargo are piston aircraft originally designed to carry passengers. These aircraft have high operating costs compared to some of the new jets, but they can be obtained for a much smaller initial capital outlay. In the United States they can move freight at average charges of about 21 cents per ton-mile, but this figure is considerably reduced when the aircraft is purchased as used equipment.

It has been estimated that in less developed countries used aircraft should be able to move cargo for about 14 cents per ton-mile, even when the cost of airports and of local pick-up and delivery services are included. The reduction stems in part from the better load factors possible where alternative methods of transport offer less competition. In addition, densities as high as 20 to 100 pounds per cubic foot can be achieved by carrying agricultural and mineral cargo, compared to the 10 pounds per cubic foot typical of moving by air in the United States.[10]

But conventional aircraft purchased secondhand are quite different from aircraft that might be specifically designed for developing countries. What is needed for them is an air vehicle that moves at relatively slow speed in order to reduce the cost of ground and navigation facilities, increase safety, and reduce operating complexity. Slower planes are acceptable because the differential between air speeds and the speed of surface travel is so great that some slowing down in the air would be relatively unimportant. A special requirement would be ease of loading and unloading and the ability to take off and land at small airports and on rough runways.

The problem of developing a short-haul plane that provides economical and safe service is complicated by different requirements for different geographic areas and different stages of development. In North Central Africa, traffic requirements, might call for large passenger transports that can operate over long distances in high temperatures and gusty winds. In South Central Africa, capacity for about six passengers and five hundred pounds of freight, adding to a third as much gross weight, might fill the need.

[10] Philip R. Carlson, "Application of Air Cargo Transport to Feeder Operations in Less Developed Areas," in *Transportation*.

This airplane would have to operate from landing strips cleared in tropical forests, with high temperatures and humidity. Southeastern Asia probably requires an air freighter with a ten thousand pound payload and good navigational aids to cope with monsoon conditions, and in much of South America an important requirement is high cruising altitudes to cope with difficult mountains.[11]

This variety of conditions does not permit a single answer, then, to the question of aircraft design for developing countries. But new aircraft to provide local or feeder service might have some characteristics in common. Because of the absence of competing surface carriers, it should be possible to move cargo by air over much shorter distances than in developed areas. If aircraft are designed for a four hundred mile instead of a thousand mile range the ratio of payload to gross weight will be higher, with consequent reduction in ton-mile costs.

Taking these factors into account, it has been suggested that a plane with a payload of 30,000 pounds could be designed that would in effect do the job of a truck. The flying truck would be powered by two turboprops, with a range of 450 miles and a cruise speed of 160 knots at 10,000 feet. At 75 percent load factor, it could carry cargo at 8 cents per ton-mile, and provide a superior service at lower cost than could be achieved by road transport.[12] If such an aircraft could be built, it might appreciably alter the character of the transport investment program.

Another possibility for expanding the use of air transport is vertical takeoff and landing. Helicopter operating costs are still high, but the introduction of jet power has been an important breakthrough. The helicopter introduces important economies by eliminating costly ground facilities and reducing the problem of pick-up and delivery. Recent helicopter models can move cargo short distances for about 16 cents per ton-mile, with a load factor

[11] David Rendel, "Design Characteristics of Aircraft for Safe and Efficient Operation in Less Developed Areas," in *ibid.*.

[12] Carlson, *op. cit.*, p. 70.

of 75 percent. For hauls over fifty miles, however, some combination of direct lift and fixed wing would be necessary at this stage of aeronautical development to achieve an economical transport that would take off vertically. It is estimated that convertiplanes of this type could be produced within a few years and that their total direct and indirect costs will approximate 10 cents per ton-mile.[13]

Present and prospective aircraft can do much more than has been the case to date to provide the mobility and access necessary in developing countries. Local air service can stretch the supply of scarce technicians by enabling them to visit more people and more places than would be conceivable by surface travel. Aircraft can move doctors and medical supplies to areas in need, and can deliver government and business officials quickly to where they have to go.

The airplane is more than a method of transport, however. It can help discover and map a nation's resources, can spray, dust, and fertilize crops, and can fight insects and disease. It can survey sites for new construction projects and carry critical supplies to remote locations. The need for these and many other local services points to the important role that aviation might play in the future development of poorer nations.

Today air transport in developing countries is often focused on trunk and international route services, and on the task of keeping pace with the upward trends in aircraft size and speed. This emphasis continues despite an ample world supply of high-speed international jet services and a shortage of regional and intermediate range air transport. The economic argument for flying international routes is that the ability to tap the long-distance traffic helps to support the rest of the operation. In addition, reliance on foreign flag carriers often causes a substantial drain of foreign exchange. It is argued that a net saving is realized when a country operates its own international air carrier. For these reasons, a nation may allocate funds to purchase jets to serve London

[13] *Ibid.*, p. 71.

and New York, although no support can be found for short-haul transport urgently needed at home. The result of these policies can be the encouragement of air transport that is least needed, and the neglect of services that could be expected to contribute most to development.

Short-haul air service for both business and government officials is a significant need in most underdeveloped countries. Without such a means of integrating the economy, it is difficult to conduct business or to maintain effective governmental machinery. But the equipment now available for the accommodation of light-density movements on short-haul domestic routes is costly to buy and to operate. Research and development aimed at providing equipment to perform these functions economically could be highly effective in aiding economic development.

Pipeline Transport

Among the relatively new transport media, the pipeline has an important bearing on the whole transport investment picture. It provides a means of substituting oil or gas movement for the hauling of coal and other fuel in wheeled vehicles, especially by rail. Continuing improvements in the quality of pipe and in the ease of installation and operation have resulted in the rapid expansion of pipeline transport of liquids and gases, and there are important potentials for moving solids by pipeline.

The feasibility of pipelines for developing countries lies in their ability to traverse even the most difficult terrain, to be practically unaffected by weather, and to furnish transport of petroleum and petroleum products at low unit costs. Where volumes are sufficiently great, the pipeline is more economical for these purposes than other forms of transport. Land costs are held to a minimum by burying the pipe three feet underground, or deeper to avoid interference with other land uses. About 70 to 75 percent of the cost of a typical pipeline system, including installation, is the cost of the pipe itself, which is made of strong but relatively thin steel. Pumping stations are located at intervals of 30 to 150 miles. If fuel is being carried, the pumps can be powered by tapping the pipe. Annual operating costs run about 3 to 10 percent of the original cost.[14]

On the basis of experience in the United States, it is a general rule that 1,000 miles of 10-inch pipe will cost $37,000 per mile, excluding right of way, while a comparable length of 20-inch pipe (with three and a half times as much capacity) will cost $66,000 per mile. Operating costs per unit of traffic are one-third as much for the large pipe as for the small.[15] Large volumes of any liquid with the approximate characteristics of petroleum can be moved through a pipeline at a cost one-fourth to one-eighth the cost of railway transport and one-sixth to one-eighth the cost of trucking it as shown in the following table. Under some conditions pipeline and barge transport may have the same costs, but for very large volumes pipeline costs are much lower.[16]

METHOD	UNIT COST
Pipeline	1.0
Ocean tanker	0.5–0.8
Barge	1.0–3.0
Rail	4.0–8.0
Truck	6.0–8.0

These cost figures explain why over a million miles of pipeline are now moving 70 percent of the energy resources of the United States. The transportation of oil has shifted almost completely from rail to pipe, with local distribution by truck. All of the major populated areas of the United States are served by gas pipelines, which cover twice as many miles of routes as the nation's railroads. Whether this trend heralds similar developments elsewhere de-

[14] J. L. Burke, "Movement of Commodities by Pipeline," in *Transportation*, p. 81.

[15] *Ibid.*, pp. 82–83.

[16] Where traffic moves distances ranging from 50 to 1,600 miles. Pipeline = 1.0. *Ibid.*, p. 81.

pends largely on the future of oil and gas both as sources of energy and as the raw materials for new industry.

For newly developing countries, an advantage of pipeline systems is the relatively routine nature of operations. They can be performed by the novice after a short period of on-the-job training. Periodic inspection and overhauls requiring greater skills can be accomplished by a small number of technical personnel moving over the system at regular intervals, generally by airplane or helicopter. Aerial inspection makes it possible to keep a close watch for leaks or other difficulties. The pipeline also has the advantage that its construction is not disassociated from the purpose it is to serve. Investment in this form of transport is decided by known needs rather than probable or imaginary needs. Finally, the pipeline must be in good working order if it is to function at all, with the result that the economic drain from poor maintenance and low operating efficiency typical of road and rail transport is not experienced.

Further potentials for pipeline transport are indicated by the experience with moving bituminous coal through a 108-mile pipe in the United States. The 10½ inch pipe has delivered coal in volumes exceeding by 40 percent its design capacity of 1,200,000 tons per year. The coal is ground to the consistency of coarse sand, mixed with an equal share of water, and moved by three pumping units that push it the entire distance in thirty hours. Cost of the coal pipeline, including land, was about $125,000 per mile.[17]

The promise of the coal pipeline is shown by the fact that in the United States transporting coal more than 500 miles from the mines costs as much as the coal itself. Coal transport costs, which are often one cent a ton-mile by rail, could be substantially reduced on some routes by moving the coal through pipes. It is also possible, however, for improvements in rail transport techniques to lower coal hauling costs, notably through integrated trains that double present capacity to 25,000 tons a train.

[17] A new low rate on coal agreed to by existing rail facilities has shut down this pipeline in Ohio.

What can be done with coal is also possible for a wide variety of other materials. It is clear that any substance that can be broken into small pieces and suspended in a liquid can be moved by pipe. Thus far the technical drawback has been the cost of preparing solids for the trip and reclaiming them at the other end. Engineering advances will undoubtedly overcome these problems. The mixing of coal and oil, piping them together, and using both as fuel, is one possibility for overcoming the problem of preparation and reclaiming.

New Horizons for Transport

The world is on the threshhold of a new revolution in transport technology, and for the first time in five thousand years, the wheel is being displaced as the symbol of transport progress. Already there are many experimental but potentially significant methods of movement that could have a major impact on developing countries. One of these is the ground reaction vehicle, which operates just off the surface of the ground or water on a cushion created by downward jets of air. These vehicles do not fly in the strict sense of the word, but use the air for support. They have special applicability for travel over unstable ground or difficult waters where shoals or other obstacles impede navigation. Development of the ground-reaction principle may lead to the production of vehicles several hundred feet in length that would rise as high as thirty feet off the ground and attain a speed of one hundred miles per hour.

The significance of the ground-reaction vehicle to newly developing areas is apparent. It would provide transport service over cleared land without a heavy investment in roadways and bridges, and it would likewise be able to operate in the rainy season where existing roads and tracks are impassable.

The hydrofoil ship represents another significant move toward a new type of transport for river and coastal service. This new vehicle increases the speed of water-borne craft from the normal ten knots on inland waterways to rates of 45 to 100 knots. Its load-carrying capacity may ultimately be as high as 5,000 to 20,000 tons. These vehicles will provide economy plus the capacity to carry masses of people and cargo.

Changes are also taking place that will alter the competitive advantage of conventional forms of transport. Development of the fuel cell, which produces electricity directly from chemical reactions, may be the key factor promoting a revival of electric propulsion. Electric power has a number of important advantages over the gasoline engine, including the elimination of transmission, propeller shaft, rear axle, and, of course, the need for petroleum.

Gas turbines are also reducing the complexity of motor vehicle engines and introducing further economies in vehicle operation. The turbine engine contains fewer moving parts and can operate on a variety of liquid fuels. Truck tests have been run over an extended period with turbine power plants that weigh less than a tenth the weight of a diesel engine with equivalent power. Other possibilities of cost reduction lie in the development of new synthetic tires with wearing quality approaching the life of the vehicle, and new light-weight materials that will further reduce operating costs and increase payloads.

In developing countries the highway itself will be increasingly effective in reducing transport costs as roadbuilding efforts proceed. The road program may be accelerated by greater use of local materials that can provide good low-cost surfaces, and by improved techniques for soil stabilization, using sand-clay and soil-cement mixtures as well as oil and chemical binders.

Further breakthroughs in transport technology are to be expected. While the developing nations are preparing to invest billions of dollars in conventional transport methods, renewed efforts should be made to accelerate current research and development to hasten improved performance and more desirable alternatives. Such a strategy might be far more effective in breaking the transport barrier than current programs directed mainly toward duplicating conventional systems.

Net Effects on Development

In addition to the cost and service characteristics of transport methods, another factor that needs to be weighed in making a wise choice of alternatives is the effect the choice will have on the economic activity of a country and on levels of living generally. Different methods of transport require different inputs of capital, foreign exchange, managerial talent, and technical skills. They take different lengths of time for completion, and afterwards they require varying inputs for maintenance and operation. The outputs resulting from these efforts will also differ, including the ability of different transport media to create capital, to earn foreign exchange, to train entrepreneurs, to foster supporting economic activities, and to provide jobs.

For road transport, substantial public capital is required to build the highway, but the amount can be tailored to the need by designing low-type roads for light traffic. Equipment for road transport may require more capital than the roads, but there is some advantage in the fact that rolling stock is generally provided by the private sector, and that a relatively small amount of investment for the purchase of a truck or bus is all that may be needed to start a road transport service. On the other hand, public funds provide the entire investment in railways, and the initial amounts of capital required are high.

Transport operations also create capital, and this may or may not be used to support further development. If transport services can be made to earn an excess of revenues over costs, the net return may be used for improvements and additions, or paid into the public treasury to support other development activities. In practice, however, railway earnings are generally insufficient even to finance replacements, let alone make a net contribution to other public enterprise. The same is true of highways, whose users rarely pay enough taxes to cover the annual cost of the road. But private operators of trucks and buses often do make a profit, which may be invested in additional equipment to expand operations or in other business activities. Generally speaking, improved transport makes profits for other economic activities, and the financial returns from providing greater mobility may not appear on the books of the transport facility.

Transport operations may thus have limited control over the financial return from their operations, but different transport methods have varying capabilities for governing their costs. It is important for a transport facility to be made available quickly and for unused capacity to be held to a minimum. For some methods of movement, large amounts of capital have to be committed at the start, and the resulting plant will be underutilized during the period between completion of the facility and the gradual traffic build-up. The "lumpiness" of investments in transport means a long waiting period before unit costs can be reduced to satisfactory levels. Because of the large initial outlays of capital required for a new railway before a single train can move, and thereafter until large traffic volumes have been generated, what has been invested is contributing little to development. Stage construction of highways and low-type surfacing can reduce the amount of this unproductive investment in highways. But air transport, with a minimum of fixed plant on the ground, offers the best means of avoiding a needless freezing of scarce capital resources.

The amount of foreign exchange needed for transport also ranges widely, depending on the type of facility and the domestic resource endowment. Many countries in early stages of development have to import nearly all the mechanized equipment they use, as well as building materials, construction equipment, and fuels. Most countries have to import all their motor vehicle requirements, or at least the components for final assembly. Tows and barges as well as dredging equipment for inland water transport may have to be purchased abroad, but many smaller river craft create no foreign exchange requirements. The opposite is true of rail transport, which in early stages of development is almost wholly dependent on outside sources of supply for everything from rails and structural steel to locomotives and cars. Aircraft and air navigation facilities must also be purchased from the economically developed countries. Only low-quality roads built with indigenous materials and local labor may be relatively independent of imports.

Transport facilities also earn foreign exchange, however, by facilitating exports and tourism. A railway that makes it possible to move ores to port, a road that increases the sale of coffee, or air transport that makes travel from other countries possible, may mean a net inflow of foreign currencies. Industries created to substitute domestic for imported transport equipment and materials add to this possibility, and these potentials should be considered in the selection of transport alternatives.

Choice of transport will also affect requirements for managerial talent, and potentials for the creation of new entrepreneurial capacities. A railway system is often the largest business in the country. Accordingly it requires an extensive management staff for effective operation. The opposite is true of road transport, which is generally conducted at the start by an individual with a single vehicle. Managerial skills for this scale of operation are modest, but running a truck affords the opportunity of acquiring business talents. Once a man has learned the art of operating a truck, he may either expand his activities to a fleet of vehicles or apply his capabilities in other enterprise.

Below the managerial level, different methods of transport also require different technical skills, some of which may be readily acquired and others less readily. Air transport calls for extensive training for pilots. Truck and bus drivers can learn more readily. A wide variety of skills are called for in the many types of railway work, while pipeline operations require technical competence but small numbers. The availability of these skills, the demand for them elsewhere, and the time, cost, and feasibility of providing the training for them should be taken into account in weighing the advantages or disadvantages of different types of transport.

The total direct and indirect employment provided by transport decisions is also a major factor to be considered in weighing alternatives. The great majority of transport workers will be unskilled or semiskilled, and the greatest number of job opportunities for them are afforded by roadbuilding and maintenance. How many jobs can be supplied depends on the type of roads and the degree to which operations are mechanized. The largest mileage will be of low-type or intermediate design, which requires considerable labor input relative to total expenditure, whereas paved roads involve more capital-intensive methods. The railway system may also engage large numbers of people, but many railways are burdened by a surplus of workers, which hampers the achievement of an efficient, low-cost service.

Selection of transport projects should also take into account activities created along transport routes. These activities include the cultivation of adjacent farm lands and the provision of access to forest and mineral resources. Different methods of transport have varying capacities for creating these impacts. Railway construction may promote development at or near stations, and to a lesser degree between them, while air transport can be expected to make no impact between airports. Pipelines carrying petroleum products or natural gas may support industrial activities whereever the pipe is tapped, but this generally occurs only in urban places. It is the road, and in some places the waterway, that is able to create developmental effects over a wide area and in a variety of ways. The road especially provides access to adjacent land for all types of users over the entire length of the route, and its area of influence can also be extended with relative ease by the construction of feeders. Thus road transport is the most important method of movement for bringing land and other resources into use.

A second type of developmental impact resulting from transport investment is the creation of supporting industries to supply materials and equipment for the transport system. These industries in turn may promote and support other economic undertakings. For example, petroleum refining capacity or the production of crushed stone may contribute to manufacturing and construction as well as to transport. Roadbuilding will create a demand for cement production, and road transport may introduce tire manufacturing, the production of parts, and the assembly of vehicles. A number of countries have undertaken the production of their own railway equipment.

The production and employment opportunities arising from the equipment and materials requirements should be reviewed in arriving at transport decisions and steps should be taken to encourage these activities. For as seen in the development of the European and American transport systems, the indirect impacts of improved mobility play a substantial role in the economic progress of more advanced countries.

Moving People

Many of the same cost and service factors that govern the selection of freight hauling methods pertain to the movement of people. Human beings, however, are more sensitive to the speed, safety, and convenience of the trips, and, unlike inanimate objects, they make up their own minds how they will go. Their decisions have considerable influence on the types of facilities and standards of service provided for freight transport, since most methods of movement accommodate both. In many cases, too, the line between passenger and freight business in developing countries is difficult to draw, since many people carry their goods to market, in their own conveyances or on public carriers, thus combining passenger and freight movements.

In developing countries, rail transport often involves as many passenger-miles per year as ton-miles of freight service. In India in 1960, for example, there were 69 billion ton-kilometers of travel on the railways and 75 billion passenger-kilometers. Passenger travel exceeded the movement of freight in many other countries, including Burma, Malaya, Pakistan, and a number of Latin American countries.[18] At the same time, there has been a universal trend to bus transport for short trips and for travel on lightly traveled routes. The airlines are supplying much of the long-distance transport between major cities.

With a selection of public carriers available, plus the alternative of private transport, what are the factors to be taken into account in choosing among available technologies to meet travel requirements? In nearly all developing countries, rail passenger equipment is ancient, uneconomical, and uncomfortable. Trains are invariably slow and overcrowded. Low fares and inability to collect fares have contributed to the magnitude of railway deficits. In some countries, an estimated one out of three passengers rides without paying. The obvious need for new equipment and modernization of the service remains unmet because of the political obstacles to upward rate adjustments that might reduce passenger service losses. As a result, the railways of the world, with only a few exceptions, suffer a cycle of poor service, low fares, increasing deficits, and still poorer service.

But the solution to these problems does not lie solely in more realistic fares. For even if modern passenger equipment could be financed, poor service would still result from the slow speeds imposed by inadequate road beds and light rails. Most railways were not designed to accommodate high-speed passenger trains. In addition, where goods movement is heavy, it may be difficult to avoid interference between passenger and freight schedules.

The task, then, is to view the intercity passenger problem as part of the total transport problem. The goal is to make the investments needed to provide a national system of passenger transport that permits effective use of rail, air, road, and water transport. To achieve this objective requires the projection of travel demands and an assessment of the economy of alternative methods of travel under different demand conditions.

[18] See Tables A.6 and A.7.

An indication of travel costs for various traffic densities is demonstrated by the difference between costs at capacity and costs under load factors in the United States. Railways provide passenger service at the low cost of 1.9 cents per seat-mile. This economy, however, can be realized only on main routes carrying heavy traffic. Actually, the low average load factor raises cost per passenger-mile to 6.9 cents, which is higher per passenger-mile than the more popular trunk airlines. Motor bus transport is the cheapest of all methods, totaling 1.3 cents on a seat-mile basis, and 2.7 cents on the basis of passenger-miles, as shown in the following table.[19]

METHOD OF TRAVEL	COST IN CENTS	
	PER SEAT-MILE	PER PASSENGER-MILE
Railroad	1.90	6.93
Motor Bus	1.29	2.73
Private Auto	2.15	4.50
Airline (trunk)	3.81	6.20
Airline (local)	5.45	12.30

These differences between passenger-mile and seat-mile costs are significant guides to policy, but the figures cited result from conditions peculiar to the United States. One of these is the fact that buses share the roads with a large number of other vehicles, and accordingly, their tax payments for highways cover only a small part of the total cost of the roads they use. Air transport cost, too, may be understated to the extent that airport and airway investments are not reflected in payments to government. But for the developing countries, the data illustrate a consideration that is universally applicable, namely, that the choice of technology depends not only on performance characteristics but on the traffic to be moved.

Time is also a primary consideration in the choice of travel methods, and with the advent of air transport this factor is of in-

[19] Class I roads including suburban. *ICC Transport Statistics in the U. S.* (1959); CAB, *Quarterly Reports of Air Carrier Financial Statistics* (December 1959); ATA, *Comparative Statement of Air Carrier Income and Expenses* (1959); *Wall Street Journal* (Aug. 23, 1960).

creasing importance. In the United States, for example, a trip of between 500 and 749 miles takes 12 to 14 hours less by air than by rail or bus, and when the trip is 750 to 999 miles the saving is 20 hours. (See Table 4.4.) In developing countries it is probable that air speeds will be the same as in the United States, since the equipment used is usually the same; but surface transport will be much slower. Thus the gap between the two types of transport may be substantially greater in newly developing areas.

TABLE 4.4. *Comparison of Average One-Way Travel Time in the United States, by Air, Rail, and Bus, 1962*[a]

Distance Between Cities[b]	Hours Consumed for Traveling			Air Time Advantage in Hours over	
	Jet Aircraft (City center to city center)[c]	Railways[d]	Bus[e]	Railways	Bus
Under 250 miles	3.2	5.1	5.3	1.9	2.1
250–499 miles	3.6	10.9	11.3	7.3	7.7
500–749 miles	4.4	17.1	18.3	12.7	13.9
750–999 miles	4.5	25.0	26.8	20.5	22.3
1,000–1,499 miles	4.9	29.8	36.1	24.9	31.2
1,500–1,999 miles	6.4	40.7	54.1	34.3	47.7
2,000 miles and over	7.3	59.9	71.6	52.6	64.3

Source: Based on the table "Comparison of Average One-Way Elapsed Trip Times by Air, Rail, Bus, and Automobile," compiled by the Office of Carrier Accidents and Statistics, Civil Aeronautics Board, December 1962.

[a] Elapsed trip time is the average of the fastest trip times for each mode of common-carrier transportation for each city pair.

[b] Each category includes four pairs of major U. S. cities.

[c] Includes estimated time consumed traveling from city center to airport at the beginning of a journey and from airport to city center at the end of a journey, including ticketing and baggage handling time.

[d] Based on schedules permitting the fastest elapsed trip time.

[e] Elapsed trip time assumed that no overnight stopovers were made.

The value placed on speed may be less in a developing country, however, than in a society that is always in a hurry. While this may be true, the value of time derives not simply from the savings to individuals, but from the ability to make more intensive use of transport equipment. An airplane may cost much more than a bus, but its speed will permit the generation of many more passenger-miles of travel.

Experience indicates that expanding total national output results in at least a proportionate increase in passenger travel in developing countries, and that the achievement of a more equitable distribution of income will effect a much more rapid rate of growth for personal mobility. American experience may indicate the general direction of future trends in other parts of the world. As families have moved up the income ladder, their outlays for transport have moved upward even faster. A study made twenty-five years ago showed that expenditures for public transport among families in middle income brackets were three to seven times greater than those of low income families, and the most affluent families spent at least twenty times as much as the poorest. Differences in outlays for private transport were even more pronounced as incomes rose.[20]

In densely populated countries such as India, with the upward trend in population and income, the railways can be expected to continue accommodating heavy volumes of passenger traffic, including substantial numbers of urban commuters. Rail passenger service under comparable conditions of population density in parts of Western Europe is substantially above the levels of two decades ago, despite high personal incomes and the rapid growth of automobile use. Traffic volumes have more than doubled on the railways of Austria, Italy, The Netherlands, Norway, Portugal, and Switzerland, and only Great Britain has registered a decline in rail travel. Japan's railways are moving ten times as much passenger traffic as those of the United States, and the new high-speed rail line between Tokyo and Kobe has initiated a revolutionary step toward modern surface carriage. But the case for an expansion of rail travel is not clear in less populated areas. The United States, Argentina, Colombia, and others have been experiencing a long-term decline in railway passenger traffic. Everywhere the improvement of roads and the introduction of bus transport have caused a significant growth in the volume of highway travel.

[20] National Resources Planning Board, *Family Expenditures in the United States: Statistical Tables and Appendixes* (June 1941), Table 11, p. 4.

In the future, air transport will also assume a larger role. In the present state of the art, vertical take-off and landing craft provide impressive possibilities. Shorter airline distances made possible by getting above surface obstacles, plus the much higher speed and better use of equipment, can save considerable time and resources. In East Pakistan, where a network of unbridgeable rivers cuts the rail system in half, surface transport is exceedingly difficult and in the monsoon season often impossible. From Dacca to Bagerhat, eighty-four airline miles, takes three days by river and rail. The trip can be made by small plane in thirty minutes. Helicopter service now provided in East Pakistan is costly on a commercial basis, but from the standpoint of providing greater mobility for government and industry personnel the economies may be substantial. The impact of aviation on travel patterns, however, is still less than its potential because aircraft manufacturing countries have focused on planes that are too big, too fast, and too expensive for local service. As a result, the 10,000 miles from New York to Southeast Asia are easy, but it is often the next fifty miles that are the hardest.

What combination of transport services will best meet the needs of a given country, then, will depend, as in the case of freight, on costs in relation to traffic volume and trip length, and on service factors that may make higher costs economical in relation to ultimate objectives.

Available technology plus the prospects for further innovation hold increasing promise that the economic and social disadvantages of immobility can be overcome. These technological possibilities should be taken into account in countries embarking on extensive programs of transport investment, for they are in the best position to break with the past and to adopt fresh approaches with a minimum burden of obsolescence. The important requirement is to maintain awareness of what technological capabilities are offered, and to seek maximum flexibility in the investments now being made in order to take advantage of innovations that are imminent.

The fact that limited progress has been made toward the fruitful application of what is technologically possible can be attributed to three major factors: the absence of institutional arrangements equipped to make the necessary choices; the reluctance to try what is new and untried; and the neglect of research and development.

Many of the plans for future transport development seem to deny the transport revolution and favor instead a reconstruction of the past. Research and development programs need to accelerate innovations that could be most helpful to developing countries. Many emerging techniques within and outside the transport field promise new approaches to solving transport problems. Their development should be promoted and funds and talents focused on getting early results.

CHAPTER V

Mobilizing Resources

SATISFACTORY INSTITUTIONAL ARRANGEMENTS are necessary preconditions for an effective transport program. Requirements include both public and private agencies capable of constructing, maintaining, and operating the system, and financing methods that are adequate and consistent with development goals. Domestic resources represent the major source of support, and the manner in which they are used will determine the success of the transport effort and the progress of development in other sectors.

The Question of Self-Support

Every country, regardless of its state of development, is burdened by the high cost of moving. In addition to the heavy initial investment required by the transport sector, there are continuing needs to maintain and operate the system, and heavy periodic expenditures for motor vehicles, ships, aircraft, and other equipment.

The most difficult problem is to finance the initial investments. Roads, railways, ports, and airports call for large capital outlays to achieve useful results. But the benefits of such expenditures are often slow to be realized. The capital needed ten years hence has to be committed now. The return from current investment will thus be realized only gradually. The situation is aggravated by the fact that traffic may increase at a slow pace while development is getting under way.

Other difficulties stem from political considerations. Funds available for public facilities must often be spread thinly over a wide geographic area in response to local demands. Often the dissipation of resources over many projects or many miles leads to unimpressive results. The critical need for new facilities also results in a tendency to neglect those already built, which quickly fall into disrepair. The cost of reconstruction then adds to the financial burden. There is also constant pressure to hold down the price paid for transport by consumers. An increase in passenger fares, gasoline taxes, or freight rates to keep pace with rising costs is almost always resisted.

Although most countries of the world operate their transport facilities at a deficit, the losses impose a heavier drain on less developed economies. In some of these countries, for example, transport losses absorb a large share of government tax revenues, thus limiting the capacity of government to meet urgent needs in other sectors. There is an endless backlog of things to be done, including the replacement of worn out rail locomotives, the repair and rebuilding of large mileages of roads, and the replacement of obsolete rolling stock. These demands generally precede the development that, in the long run, can help defray their costs.

Financial policies to cope with these problems not only determine the level of support for the transport system, but they also have a significant impact on growth in other sectors. Low rates may encourage desirable economic growth or promote types and locations of industrial activity that prove to be uneconomical and harmful to development in the long run. The opposite danger is that an effort to achieve self-support will lead to high rates that have the equally unfavorable effect of discouraging the use of facilities already provided, thus wasting resources.

Pricing policies also have an effect on the allocation of traffic among competing transport methods. The result of underpricing one form of transport or overpricing another will ultimately influence the way goods and people move. This in turn will influence the allocation of investment to accommodate these demands. Thus financial policy rather than economic and technological potentials may dictate the kind of transport system that is provided.

Where self-support is feasible, it has significant advantages. Many other vital public services cannot be financed through user charges, notably public education and other social programs. Advantage should thus be taken of levying direct charges on users wherever this can be done, in order to reserve general funds for other public facilities where pricing is impossible. Another reason for user charges is that transport is part of the cost of production and should be included in costs as an aid to resource allocation and the desirable location of economic activities. User charges also provide for greater equity when there is competition among transport agencies.

The payment of user charges or rates to defray the cost of providing transport also offers the advantage of supplying a reliable and predictable source of revenue, which can be an important aid to long-term physical and financial planning. In addition, user payments have a high degree of acceptability when the amount paid is less than the benefits received. The road user is willing to pay more for better roads because by so doing he pays less for transport. The savings are realized in the reduction of fuel consumption, vehicle depreciation, and other operating costs. Users also benefit from the fact that adequately financed facilities are most likely to stay in good condition and to keep pace with technological change.

Failure of transport facilities to pay their way, however, does not necessarily mean that these investments are socially undesirable or that they fail to contribute importantly to national product. Railway lines built in underdeveloped territories of the United States were often unable to cover their costs, yet financial losses for the transport operation were accompanied by important social returns for the economy. These were realized in the opening up of new lands and resources, in lowered costs of production and distribution, and in certain strategic and political impacts as well.[1]

It may be neither possible nor desirable in early stages of development to pay the total transport bill through the direct payments of users. The question, then, is how to finance transport facilities in a way that will supply adequate resources to meet the need and at the same time promote overall development objectives. This is a dilemma that confronts all methods of transport, but its importance focuses particularly on road and rail facilities, which involve three quarters of all transport expenditures.

Covering Railway Costs

In the railway field, the global picture is one of chronic deficits. Many railways in developing countries barely cover their operating costs. In the early sixties, the revenues of the Turkish railways covered only 77 percent of total expenses. In Syria, the figure was 72 percent and in Algeria 26 percent.[2] In some countries, the gap between costs and revenues on the railways has been so great that it has undermined the financial position of the entire national economy.

Part of the reason for the deficits is historical. It was noted earlier that rail systems in many developing countries were built

[1] An illustration is the estimate made of the increase in national income brought about indirectly by the greater productivity of labor and capital on lands opened up for development by the Union Pacific Railway. The increase in the value of the land due to the railroad was $152 million. Multiplied by the rate at which land was capitalized, the estimate of the increase in national income in 1880 created by the Union Pacific, but not reflected in the company's receipts, was $15.6 million. Thus the railway was operating at a deficit, but from the standpoint of the country the operating deficit was justified. See Robert W. Fogel, *The Union Pacific Railroad: A Case in Premature Enterprise* (Johns Hopkins Press, 1960), pp. 98–99.

[2] International Union of Railways, *International Railway Statistics, Year 1961* (General Secretariat of the U.I.C., 1962), based on Tables 3.3 and 3.5. Data include capital costs.

when military objectives or raw material exports were the principal factors determining location. The result was typically a rail pattern that tapped the hinterlands, converged on the principal ports, and avoided connections with other countries. Today these railways often prove ill-suited to the needs of both internal and regional development. Current demands for moving a diverse assortment of goods over a wide area cannot be met by specialized facilities designed for the export of primary products. This export trade may be of considerable importance to the development program, but the railway pattern is not suited to the transport demands generated by internal growth.

Even where railway location is satisfactory, the physical plant may be poorly designed to meet the need. Different gauges adopted in earlier times to discourage trade among rival states result in high costs, transshipment delays, and the frustration of potential economic integration with neighboring countries. Often the main obstacle to making the railways pay is that they are old and in a state of disrepair. The physical life of railway equipment is generally much longer than its economic life, and thus ancient and uneconomical rolling stock is kept in operation beyond its time.

To these historical reasons for railway troubles, a number of current difficulties are added. The business of running the railways is thwarted by rigidities in management, labor, and government. Railway policies do not respond readily to the need for change, especially to the possibilities of new transport techniques. Everywhere the process of abandoning a railway that is no longer needed is tortuous. Obsolete lines and uneconomic services are kept in operation because of inertia, community pressure, or refusal to substitute cheaper truck or bus service. Accordingly, lines that were originally built in the wrong place, of the wrong design, or on the mistaken hope that traffic would eventually materialize still serve. These parts of the system may contribute disproportionately to the poor financial condition of the whole.

Railway deficits have often been allowed to persist as a conscious policy of government, on the assumption that low rates will stimulate traffic and further economic or social goals. This assumption can prove to be a mistake where low rates induce unnecessary transport, pre-empt space that is needed for other traffic, and perpetuate the financial stringencies that have been the underlying reason for obsolete equipment and poor service.

The importance of railway travel to low-income groups has made many governments reluctant to increase fares to cover rising costs. The resulting mobility can have valuable social effects, but the purpose may be defeated where promotional rates are applied without adequate provision for maintaining the service. Overcrowding, inadequate equipment, rapid deterioration of travel standards, and excessive congestion often result from price policies designed to produce social benefits because financial support from other sources is not forthcoming.

Low rates on coal may have similar effects. Industries may locate at excessive distances from sources of supply because the longer haul does not enter into their cost calculations. As a result, railways may be burdened by carrying coal at a loss, while other traffic cannot be accommodated. Or low rates may discourage the supply of alternative methods of carrying coal that might be more economical, such as coastal shipping or pipelines.

The persistent idea that railways are capable of providing every type of transport service with maximum efficiency and economy seems to encourage them to engage in unremunerative traffic. Included in this category is traffic moving short distances or in small quantities, which not only puts the rail system at a financial disadvantage in these particular categories, but interferes with the conduct of other services that railways ought to be able to provide effectively.

Some categories of traffic that once moved only by rail are now being lost to trucks, however, and this loss has often dealt a serious financial blow. For the traffic that shifts from rail to road is relatively high-valued commodities that contribute disproportionately to revenue. Under rate systems based on what the traffic would bear, these commodities have always been charged high rates to help compensate for low rates on cheap bulk commodities. It is this rate-making practice that has made the railways especially vulnerable to the competition from innovations in road transport, for the truck is especially well suited to providing precisely those services that the railways overpriced. The result, then, is that the railways of the world are doing more business than ever before, but they are working harder for less money.

If rail deficits are to be reduced, the remedy will have to include a combination of approaches. In some countries, uneconomic lines and services will have to be abandoned where present or anticipated traffic volume is clearly insufficient to support them, but where alternative road services could be economically provided. Where the railways are losing money on short-haul traffic and on types of shipments that are costly to handle, this traffic should be permitted to shift to other carriers. It would be a mistake, however, to abandon a rail line already built on the sole ground that revenues are insufficient to cover expenditures. The cost of continuing rail operations at a deficit must be compared with the added road transport costs that would have to be paid if rail traffic were transferred to the highways. The shift might mean substantial additional capital investment to provide additional roadway and vehicle capacity, whereas the capital in the railway has already been invested and is still usable.

The fact that road deficits are accepted as a matter of course, whereas a railway deficit often leads to suggestions for abandonment, reflects a basic difference between the two. Roads are needed regardless of whether there is a railway because they provide access to land and resources throughout their length, and they accommodate all types of movement, including animals and pedestrians as well as mechanized and non-mechanized vehicles. They can be designed to carry a wide range of traffic volumes and are used to move people and goods on the great network of routes where traffic is light. The railway, on the other hand, is a special-purpose, high-density transport agency designed to serve a limited mileage of main routes. Even along the rail line, access to property that is not close to a train stop must be supplied by roads. For this reason, roads are built parallel to railways. The decision to build or retain rail transport depends on whether roads can perform the total transport task by themselves.

When both the railway and highway systems are operating at a deficit, the community is supporting two transport facilities that do not pay their way. Since it is not possible to abandon the all-purpose road system, the only deficit operation that can be dropped is the railway. To do so makes sense if the result will be a net reduction in transport costs without loss of needed transport service.

Pricing policies may also have to be revised to reflect the economic advantages or disadvantages of rail operations. Typically rail rates are too low for short distances and too high for the long haul. When a railway has a large amount of unused capacity, the waste of this resource may be reduced if rates are lowered to encourage more traffic, while conversely a level of rates too low may waste resources by aggravating congestion. It is important, therefore, that railway management should be empowered to determine what price policy is appropriate in the light of the particular circumstances. The practice of detailed government regulation of rates almost always leads to waste and inefficiency. The role of government lies primarily in helping to plan physical facilities for rail transport in relation to other transport and development programs and to determine overall financial policy. Pricing transport services is not the type of activity that government machinery is designed to do well.

Paying for Highways

In most countries, special taxes or tolls are collected to compensate in part for road expenditures. But the deficit, if one were to look at road finance the same way as railway finance, is often very large. Few countries come anywhere near the point of raising sufficient revenues to meet the annual cost of the facilities.[3]

The amounts necessary to finance an adequate road program are large because of the extensive mileage needed to cover the entire area of a country. Yet the amounts being spent in developing countries are small in relation to population and area compared to what is being done in the more developed economies. Even this small outlay constitutes a heavy burden, however.

Road outlays per capita are less than a dollar per year in Peru, Tanganyika, India, Iran, Indonesia, and Egypt. They are as low as thirty cents in Pakistan and Afghanistan and ten cents in Nyasaland. Most West European countries spend fifteen to thirty times more. Despite the low expenditure per capita in the less developed countries, outlays per vehicle are high because the number of vehicles is low. In many developing countries, the current cost of providing roads is ten times as much per year per motor vehicle as the outlay per vehicle in Western Europe. (See Table A.1.) Roads in less developed areas have users other than motor vehicles, however, including both pedestrians and animals, which reduces outlays per unit of traffic. But the non-vehicular use is generally local movement that could not be charged to help finance the highway program.

Motor vehicle, gasoline, and other charges related to road use are providing substantial help in financing the road programs in several countries. User taxes in Nigeria are paying more than 40 percent of what is spent for roads. These funds include part of the price obtained for exported raw materials moving over the roads. Marketing boards control the prices of such commodities as cocoa, oil palm, ground-nuts, and cotton, and allocate some of the revenues to regional production development boards, which in turn make loans or grants for roadbuilding and other develop-

[3] In a developing country, annual costs may be considerably lower than annual expenditures, since the latter include a high proportion of new investment with a useful life beyond the year in which the funds are expended.

ment projects.[4] In Kenya an independent road authority collects driver and vehicle licenses and fuel tax receipts. These combined with some general tax money are used to finance roadbuilding projects.[5]

Motor fuel taxes and registration fees have been supplemented by cash tolls on a limited mileage of roads in a number of countries, including Colombia, France, Italy, the United States, Mexico, Venezuela, and Japan. Considerable volumes of traffic are required to make the collection of tolls worth the effort, and only on heavy traffic routes has it been possible to cover total costs. But in most countries tolls are collected only as a supplement to other sources of revenue. The economic advantage of paying the toll is that while users pay more for roads, they pay less for transport service when roads are adequate.[6]

The approach to toll financing in Japan may have application elsewhere. Toll roads operated by the Japan Highway Public Corporation include some 500 miles of facilities, most of them short stretches to facilitate tourism or to bypass urban congestion. In addition is a long-distance toll facility between Kobe and Nagoya and thence to Tokyo that will provide a continuous toll route of 320 miles.[7] Because tolls by themselves are insufficient to pay the cost of those roads, their collection is combined with other financial support from a variety of sources. Fifty percent of the initial capital available to the corporation was provided by the Ministry of Finance, 20 percent by foreign bonds, 10 percent by road bonds, 10 percent from general funds, and only the remaining 10 percent from toll revenues.

[4] International Bank for Reconstruction and Development, *The Economic Development of Nigeria* (Johns Hopkins Press, 1955), p. 165.

[5] S. F. Bailay, "Contractor Finance in Kenya," *Road International* (Autumn, 1959).

[6] See Charles L. Dearing and Wilfred Owen, *Toll Roads and the Problem of Highway Modernization* (Brookings Institution, 1951), pp. 63–87.

[7] Information from Nihon Doro Kodan, Tokyo. See also Ralph J. Watkins and Associates, *Kobe-Nagoya Expressway Survey* (Ministry of Construction, Government of Japan, 1956).

The acquisition and sale of land along proposed new highway routes provide another potential source of highway revenues that might be tapped in developing countries. Sale or lease of the land after development permits the public to recoup part of the added value resulting from the road improvement. This approach to financing part of the road bill is a variation of the nineteenth century policy of federal land grants made to the railroads in the United States to provide a financial incentive to build ahead of the traffic. Consideration should be given to obtaining sufficiently wide rights of way at the time a new road is constructed to permit sale or lease of the land along the highway after it has been completed. Such a policy would also permit control of adjacent land uses to protect the traveled way from the encroachments of undesirable developments that create traffic hazards and congestion.

Financing Local Roads

The task of marshaling resources for local roads presents a different financing problem from that encountered on main highways carrying an appreciable volume of motorized traffic. Secondary and feeder roads may comprise as much as 90 percent of the highway system in underdeveloped countries and are used principally by pedestrians, animals, and non-mechanized vehicles moving short distances. They are not susceptible to financing through motor vehicle user taxes or tolls. Yet the development and improvement of these out-of-the-way rural roads is highly important to the economic development of rural agricultural economies. To a large extent these roads are the communications network—the only contact with the outside world. They provide the means by which the knowledge of a better life can be transmitted, together with the know-how. In densely populated countries, the principal possibility of building and maintaining the almost endless mileage of these roads lies in a plentiful supply of workers who are either partially employed or unemployed. In many countries, large numbers of workers engaged in subsistence agriculture are making no contribution to output and could be withdrawn from farming to work on other projects without any loss of production. In Pakistan, in the Second Five Year Plan, three million new jobs were needed to take care of new entries into the labor market, in addition to the even greater backlog of unemployment and of underemployment that had accumulated before the Second Plan began.

The need for useful jobs in much of the developing world, and the tremendous task of roadbuilding to overcome the isolation of rural areas raises the question how the demand for labor and its plentiful supply can be matched to achieve development objectives. The desirability of redirecting unproductive human effort and wasted human lives into channels that would create needed public facilities seems clear. The possibilities of doing so in the transport field are impressive because usable local materials are available, and extensive geographic areas can be covered by transport systems. In addition, much of what needs to be done can be accomplished by unskilled and semiskilled workers.

The size of the task seems overwhelming, but it should be recalled that the unemployment problem in the United States during the depression of the 1930's was also staggering, and that something effective was done about it. With one out of every three American workers jobless, an emergency program of public works was undertaken by the federal government to put three million people to work on useful projects. During this work-relief program, more than 651,000 miles of highways, roads, and streets were constructed or improved, including many miles of farm-to-market roads and new roads in areas previously inaccessible. About four-fifths of the people employed were manual workers, unskilled or semiskilled. Roadbuilding in particular proved to be a type of work they could do effectively. The building of roads could be spread over a wide area of countryside to reach the men available, and it could be expanded or contracted to meet seasonal conditions imposed by farm operations. It was this program that provided the first all-weather transportation for hundreds of thousands of farm families and got large parts of the United States out of the mud.[8]

To what extent could the same large-scale effort be made in less developed countries to provide useful jobs, to develop skills, and at the same time to create and maintain needed transport facilities? Obviously, there are important differences between the circumstances of America in depression and of the developing world in its present need. The people involved have different backgrounds and training, and the financial support made available through deficit financing in the United States cannot be made available by the poor countries. Another difference is that large numbers of the unemployed in the 1930's were trained in management, engineering, and other skills, and thus could fill the administrative posts. They helped to develop the state and local project plans, and they provided the capabilities necessary to organize and carry out the program. Excess capacity in industry also made available materials, tools, and equipment at reasonable cost.

The effort today to launch a program of construction to provide improved transport for developing countries suffers from the lack of these prerequisites. An attempt is being made to fill some of the gaps through international assistance efforts. A principal difference in the current picture is that the magnitude of the global problem of idle workers is infinitely greater, whereas the determination and effort being made to remedy the problem are infinitely less.

A major public works program in East Pakistan demonstrates the possibilities of organizing and applying available labor and other resources for the construction of community projects. This program is financed through the sale of surplus wheat from the United States, with the proceeds being used for wage payments and materials and tools. Major emphasis has been on the repair and renovation of roads, canals, and embankments to provide irrigation, flood control, and transport. Seventy percent of the effort has been directed to improving roads. Thousands of men were

[8] See U. S. Works Progress Administration, *Inventory: Appraisal of Results of the Works Progress Administration* (Government Printing Office, 1938).

given this extra source of income who had always been idle when they were not needed on the farm. In one year, 20,000 miles of road were included in the program.[9]

On many road projects, however, labor-intensive methods may not be desirable as a means of maximizing employment. Since the objective of providing transport is to further other objectives, it is necessary to consider whether the early completion of a transport project through capital-intensive methods is to be preferred. If rapid completion of a new transport facility will make it possible to introduce new industrial activities or to open the way for expanding agriculture, mining, or forestry, the effect on living standards created by these activities may exceed the impact created by maximizing jobs, through labor-intensive methods, on the transport project itself. In these circumstances, it would be more desirable from the standpoint of employment to use modern machinery to complete the transport improvement as quickly as possible.

The point is illustrated by a survey of the Turkish economy, which estimated that a simple rock crusher driven by an oil engine would save the manpower of a whole village, and that an elementary concrete mixer to go with it would eliminate the need for another village full of workers. With large numbers of people idle one would be tempted to recommend hand labor rather than machine technology. But the conclusion of this study was the opposite, on the grounds that the real intention should be to benefit twenty million Turks, and not merely a few thousand employees working on the roads.[10]

Secondary and tertiary road systems can be improved and maintained effectively, however, with the appropriate combination of

[9] Experiments in rural development are being undertaken through the Comilla Academy, a Government of Pakistan institution financed in large part by the Ford Foundation and aided by a Ford grant to the Michigan State University which furnishes advisers. See Pakistan Academy for Village Development, Comilla, "A New Rural Co-Operative System for Comilla Thana," July 1962.

[10] Max Weston Thornburg and Associates, *Turkey: An Economic Appraisal* (Twentieth Century Fund, 1949), p. 86.

hand labor and such tools and machinery as are needed. The degree of labor-intensive or capital-intensive methods depends on the circumstances. The possibility of marshaling available human resources for such public works is not yet being realized on a sufficiently large scale.

Reducing Transport Costs

The difficulty of obtaining resources to meet the seemingly endless demands for transport focuses attention on the need for reducing costs in every way possible. The effort to achieve such savings, however, calls for a broader view of costs than is generally taken. A low-cost road economically designed to save money may result in excessive costs of vehicle operation and a wasteful use of motor vehicle equipment. The cost of the road is lower, but the cost of transport is higher. A road may be built to standards inadequate to accommodate traffic in all weather, with the result that it will not be used, it will not contribute to development, and it may nullify the effectiveness of other investments depending on adequate transport for their productive use.

But the opposite errors are also common. They include the over-design of facilities, the failure to use capacity effectively, and the absence of maintenance. What seems to be a shortage of transport is often wasteful use of what there is. As already noted, many rail lines are without economic justification and should be abandoned rather than improved. Provision of storage facilities and more efficient scheduling of deliveries can make additions to transport capacity unnecessary. Port facilities are notorious for the congestion that results from excess paper work and other administrative inadequacies. These rituals tie up facilities that would otherwise be more than adequate.

There are other ways of adding unnecessarily to transport cost. They include poor supervision of loading and unloading, poor land transport connections to the ports, or the failure to program ship arrivals to avoid congesting available facilities. The absence of efficient port management can convert a satisfactory port into a major bottleneck. And congestion in the port can adversely affect a whole system of transport. The remedy first sought is often the expansion of port capacity rather than the correction of port operations.

Highways provide the greatest latitude for wasteful use of resources. Throughout the world they pose the difficult political problem that all sections of a country wish to share in the road improvement program at the same time. The result is that economic criteria for determining the best use of limited public funds must often give way to political considerations. The frequent result has been a dispersal of roadbuilding efforts over a series of widely separated and disconnected projects. Preoccupation with raising money has diverted attention from the equally important task of spending the money wisely.

The temptation to overdesign highways is global. Sometimes the error is unconscious. In one tropical country, the practice of designing low maximum grades in rugged topography was the result of adopting North American specifications originally conceived to cope with snow. As a result, unnecessary and costly earthmoving work was being undertaken. But more commonly the construction of high-type pavements where low-type designs would suffice is a foible that engineers from more developed countries find difficult to suppress. The tendency is encouraged by the fact that developing countries often neglect maintenance, and by the assumption that without appropriate maintenance, a good road will last longer than a poor one. But if maintenance is neglected, the loss may be greater on a high-type road because the investment is larger.

Overdesign is also encouraged by a belief among officials in some of the less developed countries that the more developed nations rely on higher standards than is the case. This illusion has been nurtured by the custom of introducing visitors from emerging countries to the New York Throughway instead of the secondary roads of Texas. The result is an erroneous impression of the nature of the highway network.

The fact is, however, that despite its expressways, the United States depends heavily on low-cost roads of simple design. In 1961, close to a million miles of highway were unsurfaced. Nearly half were primitive and unimproved roads. In some states, the majority of roads are unsurfaced: 78 percent of the mileage in Wyoming, and 74 percent in New Mexico. More than 40 percent of the mileage in ten other states is unsurfaced. Even the roads that have been surfaced are mostly of modest design. There are 1.3 million miles of soil-type, gravel, or stone surfaced roads and another 683,000 miles of intermediate-types with either bituminous surface-treated or bituminous mix or penetration surface.[11] Altogether, therefore, 2.3 million miles of roads in the United States are either unimproved, graded and drained only, or surfaced with gravel, stone, or stabilized soil. These roads make up almost two-thirds of the total United States road mileage. More than half of the remaining third are intermediate type roads, and only one mile out of every six is a high-type paved road.

Another way of reducing costs in addition to modest design standards is to maintain existing facilities. Development plans typically focus on the capital investment required to provide new transport facilities and overlook the continuing obligation of maintaining plant and equipment already provided. A new highway rapidly disintegrates for lack of upkeep, and construction equipment soon becomes inoperable when left without maintenance and unprotected from the weather. Signs of neglected maintenance are seen repeatedly in developing countries. Large capital savings and higher standards of transport could be achieved if the care taken to justify, plan, and execute a construction project were extended to organizing and financing an effective maintenance program.

Many miles of road surfaces that have received little or no attention since their original construction will ultimately be lost, and

[11] U. S. Bureau of Public Roads, "Table M-2," (1961).

new capital will have to be allocated to build the same facility again. In some countries the law encourages this neglect. Wherever aid to local governments is confined to construction, local governments permit roads to deteriorate until they become eligible to receive additional aid for reconstruction. Meanwhile, lack of maintenance has resulted in loss of much of the original investment, transport service is poor, and vehicle operating costs high.

The importance of an adequate maintenance program has been amply demonstrated by experience in the more highly motorized countries. In the United States, for example, one-third of all road expenditures is used to keep existing facilities in adequate condition. For local rural roads, which are comparable to most roads in less developed countries, more than half of all expenditures in recent years has been for maintenance. While the distinction between construction and maintenance is often blurred, it is clear that keeping roads in good condition is a major cost of any road program.

The emphasis on maintenance in the Turkish road program sponsored by the United States set a useful example. To stretch available funds as far as possible, two principal policies were followed. At the very beginning, the program was focused on training personnel in both the operation and maintenance of equipment and in the mechanized maintenance of the roads to be built. A training shop for maintenance operators was established to produce six hundred graduates per year, and additional assistance in training engineers was furnished through the United States Bureau of Public Roads. In addition, the program called for relatively low-cost all-weather facilities to accommodate light traffic for a ten- to fifteen-year period. It was calculated that a stabilized soil road would not qualify for asphalt surfacing until traffic had reached three hundred vehicles per day, while a concrete pavement was warranted only for traffic of a thousand vehicles per day.

Efforts to organize road maintenance operations on a continuing basis and to assure their financial support were made in Latin America some years ago through the *servicios* sponsored jointly by the United States and Latin American countries. The maintenance problem was tackled in Bolivia by the establishment of the Bolivian-American Cooperative Road Service. Three years after this program of road upkeep and improvement was initiated in 1956, traffic quadrupled. Roads maintained by the *servicio* were kept open throughout the rainy season for the first time, despite annual rainfall of over twenty-two feet per year. Good maintenance made it possible for a truck to make three times as many trips as before, and to move meat, fish, and other perishables to market with a minimum of spoilage.[12]

Organizing to Get Things Done

The problem of financial support is closely related to organizing and administering the transport program. Developing countries often have no suitable institutional arrangements for planning and constructing transport facilities, or for the continuing operation and maintenance of what is built. Even where administrative bodies are handling particular aspects of the transport problem satisfactorily, different types of transport are being separately provided, with neither satisfactory physical connections nor arrangements for through traffic and through rates. Neither physical nor financial problems are viewed in the context of a total system.

The disorganization of the transport sector is the natural outcome of transport evolution. As new methods of transport made their appearance, they were challenged by established methods that were fearful of losing patronage. A state of rivalry and often hostility among transport media resulted. Regulatory measures restricted the operations of some carriers, and allocations of public funds gave some parts of the transport system an advantage over others. These conditions have not encouraged the integration of

[12] International Road Federation, *World Highways* (Sept. 1, 1957), p. 3; (Nov. 1, 1957), p. 3.

facilities or the weighing of transport alternatives on economic grounds.

In Nigeria at one time, it was the law that motor vehicles operating on roads parallel to the railway had to pay double the ordinary rate of road tax. In the former Gold Coast, there were instances in which road bridges over rivers were removed to discourage truck transport. Cocoa traffic was diverted to the railways by excluding trucks from government-controlled ports. In Pakistan, goods moving on the road must often be transferred from one truck to another at district boundaries. In many countries, the availability of trucks and buses has been severely limited by import quotas, and repair parts are frequently at a premium. Cannibalizing two or three trucks to keep one operating is not uncommon. Ostensibly the reason is to save foreign exchange, but the desire to protect the railways is often a factor. In India, the permissible length of truck haul was at one time only fifty miles, and later seventy-five. In practice, the issuance of operating permits still prohibits truck operations in excess of three hundred miles.

Problems created for the railways by technological change might be avoided in the short run through the imposition of restrictions. But if the newer forms of transport are discouraged, both shippers and the railways will suffer in the long run by efforts to maintain services that railways are not capable of performing. Most importantly, the failure to take advantage of scientific innovation will have a detrimental effect on development.

The desire to provide a more satisfactory organizational and administrative environment has led some developing countries, with prodding from the World Bank, to take steps to alter their administrative approach to transport. One trend has been toward a public authority or semiautonomous public corporation, especially for the operation of railways and ports. Such an organization has been favored because it can be relatively independent of the political pressures encountered in government ministries, and because its financial accounts can be separately maintained. Thus far, however, most of these independent bodies have assumed responsibility for only individual sectors of the transport program. This has posed a dilemma. From a financing and administrative point of view, the authority has provided an effective solution. But there are disadvantages to dividing into tighter compartments a field of activity that already suffers from excessive fragmentation.

Extension of the responsibilities of the public corporation to include two or more types of transport investment is one direction in which further administrative innovations could lead. A more feasible approach is to lodge all public transport responsibilities in a ministry of transport, which would have its own research and planning staff to assist in policy and program coordination. If neither solution is adopted, and the railway, port, highway, airport, and other public agencies are left unrelated and independent, the national planning commission could exercise coordinating powers. The planning commission, however, has the difficult task of relating goals in various sectors of the economy to the total transport plan, which in itself is a major effort. The added task of making sure that choices of technology have been wisely made at the project level cannot be effectively carried out at this stage of the planning process.

In addition to the problem of integrating plans and policies for public transport investment and operation, a second major management problem is in the provision of transport services. In most countries, each transport service is separately supplied, and the result is often the lack of a complete system providing maximum standards and economy. In Canada, an effort to achieve this goal is being made through the organization of transport companies under both public and private auspices. There are two major rail lines in Canada, the privately owned Canadian Pacific Railway and the Canadian National Railways, a public corporation. Each of them has embarked on an effort to develop a total system of transport, one in the private and the other in the public sector. The public corporation, the Canadian National, has the largest railway in the non-Communist world, with 24,000 miles of routes operating throughout Canada and into ten states of the United States as well. The CNR also operates an airline, ocean shipping facilities, communications, and motor transport companies.

Competing with the government-owned CNR is the Canadian Pacific Railway, which also operates a variety of transport facilities. Canadian Pacific has 17,000 miles of rail routes in Canada and controls another 5,000 miles in the United States. The company operates steamships and airlines that serve five continents, plus Canada's largest fleet of for-hire trucks covering 10,000 miles of highway routes. The Canadian Pacific transport network adds up to 85,000 miles. It provides an integrated service for small shipments, using all forms of transport under its control.[13]

The Canadian systems are moving in the direction of assuring a total approach to providing transport services, and investment decisions in the public sector are aided by this effort to allocate traffic on a more rational economic basis. The total system concept has led not only to the physical integration of services but to the abandonment of outmoded rate and regulatory policies. One rate innovation has been to increase air fares for short hauls and to reduce them for long-distance travel. These changes reflect the economies of air transport and place rail passenger service in a better competitive position in the shorter distances where it has an economic advantage. Rate policy for freight movement also encourages short haul trucking.

The logic of coping with transport as one problem rather than as a series of unrelated problems seems clear, but there are strong reservations on practical grounds to an integrated approach. The principal misgiving is that the dominant carrier in many countries is the railway, and rail management might seek preferential treatment that would stifle the development of alternative water, road, or air services. If the government's transport investment were heavily committed to rail, for example, a government-operated transport company might favor this method over truck

[13] "Canada's Railroads," *Railway Age* (Nov. 2, 1959), pp. 20 and 27.

transport even if the railways were unable to provide acceptable standards of service. Obviously, this objection should be surmountable. Newly developing nations starting from scratch with a new generation of public officials, can lead the way toward an effective unification of transport management.

If a public agency were to provide freight and passenger services through unified ownership of all forms of transport, rivalry among transport agencies would be eliminated by establishing responsibility for a complete transport service. There would be a real incentive to route traffic by the most efficient way in order to achieve the most economical total operation.[14] Private transport would continue, of course, to operate along with the public carrier system.

Organizational arrangements for the provision of transport services have important implications for transport financing. A total system approach could reduce uneconomic competition among carriers because revenues could be pooled. Traffic could be encouraged by rate policies to move in ways that would lead to allocations reflecting relative economy and service. The precise arrangement by which a national network of transport services could be supplied would obviously vary among countries. Establishing a transport company would raise the question whether intercity common carrier service by truck and bus, now almost invariably in the private sector, should be included in the public agency operating the integrated transport service. The advantage stemming from privately operated common carrier services is that capital requirements for trucks can generally be met by private investors, and that the drain on public capital is reduced accordingly.

If a transport company were established, it is logical to assume that over-the-road common carrier services would be run by the government agency or public corporation created for the purpose. The fact that Canada has both a public and a private system, however, suggests that it is the system approach that counts, and not how it is operated. In any event, private ownership and operation

[14] Lee J. Melton, "The Transportation Company: An Economic Inevitability," Reprinted from Highway Research Board *Proceedings*, Vol. 39 (1960), p. 42.

in the transport sector would continue to play an important role since many industries operate their own trucks or contract for the road transport they require. In addition, a transport company would serve primarily nationwide rather than local needs, and local hauling would remain largely in private hands.

Another organizational solution is the operation of mixed public and private enterprises. This approach has been taken to provide airline services, such as in Ethiopia, and in joint state-private trucking operations in Afghanistan.[15] A compromise suggestion to overcome the disadvantages of public-private competition in West Pakistan has been to sell shares of government bus enterprises to private investors, thus reducing the need for public capital and providing an outlet for private savings. Such a plan has important service as well as financial advantages, for it eliminates the problem created by small private operators whose competition for riders often results in inadequate service.[16] Similar innovations are occurring in the construction of roads jointly by public and private agencies. In Brazil, for example, a state highway department has provided road plans and specifications and purchased right-of-way, and building and paving costs were defrayed by a private company.[17]

These examples suggest that the conventional division of transport functions between the public and private sector do not necessarily provide the most satisfactory solution. Developing countries have challenged some of the conventional approaches by a combination of public and private enterprise in the provision of highways, air transport, and bus and truck operations. The possibility that more railways should be in the private sector or operated by private management firms on a contract basis might also be considered. As will be noted later, the operation of a gov-

[15] Donald N. Wilbur, Country Survey Files, *Afghanistan*, Human Relations Area Files (New Haven, 1956).

[16] On one route in West Pakistan, for example, there are forty operators serving one thirty-mile route. R. D. Mallon, Planning Commission of Pakistan, "Memorandum," dated Oct. 15, 1959 (mimeo.).

[17] International Road Federation, *Road International* (Autumn 1961), pp. 49–51.

ernment airline through a management contract with a private firm provides a good example of the benefits of joint undertakings of this kind.

International and Community Organization

The technological changes that compel developing nations to look at the parts of their transport systems as a national whole also suggest the desirability of regional transport systems for groups of nations. Many parts of the world have already embarked on programs for planning, financing, and administering transport on an international basis. This expanding view of the transport problem and its solution has resulted in part from the increasing radius and speed of transport operations made possible by technological change. These improved methods of transport have created pressures for international arrangements due to the high cost of modern technology and the necessity for sharing financial burdens wherever possible.

Air transport requirements dramatize the need for international administrative arrangements. Joint provision of air traffic control facilities and joint purchase, operation, and maintenance of costly aircraft are growing necessities in the jet age, and the need for solutions on an even wider geographic basis is indicated for supersonic jets. The construction and maintenance of international highway routes is another obvious area for cooperation among countries. Reciprocal arrangements with respect to vehicle size, weight, and safety regulations are also growing with the extension of road services across international boundaries. International arrangements for rail and water transport have had a longer history, but their potential is increasing with the trend toward international economic integration.

Europe established many of the precedents long ago. The Danube and Rhine Rivers have been under international administration for a hundred years. These arrangements provide for freedom of navigation to vessels of all nations, and promote uniform maintenance of waterways.[18] European railroads acted to reduce the effects of national boundaries three quarters of a century ago when the Bern Conventions provided for such matters as international tariffs, interchange of equipment, procedures at frontier points, and the maintenance of collective responsibility by member nations.

More recently, with a million railroad cars crossing national boundaries in Western Europe, the interchange problem has been further resolved by establishing a ten-nation pool of freight cars that has greatly facilitated international movement, and an international financing agency makes capital available on favorable terms for the purchase of equipment by member countries of the Council of Europe. In the passenger field, express trains ignore political boundaries to provide fast international service to seventy cities.

The development of air transport has seen comparable efforts to ease the flow of international traffic. The desirability of such an arrangement was demonstrated long ago by the Scandinavian Airlines System, a joint enterprise of Norway, Sweden, and Denmark. Middle East countries have joined in a similar arrangement to provide an all-Arab airline service. Another move toward internationally integrated air transport is Europe's air navigation control system, Eurocontrol. And arrangements have been made under the European Economic Community for pooling airline operations, joint use of ground facilities, and joint maintenance of equipment.

Other examples of transport as an integrating force are the work of the European Coal and Steel Community in facilitating international movements of steel, coal, and other materials by establishing through rates and eliminating rate differentials that discriminate against international trade; the activities of the European Economic Community in overhauling transport rate systems

[18] H. Osborne Mance, *International River and Canal Transport* (Oxford University Press, 1945), pp. 1–79.

to reduce distribution costs and to promote international trade; and provisions for financing transport facilities in undeveloped areas of Europe through the European Investment Bank.

Africa, Asia, and Latin America have made less progress in providing transport on an international basis. The countries involved are generally much larger than those of Western Europe, and to date their lack of development has limited the trade and contacts that build up pressure for international cooperation. But lack of trade and contacts are in turn the result of an absence of international transport connections. The transport modernization program that is going forward will have to be viewed on a regional basis if the potentials of integrated economic development are to be realized, and cooperative arrangements will have to be worked out to help keep pace with new transport technology.

In Central America international maintenance of the 21,000 mile Inter-American Highway System has been under study, involving an inter-American maintenance authority which would be jointly supported by the affected countries. The practical value of a centralized agency lies in pooling financial support, central purchase of equipment, effective use of trained personnel and machinery, and the establishment of uniform regulations. A similar arrangement is under consideration for the international operation of air navigation facilities.[19]

In Africa, the railways of Tanganyika have been operated with those of Kenya and Uganda as one system for a decade and a half. The East African Railways and Harbours Administration, with headquarters in Kenya, provides for the administration of this unified system. The railway net is financially stronger, the utilization of its rolling stock and equipment is more efficient, staff and administrative costs are lower, and tariffs more reasonable than would have been the case if the systems had continued as separate entities. Air services of the three countries are also jointly operated by the East African Airways Corporation.[20]

[19] International Road Federation, "The Pan American Highway in Central America," *World Highways* (June 1960).

[20] International Bank for Reconstruction and Development, *The Economic Development*

The need for internationally integrated transport facilities becomes more pressing as individual countries proceed with development programs that clearly need to be related to the plans of their neighbors. Central review of country plans in connection with foreign aid programs provides an opportunity to focus attention on the potentials for regional development and the need for international transport connections to implement a broader basis for effective resource use.

In addition to regional arrangements on an international level, there is also need for organizing transport services effectively at the local level. An attack on this aspect of the transport problem has been made through various types of cooperatives. These organizations can assist the small-scale operator to achieve some of the economies of large-scale enterprise in the sale, storage, and transporting of produce, as well as in the purchase and use of equipment and the financing of seeds, fertilizers, and other supplies. The ownership of motor trucks by cooperatives provides the means of marketing crops that would otherwise never reach consumers. The fishing industry can be aided by joint ownership of boats. Cooperatives help deliver raw materials to small-scale operators on favorable terms and provide information on markets and prices. All of these aids reduce transport costs and free isolated suppliers from dependence on middlemen. These cooperative efforts also provide a useful outlet for local savings.

It is apparent in most developing countries that the problem of providing transport is magnified not only by the absence of needed resources but by the failure to use effectively what resources are available. Surplus labor that could be used for community development seldom is productively employed. Indigenous materials that could serve admirably for low-cost roads are often overlooked.

---

of Tanganyika (Johns Hopkins Press, 1961), pp. 283–84 and 291–93. The East African Railways and Harbours Administration operates as an Agency of the East Africa High Commission, made up of the governors of Kenya, Uganda, and Tanganyika. This commission is assisted by the Central Legislative Assembly, empowered to legislate for specific common services, including railway, civil aviation, ports, and telecommunications.

The organization needed to put idle men and materials to work may also be lacking, together with the public and private entrepreneurs to direct useful projects. It is even commonly the case that transport facilities are available but that pricing policies or regulations are such as to discourage or prevent their use. Transport facilities are often overdesigned for the task to be accomplished, and underutilized for lack of satisfactory maintenance. Since the major effort to provide transport facilities involves the application of a country's own resources, the key problem is obviously one of organizing, strengthening, and using these resources as effectively as possible.

CHAPTER VI

New Directions for Foreign Aid

DEVELOPING NATIONS depend primarily on their own capabilities to provide an adequate transport system, including their ingenuity and labor, the institutions they are able to create, and the materials available at home or obtainable from abroad through foreign exchange earnings. But most of these countries also need help from the outside, including capital, entrepreneurs, and technical skills. These resources, provided by countries farther along the road to development, are increments that often prove critical. To what extent and in what ways can foreign aid provide the extra margin of money, men, and management necessary to achieve the transport systems required?

The Decade of Development

The 1960's have been designated by the United Nations as the Decade of Development. This is a period in which extraordinary efforts are to be made to help nations willing to help themselves. An important step was the launching of the Alliance for Progress, aimed at delivering $20 billion of foreign capital to Latin America from the United States, Western Europe, and the World Bank, supplemented by $80 billion of Latin American development capital. The Alliance was conceived not only as an instrument for marshalling outside assistance on a global scale, but for urging social and economic reforms on participating nations. It provides a means of integrating external assistance and promoting regional development through the preparation of development plans and their review by an international panel.

The Decade of Development has promoted considerable soul-searching about the efficacy of foreign aid. Some of the aid-giving countries have been taking a closer look at what they have been doing for the poor, and the United States has concluded in a significant report to the President that it may be trying to do too much.[1] Before a third of the decade passed, there were already signs that some people were becoming disillusioned and impatient with the results. But the warning had also been sounded that telescoping centuries of pioneering into decades would not be easy, that the Decade of Development was not a slogan but a call for endurance, and that this was a time for vision, patience, work, and wisdom.[2]

In the transport field, the exercise of vision and wisdom has been less than spectacular, and the work yet to be accomplished to bring down transport barriers is formidable. But the fact remains that extensive transport assistance has been provided by the more affluent nations, and that in the short period since aid to developing countries began, many of the results have been impressive. The question is not whether the effort has been worthwhile, but how to make future programs more effective. For this purpose a clearer picture is needed of what has been done, how much it has cost, what has proved useful, and what changes experience has taught are needed.

[1] U. S. Department of State, Committee to Strengthen the Security of the Free World, "The Scope and Distribution of United States Military and Economic Assistance Programs" (Clay Report), March 20, 1963.

[2] Message from President Kennedy to the Congress on Foreign Aid, April 2, 1963.

Money and Materials

Countries in early stages of development have no domestic supply of rails, locomotives, motor vehicles, aircraft, ships, or construction machinery. They lack steel, cement, petroleum, and many other materials. Assistance programs have supplied the capital that has enabled developing countries to obtain from abroad the materials and equipment they need.

Clearly, the task of improving transport will not be accomplished without drawing heavily on the productive capacity of the industrialized nations. Since the foreign exchange earned by developing countries falls short of the cost of needed imports, much of what is necessary for transport improvement must be obtained through loans, grants, and foreign private investment that furnish capital and foreign exchange. Help is also needed to accelerate the introduction of new technology and new techniques, to improve the quality as well as increase the quantity of transport investments. This assistance is provided by many programs financed in different ways and sponsored by a large number of national, international, and private organizations.

What the World Bank Does

Significant aid for transport in less developed areas has been provided by the International Bank for Reconstruction and Development. (IBRD). From the inauguration of bank operations in 1946 through mid-1963, transport projects absorbed 2.3 billion dollars, or 35 percent of the total loan funds made available. In Africa 48 percent of all funds loaned were for transport, in Asia and the Middle East 43 percent, and in the Western Hemisphere 32 percent. (See Table 6.1.) Approximately half of transport financing was for railways and nearly a third for roads.

TABLE 6.1. *Loans by the International Bank for Reconstruction and Development, 1946 through June 1963*
(In millions of U. S. dollars)

Purpose	World Total	*Percentage Distribution*[a]	*Transport as Percent of Total Development Loans*
Total Loans			
Electric Power	2,336	*36*	
Transportation	2,261	*35*	
Communications	27	[b]	
Agriculture and Forestry	529	*8*	
Industry	1,129	*17*	
General Development	205	*3*	
Total	6,487	*100*	
For Transport, by Region			
Africa	443	*20*	*48*
Asia and Middle East	1,023	*45*	*43*
Australia	132	*6*	*32*
Europe	103	*5*	*10*
Western Hemisphere	560	*25*	*32*
Total	2,261	*100*	*35*
For Transport, by Method			
Railroads	1,090	*48*	
Roads	741	*33*	
Shipping	12	*1*	
Ports and Waterways	297	*13*	
Airlines and Airports	57	*3*	
Pipelines	64	*3*	
Total	2,261	*100*	

Source: International Bank for Reconstruction and Development, *Eighteenth Annual Report 1962–63*, based on table p. 18.
[a] Totals do not always add to 100 due to rounding.
[b] Less than 0.5 percent.

The nature of the bank's activities is indicated by the record of the past three years. In 1961, half of all loan funds were for transport investments in eleven countries: six were in Latin America, five in Asia and the Middle East, and none in Africa. Railway improvements accounted for 62 percent of the transport total, and rail projects in Japan and India together amounted to half of all transport aid. Highway projects absorbed nearly a third of the transport program, and again two countries dominated the picture. Mexico and Argentina together received four out of every five dollars lent for roads.

In 1962, the emphasis on transport fell sharply to 27 percent of total bank loans, with nine countries participating. In this year, roads were the principal object of expenditure, accounting for 62 percent of the total, just as railway projects had done the year before. Transport projects in India, Japan, and Mexico again received special emphasis—nearly 60 percent of all transport assistance.

In 1963, transport loans rose and accounted for 42 percent of the total. Roads were again the principal object of expenditure. (See Table A.8.)

Concentration on a few of the more developed countries reflects the interest of the IBRD in bankable projects. For bank loans are generally repayable in the currency in which they are made, which nearly always means in hard currencies, and terms include relatively short maturities of fifteen to twenty years with relatively high interest rates of 5 to 6 percent. Loans must be for "productive" purposes in the sense that the income from them will cover the cost, and all credits must be government-guaranteed.

Among the major railway undertakings of the bank have been eight loans to India, comprising nearly a third of a billion dollars, the largest amount lent to any country for a single purpose. The eighth of these made available most of the foreign exchange required for the Indian railways during the last year of the Second Five Year Plan.

Colombia's Atlantico Railway was also made possible by a series of International Bank loans. The first of these helped to pay for the construction of several hundred miles of new rail line and the rehabilitation of additional mileage to connect Bogota and

Central Colombia with the Atlantic port of Santa Marta. The third loan helped to finance diesel locomotives and freight cars to be assembled in Colombia, including shop equipment and repair parts.

Another major assist to rail construction was undertaken in Nigeria following recommendations of a bank survey mission to that country.[3] It provided for four hundred miles of new railway into the remote but potentially rich agricultural areas of northeast Nigeria previously served by roundabout and inadequate road connections. The line provides a direct link from the northeast provinces to the coast and to Lagos, more than a thousand miles away.

In recent years the bank has shifted from its earlier preoccupation with railway improvements, and has devoted much more attention to road projects. The largest was undertaken in Iran, where loan funds and Iranian oil revenues were combined to finance an extensive highway network. During construction, which was designed and supervised by foreign engineering firms, the Iranian Ministry of Roads also undertook to strengthen its maintenance organization with help from the United States Bureau of Public Roads.

Port improvements financed by the World Bank often include not only the construction of deepwater ports and related dock and storage facilities, but land transport connections as well. In Ruanda-Urundi, bank financing of a modern port on Lake Tanganyika included funds for a new and shorter road connection to the central plateau, where population and economic activity are concentrated. For the port of Callao in Peru, an initial loan aided in the construction of grain discharging and storage facilities and the purchase of mechanical cargo-handling equipment. Further credits were then arranged for the construction of berths for petroleum products and general cargo, storage sheds, and improved accommodations for passengers. A series of follow-up loans makes it

[3] International Bank for Reconstruction and Development, *The Economic Development of Nigeria* (Johns Hopkins Press, 1955), pp. 476–78.

possible for the bank to influence successive stages of construction as well as maintenance and operation of the facilities.

The accomplishments of the bank have been impressive, but many countries have been unable to meet the rigid credit terms imposed. As demands for help multiplied, therefore, the need for a more flexible means of responding became increasingly urgent. The answer was to create within the bank a financially separate but affiliated agency that could provide assistance where it was needed on terms that would be financially feasible.

Extending the Bank's Work Through IDA

The International Development Association was created by member states of the World Bank in the fall of 1960 as an ancillary organization to assist countries in financing the type of project that contributes to development but cannot qualify for support under the terms established by the bank itself. In three years IDA acquired ninety members and subscriptions of close to a billion dollars.

Loans through IDA provide flexible terms that create less pressure on the balance of payments of underdeveloped countries. Credits are extended for a term of fifty years, interest free, with a service charge of less than 1 percent annually on the amount outstanding. Loans are repayable in hard currency, with amortization beginning after a ten-year period. Thereafter, 1 percent of the principal amount is repayable annually for ten years, and 3 percent in each of the final thirty years.[4]

The IDA has emphasized the construction of roads in its transport program, particularly secondary and feeder routes. More than one-fourth of its credits were extended for this purpose during the first two years of operation. The bank and IDA finance many projects jointly, such as the program to construct 800 miles of main roads in Colombia. In this case, IDA credit was extended

[4] For transport loans by the IDA, June 1961–June 1963, see Table A.9.

to help cover the cost of construction, while the bank loan was for purchase of equipment. Other IDA projects have included improvement of about a third of the Costa Rican highway system, the opening of rich agricultural lands in populous regions of Honduras, and assistance in financing half of India's national highway expenditures during the first three years of the Third Five Year Plan. One out of two dollars of assistance through IDA has gone to India.

Help has also been extended for inland water transport in Pakistan, including the installation of cargo and passenger facilities at five inland river ports. The International Bank was instrumental in getting the Pakistan government to establish the Inland Water Transport Authority, which is in charge of operating the ports as well as supervising the operation of the inland water transport system. Part of the IDA credit was used for the services of foreign personnel to assist the authority in operations and training.

Transport Financing by the Export-Import Bank

Bilateral arrangements for financing transport are made by the United States through the Export-Import Bank and the Agency for International Development. The latter is the focal point for United States aid while the Eximbank, which has been a major lending agency for nearly thirty years, is a more specialized operation with its focus on trade.

The Eximbank of Washington was established in 1934 to promote trade between the United States and the Soviet Union. When preliminary negotiations failed to settle outstanding obligations of the Soviet Union to the United States, however, the bank shifted its attention to the promotion of United States exports throughout the world. Since then, it has extended nearly $14 billion of credits to eighty-nine countries. Transport projects have accounted for about $2 billion (see Table A.10), nearly as much as the transport loans of the World Bank. Operations are on a self-supporting basis, including interest on all borrowings at a rate set by the United States Treasury, plus substantial dividends on capital stock. The Eximbank also pays its administrative costs out of earnings, and has built up a half-billion dollar reserve.

Loans have been concentrated in Europe and Latin America, but in recent years assistance to Asia has been stepped up considerably. Latin America's share of transport credits has been 56 percent of the total, while at the other extreme Africa has received less than 6 percent of the funds made available for transport. (See Table 6.2.)

TABLE 6.2. *Transport Credits Extended by the Export-Import Bank, 1934 through June 1963*

(In millions of dollars)

	Transport Credits	*Percent*
By Region		
Africa	122.6	*5.7*
Asia	418.0	*19.6*
Europe	381.8	*17.9*
Latin America	1,186.5	*55.5*
Oceania	27.3	*1.3*
Total Transport Credits	2,136.2	*100.0*
By Transport Methods		
Railways	853.2	*39.9*
Aircraft and airports	428.7	*20.1*
Highways	414.1	*19.4*
Harbor development	117.0	*5.5*
Vessels	76.1	*3.6*
Automotive equipment	97.8	*4.6*
Auto industry equipment	114.0	*5.3*
Construction equipment	35.3	*1.7*
Total	2,136.2	*100.0*

Source: Table A.10.

The Export-Import Bank program combines the objectives of expanding the export market of the lender and furthering the economic strength of the borrower. Loans are made both to governments and to private industries. They must supplement rather than compete with private capital, and must offer a reasonable expectation of repayment. United States private investors and manufacturing and export firms make substantial contributions in connection with the bank's operations through credits extended by suppliers of the equipment being financed, and by advances from commercial banks operating with Export-Import guarantees.

The major field of concentration for the Eximbank has been railway locomotives and rolling stock, which have accounted for 40 percent of all transport loan funds. Assistance to Mexico's rail system helped rebuild two-thirds of the country's main line mileage and supplied diesel locomotives to help accommodate a 50 percent increase in freight traffic over a ten-year period. Another loan has enabled the United Arab Republic Railways to buy a hundred diesel locomotives.

The Eximbank has also directed substantial resources to the sale of aircraft, chiefly commercial airliners. Altogether 20 percent of bank transport financing has been for air transport. The method of combining bank credit with private financing is illustrated by the sale of Douglas jets to Brazil. The transaction was made possible by a 12 percent loan from Douglas, a 20 percent down payment by Panair on delivery, and an Eximbank credit for the remaining 68 percent.

The Eximbank has also helped many countries to finance the dollar costs of roadbuilding, including equipment, materials, and technical assistance. One example is a credit to Iran for procurement of machinery needed for the Iranian road program, including motor vehicles, earth-moving equipment, spare parts, tools, and radio facilities. This loan was combined with World Bank financing and technical assistance from the United States Bureau of Public Roads.

A number of industrial loans have also been made to support transport equipment manufacture. Credit has been extended to Japan's Toyoto and Nissan Motor Companies for expansion of automotive production facilities, to Turkey for the production of jeeps, and to private companies in Argentina for the manufacture of machine tools used in the production of pick-up trucks.

The Export-Import Bank, in contrast to the World Bank, has been only incidentally concerned with development. It has operated extensively in developed as well as in underdeveloped countries. But in recent years, Eximbank transactions have often been tied to United States assistance projects in a way that permits the bank to carry out its traditional function and at the same time promote development objectives.

The Agency for International Development

The United States operation expressly concerned with helping the less developed countries is the Agency for International Development, which was established in 1961 to carry on the established programs of grants and loans, technical assistance, and support for international organizations. This organization is the successor to the International Cooperation Administration and the Development Loan Fund. These programs in turn succeeded the Foreign Operations Administration, the Mutual Security Agency, and the Economic Cooperation Administration.

A summary of United States assistance to transport development prior to the AID program requires a look at the ICA and the Development Loan Fund.[5] From 1955 to 1961 the ICA committed the equivalent of $4.9 billion to finance specific projects, mostly in the form of grants. One-fifth of this program, or nearly a billion dollars, was for transport. Actually, this sum was partly dollars and partly United States-owned local currencies. Of the dollar-financed projects in the ICA program, which totaled $2.8 billion, 25 percent was for transport. Other project expenditures, equivalent to $2.1 billion, were financed from United States-owned local currencies created by the sale of surplus agricultural commodities.

[5] For funds obligated by the International Cooperation Administration and the Development Loan Fund, 1955–61, see Table 6.3.

TABLE 6.3. *Funds Obligated by ICA and DLF with U. S. Dollars and Local Currencies, 1955–61*

(In millions of dollars)

	Transport Loans	*Percent*
By Region		
Far East	450.2	*29.2*
Near East and South Asia	632.9	*41.1*
Europe	205.5	*13.3*
Latin America	181.9	*11.8*
Africa	71.2	*4.6*
Transport Total	1,541.7	*100.0*
By Transport Method		
Roads	647.0	*42.0*
Railways	484.6	*31.4*
Air	186.0	*12.1*
Ports and inland waterways	93.5	*6.1*
Miscellaneous	130.6	*8.5*
Total	1,541.7	*100.0*
Total development loans	6,854.0	
Transport as percent of total		*22.5*

Source: Tables A.12 and A.13.

Of these expenditures, 13 percent was for transport.[6] Five countries, India, Pakistan, Thailand, Cambodia, and Afghanistan, accounted for 27 percent of all project obligations, while twenty-three other countries shared the remainder. (See Tables A.11 and A.12.)

The Development Loan Fund, which was the forerunner of the present loan program, was created two years after the ICA began to operate to provide a source of capital for long-term development. This was the initial departure from the previous emphasis on grants. The DLF operated through loans, investment guarantees, and other forms of financing. Repayment was either in local

[6] The picture is further complicated by the fact that some "non-project" aid was also used for transport equipment purchases. In 1961 over $40 million of transport machinery was financed this way. See International Cooperation Administration, *Operations Report, Data as of June 30, 1961*, table, p. 62.

currency, in dollars, or in other currency specified in the loan agreement, depending on the financial capacity of the recipient. Financing was provided then, as now, only when money was unavailable on reasonable terms from the International Bank, Eximbank, or private sources.[7] Under the Development Loan Fund, money made available by the Congress was available until expended and did not have to be obligated within specific periods of time, and such funds, together with repayments and earnings, were made available for further lending. The fact that these funds were drawn from a more or less permanent source formalized the commitment of the United States to long-term financing of economic development.[8]

The Agency for International Development has departed from former aid programs by focusing on loans. This new approach has resulted from the view that loans tend to minimize sensitivities among those who receive as well as those who dispense, and that the obligation to repay is an inducement to effective program execution. Another new emphasis has been to encourage developing nations to establish long-range plans. Recipient nations are also being urged to pursue sound fiscal and financial policies and to undertake social reforms. The United States itself is viewing its aid policies more closely in relation to other national objectives, and the interagency policymaking body, the Development Loan Committee, establishes standards and criteria for harmonizing lending operations with United States foreign policies.[9]

The terms and conditions on which development loans are extended differ markedly from prior practice in two major respects: all repayments are to be made in dollars, and repayment terms are

[7] The interest rate on loans was $3\frac{1}{2}$ percent for infrastructure projects and $5\frac{3}{4}$ percent for industrial type projects.

[8] U. S. Department of State, U. S. Department of Defense, International Cooperation Administration, *The Mutual Security Program, Fiscal Year 1960: A Summary Presentation* (March 1959), p. 59.

[9] Represented on the Committee are the Assistant Secretary of State for Economic Affairs, the Assistant Secretary of the Treasury dealing with international finance, the Chairman of the Board of Directors of the Eximbank, the officer of AID dealing with development financing, and the Administrator of AID, who is the Chairman.

tailored to the recipient country's financial capacity rather than to the character of the activity financed. Thus even though repayment must be in dollars, the borrowing government has forty years to pay, plus a ten-year grace period. Meanwhile, it pays a fee amounting to 2 percent per year.[10] The shift to dollar repayment reflects a consensus that the advantages of local currency repayment are outweighed by its disadvantages. In a number of countries the United States already has excessive holdings of foreign currencies.

The development financing activities of AID include three major categories: development grants, development loans, and supporting assistance. Transport projects are included in all three.

Development grants are primarily for social projects, including health, education, and sanitation, but they are also used to finance transport projects in countries where preconditions for growth are still absent, including newly independent countries in Africa. The African continent as a whole in 1962 received one-third of all development grants, and of the somewhat more than $100 million received by African nations, 13 percent was for transport. (See Table A.14.)

Development loans are made either for specific capital projects or for imports that would permit the recipient countries to carry out a general investment program. During fiscal year 1962, development loans amounted to slightly over a billion dollars, of which a little over half was aid for specific projects, aimed at improving agriculture, industry and mining, health and sanitation, and transportation.

A third category of aid, supporting assistance, is provided largely on a grant basis. Justification for this type of aid is that recipient countries need an input of resources to permit them to support the burden of their military forces, or that they require additional resources to prevent economic instability from threatening United States political interests. Usually this assistance is used

[10] The terms were altered in 1963 to raise the rate of interest on the unpaid balance from less than 1 percent.

TABLE 6.4. *Transport Financing through AID, Fiscal Year 1962*[a]
(In thousands of dollars)

	Expenditures	*Transport as Percentage of Total Project Aid*
By Type of Assistance		
Development Grants and Technical Assistance	24,411	*7*
Development Loans	95,700	*18*
Supporting Assistance	53,816	*53*
Total	173,927	*17*
By Region		
Far East	16,830	*12*
Near East	19,012	*22*
South Asia	103,560	*26*
Africa	25,465	*14*
Latin America	8,684	*14*
Europe	16	*1*
Non-Regional	360	*1*
Total	173,927	

Source: Tables A.14, A.15, and A.16.
[a] Project aid only.

to finance imports, which are sold to provide funds to meet budgetary needs resulting from either military expenditures or development projects. During 1962, when supporting assistance obligations totaled $704 million,[11] only $102 million was for capital projects. Approximately 53 percent was for transport. (See Table A.16.)

In summary, aid for capital projects in the categories of development grants, loans, and supporting assistance involved approximately a billion dollars in 1962. The share of this total made available for transport projects was 17 percent, or $174 million. Additional transport equipment was provided through nonproject type aid. (See Table 6.4.) For example, AID and its predecessors ex-

[11] Agency for International Development, *Operations Report, Data as of June 30, 1962,* graph on p. 3.

pended some $700 million, approximately $70 million per year,[12] to finance the purchase of transport machinery in the decade 1952 to 1963.

Almost all loans for transport authorized by AID during the first year of its operations carried the stipulation that transport equipment should be procured in the United States.[13] This policy is often criticized on the grounds that it increases project costs. The argument in favor of tied loans is that they are necessary to avoid aggravating balance of payments problems for the United States.[14]

Just as the World Bank and the IDA have joined forces, AID and the Eximbank often combine efforts, with equipment costs financed by the bank and the remainder of the project by AID. For example, an AID loan for two high-priority roads in Argentina covered 75 percent of the local costs of the road-improvement work and 75 percent of the cost of engineering services from the United States. Equipment credits provided through the Export-Import Bank financed most of the remaining dollar costs. Another joint AID-Eximbank project was a 60 mile highway in Guatemala. This road to the border of Honduras was made possible by an Eximbank loan to cover foreign-exchange costs and a loan from AID to cover local costs, both to be administered by the Eximbank.

New commercial jet aircraft for Ethiopia have been made available with the help of an Eximbank credit, with a loan from AID to finance equipment and parts for jet-engine overhaul. AID assistance has also included a management contract with TWA for

[12] The estimate of $700 million was derived from deducting the $400 million in transport equipment aid provided prior to June 1952 from the cumulative total of $1,103 million for all transport equipment aid extended between April 3, 1948 and June 30, 1963. This $400 million includes $371 million expended for motor vehicles, aircraft, vessels, railway cars, and related parts, and about $30 million for miscellaneous transport machinery. See Agency for International Development, *Commodity Code Book*, July 1, 1963 (Statistics and Reports Division); and Mutual Security Agency, *Paid Shipments, Data as of June 30, 1952* (Statistics and Reports Division).

[13] See statement of Frank D. Coffin before the Subcommittee on International Exchange and Payments of the Joint Economic Committee, Dec. 12, 1962.

[14] For a discussion of the desirability of tied loans for balance of payments reasons, see Walter S. Salant and Associates, *The United States Balance of Payments in 1968* (Brookings Institution, 1963), especially Chap. VI, Foreign Economic Assistance.

Ethiopian Airlines and the construction of a new airport at Addis Ababa, along with the expansion of other major airports and the improvement of smaller airfields in remote parts of the country.

Food for Peace Program

In addition to the use of local currencies generated by the sale of surplus United States commodities, American food surpluses have been applied directly to support public works through the Food for Peace Program.[15] This program has helped to promote improved transport in newly developing countries by making food available as a partial wage payment for construction workers. The effort was begun in Tunisia in 1958 to provide famine and emergency relief. The program has now been introduced in many other countries including Taiwan, Dahomey, Ethiopia, India, Iran, South Korea, Libya, Morocco, Tanganyika, and Tunisia. At one point, negotiations were under way with twenty-five other countries.

The process of using food for developing transport is illustrated by the case of Tunisia, which in 1958 was experiencing a serious unemployment problem created by the departure of French personnel and capital. In response to a request for a work-relief program by the government of Tunisia, the International Cooperation Administration helped to develop projects and provided food as a stimulus to work rather than as a dole. Surplus wheat was used for work-relief projects, which, in addition to providing wages and reducing unemployment, could be expected to increase agricultural production through the repair of roads.

Beginning in 1961, the name of the food-for-wages program in Tunisia was changed from "work relief" to "labor-intensive development" to reflect the shift in emphasis from emergency unemployment relief to long-term economic development. Labor-intensive projects approved in that country have included construction

[15] The Agricultural Trade Development and Assistance Act of 1954, Public Law 480 (68 Stat. 454). Title I permits sales of agricultural commodities for economic development, and Title II permits grants under certain conditions.

of small dams and canals, reinforcement of canal channels, construction of rural market roads, and extraction of stones for roads. The recipient government makes the major contribution to the program by supplying the cash component of the wage. Wages are about two-thirds cash and one-third United States commodity donations. The government also contributes administrative services for the program and provides for the distribution of donated commodities.

Over half of the normally unemployed labor force of some 300,000 men has been working on some 6,000 of these projects in Tunisia, involving as few as ten and as many as 3,000 men per project. Arrangements are made to permit the sale of varying percentages of the food for cash in order to purchase hand tools and to meet other local expenses. The food received is for both the workers and their families, and an estimated one-quarter of the population has participated directly in the benefits.

Since workers in the developing countries devote over half their wages to food, a considerable part of the cost of development projects, which have a high labor component, can be financed by shipments of surplus food. In addition to reducing unemployment and furthering development, food shipment can counter inflation of food prices that would otherwise accompany development projects. Thus, India's development plans depend heavily on United States agreement to supply large tonnages of wheat annually. Unwillingness to accept certain foods, unauthorized sales, and difficulties of transport, storage, and distribution all present barriers to such a program. Some difficulties may also result for the agricultural sector in countries that export. On balance, however, the program has had a favorable development impact.

Financing Through Regional Agencies

A number of regional groupings and institutions dealing with economic development have entered the aid picture to supplement or carry out the financing arrangements already discussed. One of these is the Inter-American Development Bank, which was established to finance major projects in Latin America and to provide technical assistance.

Loans are made or guaranteed by the bank from its ordinary capital resources, which are provided by subscriptions of its members. Financing is primarily for specific projects, including those forming part of a national or regional development program. The bank is a supplementary source of financing for borrowers unable to obtain a loan or guarantee from private sources on reasonable terms. Loans ordinarily cover up to 50 percent of the cost of a project. Thus far transport has accounted for an almost insignificant part of the loans provided, but the bank's operations have made a significant contribution to development planning and research.[16]

Another important regional organization providing assistance for transport is the European Development Fund of the European Economic Community. The fund finances economic and social development programs in the associated overseas countries. Contrary to trends elsewhere, it does so by grants rather than loans. Capital is made available to the fund by members of the European Economic Community. Of the amount allocated to specific projects, as of January 1963, 45 percent was for transport—more than two-thirds for roads.[17] Projects are implemented through the development programs of the associated countries. Once an agreement for a particular project has been signed, the recipient country is fully responsible for carrying out the work.

[16] In 1961, the first full year of operation for the Inter-American Bank, loans totaling $293 million were made to eighteen member countries. These were financed by the bank's resources as well as those of the Social Progress Trust Fund. The latter consists of $394 million of the $500 million that the United States made available to promote social progress in Latin America as part of the Alliance for Progress. The Inter-American Bank has been designated administrator of the Trust Fund.

[17] For the five-year period 1958–62, $600 million was made available. Approximately $438.9 million of this had been allocated as of January 1, 1963, of which nearly half was approved for transport projects—$140.9 million for roads, $22.3 million for railways and $32.5 million for ports. See "European Development Fund: Balance Sheet 1958–62," Information Memo, issued in January 1963 by the European Economic Community, Brussels.

Still another regional arrangement is the Colombo Plan, in existence since 1950. This provides a framework for mutual development assistance among countries of South and Southeast Asia, and it serves as a channel for aid to the Asian nations from the older members of the British Commonwealth and the United States. There is no Colombo Plan fund. Each Asian member has its own development plan, and assistance from its fellow members, Asian and non-Asian, is on a bilateral basis. The plan does not control or administer, but rather surveys needs and resources as a cooperative body. Large investments have been made by member governments, supplemented in many instances by other foreign assistance, but no systematic record is kept of the total capital involved. Asian members of the Colombo Plan not only receive aid but give it in the form of loans and technical assistance to other members. India has provided assistance to Nepal for the maintenance of roads and waterways, and Japan has made a substantial loan to India for a variety of development projects, including railways.

Total Financial Support for Transport

The cumulative figure, as of June 1963, of all loans and grants for transport by major United States and international donor agencies over a twenty-year period has been approximately $7.2 billion. This includes programs of the World Bank, the International Development Association, the European Development Fund of the Common Market, the Export-Import Bank of Washington, and the United States Agency for International Development and its predecessors. Transport project expenditures totaled $6.5 billion, with the balance of $700 million representing nonproject assistance from AID and its predecessors, in the form of equipment. Of the transport projects financed by these agencies, the World Bank and IDA have supplied 38 percent and the Export-Import Bank 33 percent, while AID, ICA, and the Development Loan Fund have together accounted for 26 percent. (See Table 6.5.) Most of this financing has been in the form of loans,

TABLE 6.5. *Cumulative Aid for Transport, United States and International Agencies*[a]

(In millions of U. S. dollars)

	Total	*Percent*
By Source		
IBRD and IDA	2,508.2	*38.3*
Export-Import Bank	2,136.2	*32.6*
ICA	979.9	*14.9*
DLF	561.9	*8.6*
AID	173.9	*2.7*
EEC (European Development Fund)	195.7	*3.0*
Total	6,555.8	*100.0*
By Method of Transport		
Railways	2,537.4	*38.7*
Roads	2,080.9	*31.7*
Ports and inland waterways	562.0	*8.6*
Shipping	88.1	*1.3*
Air	671.7	*10.2*
Pipelines	64.0	*1.0*
Miscellaneous	377.8	*5.8*
AID	173.9	*2.7*
Total	6,555.8	*100.0*
By Region		
Africa	862.0	*13.2*
Asia and Middle East	2,826.9	*43.1*
Western Hemisphere	2,016.2	*30.8*
Europe	690.7	*10.5*
Oceania	159.6	*2.4*
Non-Regional	0.4	
Total	6,555.8	*100.0*
Transport Equipment—AID	700.0[b]	
Grand Total	7,255.8	

Source: "European Development Fund: Balance Sheet 1958–62," Information Memo, European Economic Community, Brussels, January 1963. Others based on Tables A.9, A.10, A.12, and A.13, and Tables 6.1 and 6.4.

[a] Over the life period of the aid organization to June 1963, except for the AID data which cover only through June 1962, and the European Development Fund figures, as of January 1963.

[b] Transport equipment aid expended by AID and its predecessors under non-project type aid between June 1952 and June 1963.

which developing countries are expected to pay back. Loans by the World Bank, the International Development Association, and the Export-Import Bank of Washington have accounted for 71 percent of all the aid for transport projects.

Only a few countries have received a sufficient amount of financial assistance from all these sources combined, however, to make any substantial contribution to the solution of their transport problems. India is one of them. India has negotiated a series of loans with the World Bank, which total close to half a billion dollars. The addition of Eximbank and Development Loan Fund credits raises the Indian total to nearly two-thirds of a billion dollars. This has averaged over $50 million per year. But most countries of the developing world have received much more limited assistance.

In addition to loans, outright grants for transport by the United States have not been inconsiderable, although most of them represent past transactions through the ICA, with some AID funds added. Over an eight-year period these funds have totaled $1.1 billion, or about $140 million per year.

To date the railways of the world have received the largest part of the aid for transport projects, accounting for 39 percent of the total. Roads have been the object of nearly 32 percent of the transactions. Shipping and pipelines, generally in the private sector, have received only 2.3 percent of the total, and ports 8.6 percent. The air transport total has been nearly as great as that of shipping, ports, and pipelines combined.

Geographically, the transport program has been concentrated in Asia and the Middle East, where 43 percent of total outlays have been made. Western Hemisphere countries have accounted for 31 percent of the combined programs, and Africa 13 percent.[18]

The increasing number of independent countries and the growing demands of Africa and Latin America are creating new pressure for help. If the growing challenge of meeting the needs for

[18] A large part of the financial assistance to emerging nations in Africa has been supplied by European countries to their colonies or former colonies.

money and materials is to be met, the necessity for larger amounts of financial support is clear. To make additional help effective, however, requires not simply money but other factors, including the building of institutions and the transfer of knowledge.

Men and Management

Along with a shortage of funds, it was noted that developing countries lack skills and experience as well as organizational arrangements to perform the tasks imposed by the transport function. A large number and variety of programs to meet these needs are being conducted by international agencies, individual countries, and private institutions. They include the conduct of surveys, the dispatching of missions, the training of personnel at home and abroad, and the provision of advisory services.

World Bank and United Nations Technical Assistance

The World Bank has spent about $6 million on technical assistance programs. Bank mission reports and special sector studies have been influential in guiding transport development and in paving the way for financing specific projects. Missions organized under IBRD auspices often survey the needs and potentials of the economy as a whole, including the transport sector, to provide a general framework for development efforts. Projects recommended in these reports are often financed at a later date by loans from the bank and IDA as well as by private capital.[19]

More recently the bank has extended its overall economic survey program to special transport studies, and considerable attention is

[19] Bank survey teams have operated in twenty-two countries, including Colombia, Turkey, Nicaragua, Guatemala, Cuba, Iraq, Ceylon, Surinam, Jamaica, British Guiana, Nigeria, Malaya, Syria, Jordan, (Italian) Somali, Thailand, Libya, Tanganyika, Venezuela, Uganda, Spain, and Kenya.

being given to analysis of individual projects. Financial assistance has been given for transport studies in Colombia and Ecuador, a highway study in Peru, a railway survey in Bolivia, and port studies in Haiti and Honduras. Funds have been allocated for the study of bridging the Hooghly River in Calcutta, of building feeder roads in northeast Nigeria, and of carrying out a road project in Burma.

The bank also acts as executing agency for projects of the United Nations Special Fund. A major study of transportation problems in Argentina was undertaken on this basis, together with harbor studies in British Guiana and Thailand.[20] The Economic Development Institute is another element in the bank's program of technical assistance, organized as a staff college for senior officials from less developed countries whose work involves economic policy formulation and development programs.

As the number of countries participating in aid activities has continued to increase, the bank has arranged "consultative groups" to mobilize and coordinate external assistance. They assist recipient countries in planning their development programs, and they advise aid-giving countries on the programs and projects for which aid is being sought. Nigeria and Tunisia are among the countries for which consultative group arrangements have been made. Financing for development projects is arranged through consortia of countries, whose members discuss and advise on the relative merits of various development schemes and priorities.[21]

Programs of the United Nations include the Expanded Programme of Technical Assistance and the United Nations Special Fund for Economic Development. The Technical Assistance program is involved primarily in advisory services, demonstration

[20] The bank has also initiated a Development Advisory Service to provide economic and technical advice to member governments.

[21] As of June 1962, consortium members were Austria, Canada, France, the Federal Republic of Germany, Japan, The Netherlands, the United Kingdom, the United States, and Belgium. Representatives of the World Bank and IDA attend consortium meetings.

projects, and technical training. The Special Fund, on the other hand, supports larger pre-investment projects, with emphasis on surveys and feasibility studies to reveal natural resource potentials. Various affiliated agencies of the United Nations, such as the International Civil Aviation Organization, are the executing agencies for the projects that are selected, planned, and in many cases financed by these two technical assistance agencies.

Technical Assistance Through United States Agencies

The Agency for International Development has financed extensive country surveys of transport requirements in Thailand, Sierra Leone, and in East and West Pakistan, and detailed studies of specific transport projects in many other countries. But technical assistance efforts of the United States are focused particularly on training. This activity draws on the resources of nine hundred universities and on seven thousand private industrial firms, the former for instruction and the latter for on-the-job training. Since 1953 the United States has sponsored the training of nearly 60,000 persons at home and abroad under the Participant Training Program. During 1961, 8 percent of these trainees were in transport.[22] Complementing the Participant Training Program have been technical missions sent to less developed countries for on-the-scene guidance. As of mid-1961, 3,500 United States technicians were in the field, 10 percent of them on transport missions.[23]

A special type of overseas technical assistance at the community level has been provided in recent years through the operations of the Peace Corps, a semiautonomous agency within the United States Department of State. The corps helps the people of developing areas meet their needs for trained manpower through everyday contact with volunteer workers from the United States.

[22] AID, *Operations Report, Data as of March 31, 1962*, pp. 8, 71; *Operations Report, Data as of June 30, 1961*, pp. 14–15.

[23] ICA, *Operations Report, Data as of June 30, 1961*, p. 13.

Projects have involved predominantly social services, with particular emphasis on secondary education, health, hospital facilities, and improved agricultural methods. But considerable work has been undertaken to provide better rural and village roads, and to assist in the development of skills to operate transport facilities. The main task is to mobilize communities to handle their own problems.

In Afghanistan, a number of volunteers have helped in the development of repair and maintenance facilities for the recently mechanized transport system. In Colombia, volunteers are working with local crews engaged in building access roads. In Ecuador, Malaya, and many other countries, large areas are sparsely inhabited, uncultivated, and relatively inaccessible due to the lack of even rudimentary roads. Peace Corps volunteers are introducing the necessary skills and are working with local apprentices to get the work done.

Participating in the foreign aid program are a number of federal government agencies concerned with transport in the United States. These organizations cooperate with both United States and international agencies in extending technical help to the less developed countries. The Bureau of Public Roads in the Department of Commerce, for example, provides assistance for highway development.[24] Funds for these operations are obtained from the Agency for International Development, the Eximbank, the World Bank, and occasionally the host government. When a loan or grant for a highway project is made by one of the aid organizations, either the aided government or the financing agency may ask for highway engineering services, equipment specialists, and administrative consultants. These the bureau provides through its own staff or through engineering consultants, contractors, or state highway departments.

Typical of the projects undertaken by the Bureau of Public

[24] In 1962 it was operating in fourteen countries: Ethiopia, Iran, Jordan, the Philippines, Sudan, Nepal, Lebanon, Laos, Yemen, Peru, Colombia, Cambodia, Spain, and Brazil.

Roads has been its work in Cambodia, where overseas staff has done field engineering work and drawn up contract plans and specifications for road rehabilitation. Peru was assisted in planning and implementing highway projects financed with loans from AID and the Eximbank. In Ethiopia, the bureau has helped to implement three main highway projects financed by the World Bank. Bureau staff also administers training schools in Iran, Jordan, Lebanon, Sudan, Yemen, and at the Pan-American Highway Training Center in Colombia.

The Federal Aviation Agency provides developing countries with technical assistance in aviation. It conducts surveys of air transport requirements, and recommends priority projects. FAA participates in aviation projects financed by AID or Eximbank, by installing ground facilities, modernizing aviation equipment, and training operators and maintenance personnel.

The Role of Private Industry

The domestic supply of transport equipment is an important factor in the provision of transport services in developing countries. Such enterprises are being encouraged in the private sector by both bilateral and multilateral guarantee and financing programs. For United States industries operating overseas, the Investment Guaranty Program encourages new private investment by guaranteeing up to 75 percent of the risks of inconvertibility and loss of investment due to expropriation, war, and revolution. By mid-1963 the United States had entered into agreements for investment guaranties with fifty-three nations, and more than $1 billion in United States private investments have been guaranteed under this program.

Guaranteed private investments have included companies providing motor vehicles, railway equipment, automobile tires, parts, and accessories in such countries as Iran, the Philippines, Turkey, Afghanistan, Taiwan, Costa Rica, and Jordan. In addition to investment guaranties, the Agency for International Development extends local currency loans to United States private industries or their foreign affiliates.[25] Assistance to private investors is also furnished by the International Finance Corporation, an affiliate of the World Bank, which helps to locate investment opportunities for private business in developing nations.

Private corporations themselves are providing aid by their participation in training and other technical help. Trans-World Airlines assisted in the development of Ethiopian Airlines through an agreement by which it provided advice and supervision in navigation, communications, maintenance, accounting, financing, and customer relations. The project was made possible by a loan from the Export-Import Bank. Loans to the Iranian State Railways from the Eximbank to finance the substitution of diesel for steam locomotives, also set the stage for technical assistance by General Motors Corporation, manufacturers of the new equipment. The corporation trained Iranian railway technicians at its factory and in the shops of United States railways. These technicians then established training operations for railway operating and maintenance personnel in Iran.

In most of the less developed countries, private foreign industries are also producing a variety of products that support transport operations. These activities are undertaken on a purely business basis without government help. Their operations have been an important complement to publicly financed economic assistance. These activities have supplied capital, transplanted managerial and technical skills, and substituted domestic production for imports. They have made a contribution to improved transport that is often overlooked.

[25] The Cooley amendment to P.L. 480, adopted in 1957, requires that up to 25 percent of P.L. 480 foreign currencies be made available for lending to private American enterprise for use in the countries purchasing the P.L. 480 commodities, or to foreign business firms that help expand markets for United States agricultural products. AID inherited the administration of the Cooley Loan funds from the Export-Import Bank. See Robert E. Asher, *Grants, Loans, and Local Currencies: Their Role in Foreign Aid* (Brookings Institution, 1961), p. 11.

Effects of the Transport Aid Program

Aid for transport from the rich countries to the poor, most of it delivered during a decade and a half, has had significant impacts on development. The global system of jet air transport that has brought the world's major cities so close together was made possible to a large extent through programs of assistance for aircraft purchase, airway and airport construction, and aviation training. Extensive networks of regional air services have also been created with the help of resources from the more developed countries. The resulting communications within developing areas and between the rich countries and the poor have been a key factor in the conduct of public and private affairs and in the transfer of knowledge and skills. Without this global system of air transport, the magnitude of the current effort to improve living standards throughout the world would have been impossible.

The effects of the aid effort are also evident in the improvements to surface transport that have been made both for water and land movements. Modernized railways, expanded port facilities, and new roads and motor vehicles serving previously inaccessible areas provide impressive testimony in numerous countries of solid accomplishment.

Two things should be said about the size of the bill to get this transport revolution under way. First, seven out of every ten dollars represent loans from the Export-Import Bank and the World Bank that are being repaid with interest, and represent no net financial support from the financing countries. Second, much of the balance that is more in the category of aid is designed not simply to assist the poor countries but in addition to market the products of developed countries. When the Agency for International Development concludes a loan agreement with Ethiopia for the purchase of United States aviation equipment, the direct beneficiaries are not only the Ethiopian Ministry of Public Works and Communications, but the Kansas City Metal Products Company, the Detroit Tool Engineering Company, and half a dozen other midwestern suppliers. United States loans are restricted for the most part to the purchase of American made locomotives, trucks, aircraft, and other equipment. Aid does not represent the largesse that many people assume it to be. Actually, it is an outlay that has benefited both donors and recipients.

It is also clear that part of what has been spent has been wasted and that aid efforts for transport have often been dissipated to the point that they have produced inconsequential results. The political pressure to share available resources with as many people and as many places as possible is felt both internationally and domestically. Funds available for transport have often been spread thin to include as many countries as possible. Roads that ought to be built to cover long distances are typically built in short sections. Work may proceed in twenty or thirty different places, and for what sometimes seem to be as many years. And where there has been concentrated effort, it has not always been where transport needs were the most, but where credit risks were the least.

It must be remembered, however, that the assistance efforts of the past decade and a half represent a massive experiment in which for the first time the rich countries have tried to do something to help the poor. It is a tribute to those who have participated that, out of the confusion, the various aid programs for transport have made so considerable a contribution to development. The question is how the task can be more effectively accomplished in the future. For in light of so many unmet needs, the fact that the results were less than they might have been is unfortunate. The need, therefore, is to take advantage of the knowledge and experience gained during the first decade and a half in order to make adjustments in the long-term effort.

Goals for Foreign Aid

Four principal revisions will be necessary to achieve a more effective external assistance program for transport. (1) The trend toward providing aid for transport through international channels and multilateral arrangements should be furthered. (2) Transport development should be a continuing effort with donor countries making long-term financial and administrative arrangements that developing countries can rely on. (3) Pre-investment surveys of transport needs should be improved to avoid costly misallocation of resources. (4) A global effort is needed to carry out research and development and to analyze and distribute useful information and experience to guide all developing countries.

Strengthening International Channels

The foregoing recitation of foreign assistance efforts aimed at improving transport indicate that there are mixed motives at work. An attempt to classify the confusion suggests that there are six reasons for conducting aid programs: the pursuit of humanitarian purposes, the provision of subsistence aid, the furtherance of military objectives, the offering of bribes, the building of prestige projects, and the promotion of economic development.[26] These motivations often introduce contradictions and conflicts that either nullify or reduce the effectiveness of aid efforts in accelerating development. A transport facility built for strategic purposes may divert local resources from transport improvements needed for development, or a political decision to build a road primarily to please some one may end up carrying nothing and pleasing no one.

These categories of motives help us to see more clearly the ap-

[26] Hans Morgenthau, "A Political Theory of Foreign Aid," *American Political Science Review*, Vol. LVI (June 1962). Reprinted in the *Congressional Record*, Vol. 108, Pt. 11 (Aug. 1, 1962), pp. 15330–34.

propriate roles for international and bilateral assistance efforts in the future. The first and second categories of aid, which are motivated primarily by humanitarian instincts, should continue to be maintained for whatever contributions individual countries might care to make. International channels are also available for such assistance through the United Nations and other multilateral organizations. Aid for reconstructing the transport facilities devastated by earthquakes in Chile and Yugoslavia are examples of how both individual countries and international agencies played a role. The third, fourth, and fifth categories of assistance, however, should obviously be confined to a bilateral basis. These may or may not play a role in raising levels of living, but they are associated with an extension of military strategy or political influence aimed at helping the donor.

The sixth category of aid, for economic development, presents a different motive that requires a different treatment. Assistance to provide transport facilities for self-sustaining development should be granted on the basis of an overall economic strategy adhered to by both recipients and donors, regardless of the selfish interests of the latter. In other words, aid for this purpose should be judged by objective appraisal of what is best for the aided country. Bilateral arrangements, if they adhere to preplanned programs in the developing countries, can carry out an orderly program aimed at the goal of improving levels of living. The plans themselves, however, and the pre-investment surveys, should be arrived at without mixing economic development goals with other motivations. This suggests at a very minimum that pre-investment surveys and plans should have international sponsorship. But even with multilateral agreement on plans and objectives, it may be difficult to avoid tensions and disagreements between donor and recipient nations when aid is given on a bilateral basis. Technical requirements or other stipulations are more readily accepted when groups of nations are making the rules than when there is any hint of dictation from one country.

A good case can be made, then, for the conduct of transport aid programs through multilateral arrangements that remove the possibility of mixing development goals with extraneous motives. The United States is conducting about 10 percent of its foreign economic assistance activities through international agencies. It is the principal contributor to the technical assistance and development programs of the United Nations and the largest single contributor to the operations of the World Bank and its affiliates. A continuing trend in the direction of working through international channels will help to remove the temptation for development assistance to be a mixture of other things as well.

An internationally sponsored aid program has other advantages. It provides an opportunity for the financial burden to be shared more equitably among countries in a position to participate, including smaller countries whose resources are insufficient to support a separate foreign assistance program. International programs can also help to conserve the short supply of qualified personnel. A major weakness of bilateral aid programs is the absence of staff in overseas missions that can help to program desirable transport projects and prepare applications for loans or other assistance. The need is for people who can relate transport plans and programs to the problem of raising standards of living. The world supply of persons with these capabilities is not large, and the demand for them is expanding. The most immediate solution is to make the available supply go as far as possible through greater reliance on the international conduct of assistance programs.

The World Bank and the International Development Association provide an obvious channel for both transport survey work and for transport investment financing on a global scale. These organizations, as noted earlier, are already heavily engaged in the transport sector, and the extension of the bank's interests and influence through the IDA has given it much greater potential for dealing effectively with transport problems.

Complete reliance on a world organization, however, would be not only politically impractical at this time but would inevitably reduce the amount of assistance available. Thus, an international approach to aid should also be sought through regional arrangements such as the Alliance for Progress, the European Development Fund, and other multilateral programs. And where special ties exist between two countries, the resulting aid program may be on a sufficiently large scale to favor a continuation of bilateral aid.

Matched Grants for the Long Pull

A second new direction for improving foreign assistance efforts should be to view the task as a long-term operation. Improving transport requires a long period of time for planning and constructing facilities. These responsibilities call for appropriate government institutions, good administration, and financial planning. If external assistance is to be effective for development, all these ingredients of the transport program must be included.

Some useful lessons in continuity can be learned from the approaches taken by the United States in its program of federal aid to the states for roadbuilding. Federal aid for highways in the beginning required the states receiving assistance to match aid, to establish a highway department, to engage the services of engineers, and to designate a limited mileage of highways eligible for federal funds. It was further provided that road funds would be withheld in the future unless design standards met federal specifications and projects were properly maintained.

Aid to developing countries could also be made more effective if a limited mileage of principal road, rail, water, and air transport routes were designated as eligible for external assistance. The necessity of laying out the most important national transport routes would serve as the initial step toward developing an integrated system and programing its improvement on a long-term basis. Desirable administrative arrangements to permit the transport system to be viewed as a whole and in relation to other national objectives would be encouraged in the process. The result, in addition to making aid expenditures more effective, would be to increase the enthusiasm of financing agencies in a position to provide assistance.

The laying down of conditions under which financing is provided is not a chore that individual donors perform gracefully or effectively. The World Bank can and does prescribe changes in transport organization and administration, as well as physical and financial alterations prior to an agreement with respect to financial support. Stipulations of this kind are often necessary to make projects effective and useful, to avoid waste, and to assure that the developing country gets what it bargained for. The conditions under which financing is provided are in reality the directions for employing resources productively. Stipulations written into aid transactions can help to shift part of the burden of unpopular decisions from local officials. In addition, to the extent that aid-giving machinery is international, the prospects of obtaining compliance are better than if countries were free to shop for help from a variety of other sources as a means of avoiding restrictive commitments.

Closer controls over financial assistance through international agreements would also make practical a system of grants instead of loans. There is serious doubt that in the long run large-scale efforts to raise transport standards in less developed countries can succeed if assistance from outside results in a heavy accumulation of debt service obligations. Projects in the rapidly changing field of transport will not avoid the obsolescence of a half century. The argument that general development resulting from today's loans will provide the capacity to pay tomorrow is not convincing in the light of history. There will be even greater possibilities for transport obsolescence in the years ahead. The dilemma, then, is that short-term loans are beyond the financial capacity of poor countries, and long-term loans extend payment beyond the life of the transport provided.

In this setting, the emphasis on loans in current aid programs is supportable only if it is understood that repayment obligations are partly a fiction that spares the feelings of both donors and recipients. For it is clear that the rules will have to be altered in subsequent years to remove the burden of repayment where this proves necessary.

Many transport projects continue to warrant the use of development loans, especially for equipment purchase, and many institutions can continue to provide assistance of this kind. For other projects, however, and especially for basic facilities such as river, road, and airway improvements, the use of grants offers the only promise of stepped up efforts without future financial difficulties. Grants could be made on a businesslike basis if they were matched by the recipient countries on a sliding scale determined by financial capacity, and if eligible projects were selected on the basis of their priorities in a planned system of facilities. Year-to-year grants patterned on United States highway experience, with stipulations concerning design and maintenance, would provide closer control over the use of foreign assistance funds than if capital transfers were made through occasional loan agreements.

Where, then, is the grant money to come from? The European Development Fund made available by the Common Market countries primarily for African nations suggests the pattern for comparable efforts elsewhere. The six nations contributing to the fund provide over $100 million a year for development assistance. This example suggests that all developed nations should help to provide a source of grants for developing countries on the basis of an agreed percentage of gross national product.[27] Provision for matching these funds in the developing countries could be aided by levying gasoline taxes and other fees on transport equipment and usage. Taxes to create a matching transport fund could be initiated at a modest level, much the same as user taxes were first levied by the states to help match federal grants in the United States. These levies could be increased with the expansion of economic activity and the improvement of transport conditions.

[27] Barbara Ward, *The Rich Countries and the Poor Countries* (W. W. Norton & Co., Inc., 1959).

Pre-Investment Surveys Through the United Nations

In addition to improving the channels and methods of external assistance, a critical task is to improve the surveys and plans for transport investment programs. The pre-investment surveys being supported by the aid-giving countries are the key to effective program decisions. Good surveys increase the chances that the right amount of the right kinds of things will be done at the right time.

Transport surveys to date, and the recommendations for transport investment stemming from them, leave something to be desired. The previous discussion has made clear that most of the pre-investment studies have not translated economic goals into transport demand, that they have not adequately considered the transport alternatives offered by modern technology, and that most of them overlook solutions to transport problems to be found outside the transport sector. If pre-investment surveys are unsatisfactory, loan decisions which establish how much and what kind of transport investment will be needed must also be unsatisfactory.

The problem is not easy, and the quest for high quality will have to await more experience and more research. Meanwhile at least one condition can be met. Pre-investment surveys should be acceptable to all agencies engaged in the business of financing what is recommended. Aid-giving agencies should agree on the types of studies undertaken and on the questions to be answered, and they should make cooperative arrangements to have these surveys made.

The task of providing effective investment guidance requires a cooperative effort by all nations, developed and less developed. It would be difficult to avoid the conclusion that international auspices should be relied on. Such an arrangement avoids many of the problems that are inevitable when responsibility for the assessment of need is lodged in any one nation. The less developed countries, as members of the United Nations, also have the satisfaction of being both sponsors and recipients of assistance, and of knowing that the recommended improvements are as free as possible from the bias invited by single-country surveys.

The United Nations is the key agency. The Special Fund is already supporting extensive pre-investment survey work through the specialized agencies, and the World Bank has played a central role in transport survey work. The bank has a number of advantages that qualify it, including a permanent international transport staff, an acquired experience in this field, and the resources and reputation that allow it to draw on outside sources to help to supplement its own capabilities. An additional asset is the bank's concern for development as a whole, which has helped it to view transport in perspective. The bank also has a stake in supporting pre-investment surveys and in improving their quality because of its financial commitments.

If pre-investment surveys of transport are conducted through international channels and capital assistance shifted more and more to multilateral arrangements, the role of the United States aid program for transport could take on a new complexion. Rather than attempting to provide every type of assistance, the United States might concentrate on these aspects of economic development for which its talents best qualify it.[28] This suggestion is particularly appropriate to the transport field. The United States is being placed in the position of supporting projects rejected by international agencies. Meanwhile, it has demonstrated special talents in such activities as technical assistance and training, the work of the Peace Corps, and the Food for Peace program. American aid could make its maximum contribution to the solution of transport problems if, in addition to contributing substantially to international agencies, it were to concentrate its attention on institution building, research and development, and training.

[28] Robert E. Asher, "Multilateral Versus Bilateral Aid: An Old Controversy Revisited" (Brookings Institution, 1963), Reprint No. 66, p. 716.

Research and Education Through a World Center

Promising new directions for foreign assistance policy can be discovered through an organized research effort aimed at new and more effective ways to promote development. This program in the transport field should be designed to improve understanding of the role of transport in the development process, and to reveal effective means of overcoming transport difficulties. Attention should be focused not only on studies in the social sciences but on the possibilities of research and development in the physical sciences that can accelerate courses of action found to be desirable. The success of military research and development in creating new systems for war demonstrates the potential payoff that could result from focusing research on problems of peace.

In addition to individual country research and development, there is urgent need for establishing a World Transport Center to serve the United Nations. The center would be the focal point for research and education in a vital area that has been fragmented and neglected.[29] The world transport center would relate the work of the specialized agencies and of the regional commissions. The regional commissions could play a supporting role through regional transport staffs in Bangkok, Santiago, Dakar, and Addis Ababa. This would provide for an interchange of experience among member countries in various parts of the world, would promote regional transport solutions, and would direct research and training efforts toward the solution of common problems.

There is already a large and growing volume of information in both the developed and the less developed countries that should be

[29] The United Nations at one time attempted to focus transport responsibilities in the Transport and Communications Commission, which was the transport adviser to the Economic and Social Council and the coordinator of activities in the various U.N. organizations dealing with this subject. The potentials of the commission were never fully realized, and it has since been discontinued. See Robert E. Asher and Others, *The United Nations and Promotion of the General Welfare* (Brookings Institution, 1957), pp. 427, 450.

analyzed and made available to help guide transport improvement programs. The supply of capital assistance may be limited, and it may be necessary to concentrate efforts to get results, but no case can be made for being parsimonious with advice. The need is for machinery by which useful information on transport problems and solutions can be made known. Developing countries stand to benefit greatly from a knowledge of what others have done, successfully and otherwise.

The experience of newly developing countries themselves is especially pertinent. A primary need is to evaluate transport activities to date to find out what happened after a transport project was undertaken, to compare what happened with what was anticipated, and to observe the factors that contributed to the results.

Very little is known about the impact that transport facilities have had on development and about the factors that favor or retard maximum results. The degree of ignorance can be reduced by establishing machinery to provide before-and-after analyses of transport investments. Failure to provide this feed-back to guide foreign aid efforts is an oversight. The reason has been partly the pressure to get on with the job, but there has also been a reluctance to evaluate past decisions that might reveal errors of judgment. But refusal to learn from experience is a more grievous error than the mistakes that might have been made by those who took the initiative to get things done.

If the Decade of Development is to close with a record of real accomplishment, the strategy will have to include more adequate support through grants, greater reliance on international channels, improved survey techniques, more effective educational efforts, the retrieval and dissemination of useful information, and more imaginative efforts to innovate through research and development. These steps are all part of a broader strategy for mobility.

CHAPTER VII

A Transport Strategy for Development

THE REVOLUTION IN TRANSPORT is playing a major role in the social and economic revolution around the world. Mobility has contributed to development not only by increasing domestic commerce and world trade, but by establishing contacts among peoples and nations. In the process, it has made possible a global awareness of the problem of poverty and a global effort to find solutions. The scientific breakthrough in transport has accelerated the process of learning and extended the influence of those attempting to apply it to the task of improving man's lot. Every profession is being affected by a more rapid evolution of thought and a greater capacity to act on an international basis. Transport and communications have set the stage for man to think his way as well as work his way out of bondage.[1]

Soon the international web of communications will be drawn tighter around the world. Supersonic flight will mark a new triumph over time and distance, and all parts of the globe will be linked orally and visually through satellite communications. This will not be a world in which it can be argued that the future of countries on the lower rungs of the development ladder is of no concern to the future of those on top. No country will be able to

[1] Pierre Teilhard de Chardin, *The Phenomenon of Man* (Harper and Brothers, 1959), pp. 239–40.

escape the reality of its political and economic interdependence within the world community.

It is evident, however, that in poor countries the web of communications does not extend beyond the major cities and main intercity routes. The transport revolution has been contained in scattered economic islands where mobility and some degree of prosperity go together. There are still vast areas where immobility and poverty persist.

Experience in both the developed and the less developed countries makes it clear that transport has played a key role in helping to overcome poverty. In many instances, the failure to provide adequate transport has been the major missing element impeding economic and social progress. But often transport facilities have failed to make an effective contribution. Projects built on the chance that development would follow have led to costly disappointments, and other sectors of the economy have been denied resources that could have been put to better use. Knowing when, where, and in what circumstances transport will make a positive contribution to better living is the key question.

There are no easy guides to success or failure for the transport decision maker. Transport policies that make sense have to be derived from development objectives that also make sense. The most urgent need is to create a new state of mind in which transport decisions are clearly seen as an integral part of other policy decisions. To do this will mean giving up some global misconceptions about the transport function.

The mistake that causes the most trouble is the view that transport is a separate sector of the economy. In reality, it is not a sector but a link among sectors. As a consequence, the idea that transport should be improved for its own sake is erroneous. Actually, the only justification for providing transport lies in serving other objectives. Transport can not be planned and managed in isolation, for what is done or not done to provide mobility and access will often determine the success or failure of the development effort.

This conception has generally concealed the fact that supplying transport is different from meeting other needs. Combating hunger, for example, calls for a specific target for food, expressed in a definite number of calories per person per day. Goals for education can be expressed in plans for children to be instructed through a specified number of grades. But comparable goals for transport would be irrelevant. It cannot be specified that everyone needs to travel a hundred miles a year, or that for each person a thousand ton miles of freight should be hauled. It is impossible to say what amount of transport is enough or too much except in relation to purposes served. Food is necessary to live, and education is necessary to live well, but transport is necessary only to the extent that it helps people to eat, to become educated, or to achieve some other economic or social gain.

As a result, it is impractical to lay out a program for transport unless economic trends and objectives are known and translated into transport demand. Then the attempt can be made to determine how much transport is called for, where it is needed, and what kind it should be. The task is not easy. Providing mobility is not like producing cement. When cement piles up in warehouses, someone will see that a halt should be called to making more. But a country can go on for years providing more transport than it needs, and there will be no tell-tale surpluses to suggest a different course. When transport facilities are built that are not used, it is difficult to shut them down like a factory, and it is easy to repeat the same mistake in some other location. The payoffs from transport have been spectacular, but so have the losses.

The engineer is generally saddled with the job of determining what is required. In carrying out this role unaided, he is obviously miscast. The engineering contribution is not to determine the need but to meet the need. It is up to those responsible for food production, industrialization, and other targets to say what transport will be required. It is then the task of the builders to determine alternative ways of proceeding, to estimate costs, and ultimately to create the facilities. A systems approach to solutions is needed—

meaning not simply that the transport system should be viewed as a whole, but that transport has to be related to the economy. To do this effectively calls for a strategy for mobility.

Determining Transport Needs

During early stages of development, a given percentage increase in national product will be accompanied by a considerably larger percentage increase in freight traffic. Conversely, an increase in freight movement will be accompanied by a substantially lower percentage increase in the growth of national product. In countries that have achieved a high degree of development, however, the growth of traffic tends to parallel the growth of economic activity. Countries such as the United States and Canada have been experiencing this relationship for some time. In the future, however, the effect of further technological change, particularly in food processing, sources of energy, and techniques of communications, may lead to an economic environment in which increases in living standards will be achieved with less than proportionate increases in transport volume. A strategy for mobility in developing countries should aim at approaching more rapidly the relationship between economic growth and transport volume that characterizes developed countries. Ultimately it may be possible for poor countries to achieve more wealth with less transport through the application of scientific and technological innovations.

Investment in transport as a percentage of total investment also tends to decline with economic growth. This trend can be furthered by more effective use of existing facilities, better organization, and improvements in administration, as well as by avoiding overdesign, by construction in stages, by the selection of the most appropriate technology, and by efficient construction methods. In other words, developing countries should take measures that will cause a given investment in transport to accommodate as much traffic and add as much to the national product as possible. This should be the guiding principle in the construction and operation of individual projects as well as transport systems. The sum of individual projects will determine for the economy as a whole whether the aggregate relationships between levels of economic activity, volumes of traffic, and transport investment reflect a satisfactory degree of transport efficiency. The elements of a strategy to accomplish this goal will differ among countries in different stages of development, but in all cases the first step is to determine what transport is needed.

Surveys of natural resources are a prerequisite for providing information on what a nation has to work with—its land, water supply, soil conditions, minerals, forest reserves, and power potentials. No nation can afford to remain ignorant of its resources, which are the essential basis for making development decisions. Aerial mapping and exploration can help to discover natural wealth and to determine feasible transport routes quickly and at low cost. The entire area of the less developed continents should be systematically explored and mapped with international assistance as a first step toward a strategy for development.

To establish development goals, resources have to be compared with the needs of the people, and targets set to guide the effort toward better living standards. Goals include requirements for food and other agricultural products, for housing, schools, and health services, for jobs in industry, for power, and for transport. Development plans to help guide national, regional, and urban growth are necessary as a means of allocating capital, labor, and entrepreneurial skills effectively and consistently.

To translate traffic into transport needs, aggregate demands for transport can be estimated from the top down on the basis of economic indices, overall traffic trends, and production targets. Estimates of demand for specific routes and areas, however, require knowledge of the location of economic activities, sources of supply, and markets.

The translation of transport demand into physical needs requires a comparison of projected passenger and freight movements with the condition, capacity, and use of existing transport facilities. Physical needs can then be translated into financial requirements by determining to what extent projected use is to be accommodated by new investment, improvements in existing plant, better maintenance and operation, or measures to influence demand.

Economic justification of transport expenditures can be measured in part by increased production from reductions in transport cost and improvements in service for traffic already moving. But an additional measure is the volume of new production created by activities that greater mobility makes possible. In judging the desirability of improved transport, newly generated traffic may be the most important factor as well as the most difficult to estimate. In addition, many of the projected benefits from improved transport will be intangible and difficult to measure. They include the achievement of greater political unity, internal security, the development of cultural ties, the transmission of new ideas and new techniques, the provision of better health services, and the improvement of education. Fortunately, however, most of these benefits are realized only through the movement of traffic. Traffic measures the success of a transport service, and estimates of traffic are the key to economic justification. The decision to improve transport, therefore, depends on whether the volume of goods and passengers to be moved will add sufficiently to the wealth of the country to cover the cost.

To date, the projection of traffic has been made by predictions of what is likely to happen if the improvement is made. These happenings generally depend on a variety of private decisions that may or may not be taken after better transport has been provided. A strategy for mobility should seek to assure that such developments actually materialize. Instead of building a road in the hope that it will lead to increased agricultural output, steps should be taken to help make new production possible. This may require colonization programs, fertilizers, irrigation, or agricultural extension services. To provide only for the transport facility, leaving the rest to chance, is an unnecessary gamble. Instead of guessing about the future, it will often be necessary through a balanced regional development program to help fashion the future.

Establishing the need for transport investments has become more and more dependent on the presentation of elaborate analyses of project costs and benefits. This process has facilitated the task of decision-making, but there are two dangers in the current trend. One is that concentration on individual projects can limit economic perspectives and defeat the objective of developing an integrated transport network. Second, the concentration on project proposals has led to meticulous and time-consuming study of details, the validity of which may depend on broad underlying assumptions that depend primarily on good judgment. If the now affluent countries had put their faith exclusively in benefit-cost ratios, it is not altogether clear that they would have achieved their present state of development.

The Choice of Technology

The cost, performance, and development impact of alternative methods of transport will differ with the transport tasks to be performed, with geography, and with resource availability. Railways and water carriers will continue to be the preferred method for long hauls and heavy traffic. The movement of food grains, staple agricultural commodities, industrial raw materials, and fossil fuels make up the bulk of the traffic moving by these methods. But road transport continues to be the most rapidly expanding method of transport and accounts for the largest share of transport investments. A large proportion of transport for short hauls, high-valued commodities, perishables, and small consignments will be by motor vehicle. Roads afford the best means of providing access to land and other resources, and affect the lives of the largest number of people. The fact that road transport comprises a much larger network of routes than either rail or water transport makes it the most universal method of movement.

A common mistake is the attempt to maintain uneconomical railway services that could be provided more satisfactorily by other methods. A related policy that frustrates development is restricting the use of motor vehicles on grounds of protecting the railways or conserving resources. The railways are not protected by the retention of traffic they are not suited to carry, and the resources conserved by inhibiting the growth of motorized transport have to be weighed against the resources that as a result remain unused.

Although road and rail transport generally account for as much as 75 percent of the transport bill, other methods of movement are playing an increasingly important role. From many points of view, the airplane and helicopter are ideal transport media, since they require a minimum commitment of resources and provide the necessary services within a minimum time period. The fact that air vehicles refuse to fly without proper upkeep has also inculcated good maintenance practices in the most unlikely places. The pipeline, too, has much to commend it, being the ideal method of transport from the standpoint of economic planning. No one builds a pipeline without knowing what is to be piped. The greater use of both these forms of transport should be beneficial to developing countries.

Technological advances, especially in ground-effect machines and air transport, promise new possibilities for the solution of transport problems. The difficulty of foreseeing the future course of technological development and the certainty that innovations will continue to render existing facilities obsolete emphasize the importance of flexibility and the need for avoiding unnecessary commitments. This can be accomplished by adopting minimum standards, avoiding large fixed investments, and favoring projects with an early pay-off. Meanwhile, research and development efforts to hasten the practical use of new methods of freight and passenger movement will be of key importance and should be given top priority. The greatest hope is that science and technology will provide entirely new ways of solving old problems.

Technology outside the transport field offers important opportunities for influencing the nature of a country's transport problems. Energy sources, energy distribution, and processing techniques for agricultural and mineral output may greatly lessen the transport burden. So may the location of industries and the design of urban areas. Scientific innovations that reduce unnecessary demand for transport may prove as important as increasing transport supply.

Improvement of communications will also be important. If a nation is to emerge from subsistence, the most important trade will be the trade in ideas. An effective development program requires an understanding of what is at stake. Participants need to know that living conditions can be improved and that economic progress has something tangible to offer. A revolutionary movement toward higher living standards will not take place until the word gets through to areas and people now beyond reach. Thus a basic requirement is a communications network for the dissemination of knowledge, and this network no longer depends exclusively on transport. Communications can provide a new impetus to growth by extending the scope of technical advisory services, by compensating for the scarcity of teachers, and by expanding medical aid and other help to remote areas.

Implementing Transport Strategy

The conventional practice of planning and operating competitive transport media under separate administrative agencies has made physical coordination of facilities difficult and has introduced conflicting criteria for investment decisions. The result is often an uneconomic allocation of resources and perennial controversies over rates and government regulations. This lack of cooperation runs counter to trends in technology, which have made different methods of transport complementary. A compartmentalized approach is obsolete. Transport investment programs in the public sector need to be integrated through an appropriate single administrative agency, and principal common carrier services need to be operated as a unified system. The provision of facilities and services also needs to be responsive to the physical and social targets established by national and regional development agencies. Not many countries can yet provide the comprehensive plans on which transport decisions need to be based, but initial steps can be taken to establish a consistent set of national goals by establishing appropriate planning and programing operations.

An integral part of the problem of organization and finance is the establishment of rates and charges for transport services that will reduce the drain of the transport program on general tax revenues without inhibiting the use of transport investments. When transport fails to pay its way by a wide margin, it drains support from other urgently needed development projects and encourages transport obsolescence. When there is some degree of self-support, a predictable source of income can be counted on to permit long-term physical and financial planning. The degree to which transport charges cover total costs, however, will differ with stages of economic growth, and financial policy has to be tailored to what is most conducive to development. In all cases, one of the key requirements is to budget the amounts necessary to maintain investments already made.

The appropriate roles to be played by the public and private sectors raise important unresolved questions. More administrative and financial experimentation is called for to provide the managerial talents, financial incentives, and the partnership of government and industry that can get the job done. For example, the supply of entrepreneurial talent can be supplemented by management contracts that fill the initial void and help in the training of personnel. The success of such contracts between the airlines of developed and less developed countries suggests that railway, trucking, and other transport operations might benefit from similar contractual arrangements. Cooperatives offer another means of assisting in transport management by providing distribution services that include assembly, storage, transport, marketing, and financing.

Errors in strategy often stem from the division of responsibility between roadbuilding in the public sector and the provision of vehicles in the private sector. Large outlays are made for roads while the availability of vehicles is restricted by high duties, burdensome taxes, and punitive restrictions. Putting the main emphasis on roads and neglecting the vehicle is a reversal of the policy followed by industrial nations. In the latter it was the encouragement of vehicle ownership that created the pressure for good roads. But the ideal approach is to achieve balance. Total transport costs will be excessive if either vehicles or roads are neglected, since poor roads mean high vehicle operating costs, and restrictions on the supply of vehicles mean high unit costs for roads. The division of total outlays for road transport can be varied by trading off road costs and vehicle operating costs, and thus shifting the cost burden between the public and the private sectors. A single focus of responsibility is needed for effective decision-making in this area.

The dimensions of transport strategy also need to be extended beyond the transport system to the supporting industrial structure, and beyond national boundaries to the international economic community. In the more advanced societies, the transport sector has created a variety of industries providing materials, equipment, and services that have important spillover effects for the economy as a whole. Much of this supporting structure will fail to develop unless specific provision for it is made in conjunction with the transport program itself. A feasible program of industrial support helps to provide new economic opportunities, entrepreneurial skills, and technical competence.

Extension of the radius of transport operations has introduced the opportunity for economic development to be undertaken on a broader geographic scale. Individual countries can benefit from improved transport by developing their comparative advantages and avoiding unnecessary duplication of industrial, agricultural, and power projects. A major need is to expand the present focus on national plans to plans for international economic integration that modern transport can help achieve. At the same time, the introduction of modern transport with its heavy capital costs makes it increasingly important for nations to share the responsibility for transport facilities crossing national boundaries. Joint use of facilities, interchange of equipment, and through traffic arrangements can facilitate movement and reduce costs.

If the transport strategy of low-income countries is to succeed, it will have to be more effectively supported by the rich countries. But present approaches reflect the lack of a common strategy, and views on foreign assistance in many instances amount to self-deception. The view has been stated that aid programs are over-extending the rich countries, when in reality they have hardly begun to tap their potentials. Moreover, aid is a two-way street, with benefits to donors often overshadowing benefits conferred. The feedback includes investment opportunities, growing demands for transport materials and equipment, and prospective long-run expansion of overseas markets in countries now too poor to trade. An additional by-product is the insight that developed countries are gaining into their own problems and into solutions that could work at home. It is a misconception, then, to stress how much poor countries need help without considering how much this help can mean to countries that are rich. A strategy for mobility should view the global revolution in perspective.

The basic fact to be recognized is that capital made available through aid programs to help build transport capacity in developing countries has failed to reach a critical level capable of breaking the transport barrier. A larger international effort is needed. A voluntary levy of a small percentage of the gross national product of developed countries could create an international development fund to multiply assistance efforts. Ultimately a percentage of savings from the reduction of armaments can help to provide the funds that will boost the poor nations into sustained economic orbit.

An international development fund is called for to permit a grant program for transport to supplement long-term loans for "bankable" projects. Grants are to be preferred in a period of rapidly changing transport technology because transport facilities may be obsolete before long-term loans can be paid off. In addition, the constant accumulation of loans for transport development threatens an excessive burden on poor countries. Grants for transport should be matched, however, spent on designated transport systems, and made contingent on acceptable designs and satisfactory maintenance.

The principal role of individual countries should be the support of international programs. But bilateral arrangements also can play an important role by sponsoring special projects and programs for transport in particular countries. Bilateral aid will continue to be maintained for political and strategic purposes and between countries with special ties. Its desirable features are indicated by such programs as the distribution of surplus United States agricultural commodities and by the work of the Peace Corps. Bilateral aid also provides an opportunity to experiment with solutions to transport problems.

International sponsorship is better suited to carrying out the critical task of undertaking surveys and plans to guide transport development. Conducting surveys of transport needs and assuring plans that are sound yet imaginative are undertakings basic to the entire program. Costly surveys that are one-time efforts leading to large volumes relegated to the shelf should be avoided. Instead, emphasis should be placed on the creation of local institutions and staffs that can participate in the planning process on a continuing basis. The United Nations should be the principal sponsor of pre-investment survey work, with the aim of producing results acceptable to all, and the World Bank, which serves as the specialized agency for transport, is the logical focus for this activity.

At present the number of well-prepared and economically attractive transport investment proposals being submitted to national and international agencies for financing are insufficient to absorb the funds available. Yet a far greater effort will be necessary if a significant attack is to be made on world transport problems. What is necessary, therefore, is an acceleration and improvement in the process of transport program planning and project preparation. A first step should be the creation of a fund for the support of a continuing planning process in those countries not now equipped to make the necessary surveys of their development requirements. Donor nations should set aside 1 percent of the development funds being made available each year, to be earmarked for the support of appropriate programing efforts. This can help to assure a continuing flow of useful projects through the international financing pipeline and to reduce the excessive lag between project conception and execution. The 1 percent fund could be used for training programing personnel and for helping to finance advisory services. This would be a first approach to making capital assistance contingent on projects being part of a transport system plan, based in turn on overall development plans.

To carry out these programs, the ultimate solution is a world transport center in the United Nations. The purpose of such a center should be to further the role of transport in the development process by mobilizing talent, conducting or contracting for research, disseminating information, and furthering the efforts of the regional commissions and development institutes of the United Nations.

Finally, trade policy and aid for transport need to be linked. The potential value of trade for developing countries dwarfs the amounts available in loans and grants. Measures to increase the ease of movement need to be accompanied by measures to increase the freedom of movement and to reduce the gap between export yields and import costs.

The rich countries as well as the poor countries have a stake in the results. For the favored position of developed countries is by no means assured. Rapidly altering political, economic, and technological conditions have created uncertainty about the position of each on the development ladder tomorrow. Indeed, the problems of the poorest countries are often only a different aspect and a higher magnitude of the same problem faced by many who live in more developed countries. It is not likely that an effort to resolve either problem separately can succeed in the long run.

If the developed countries are to find outlets for their productive capacity in an age of automation, they will have to look to the limitless needs of the less developed world. They will also have to be willing to buy from these areas as well as sell. To the extent that capital and technical help can increase per capita incomes in Asia, Africa, and Latin America, large additions to the demand for goods and services and to the total volume of international transactions will result. Progress for others can mean progress for all.

Finally, what the developed countries are urging on the less developed are things they ought to be doing themselves. High costs, accidents, congestion, and the obsolescence of both transport facilities and transport policy have created many unfavorable impacts on living standards in the West. Study of transport in less developed areas has provided a laboratory in which large numbers of people have acquired a new awareness of the problems they face at home. These problems have been difficult to identify on the local scene because they are too complex, too familiar, or too easily concealed.

Yet transport still plays an important role in the rich nations, just as it did in the nineteenth century. These countries have been too preoccupied with regulating the competitive struggle among carriers to see the positive role of transport in economic growth. Now they are beginning to understand more clearly the need to establish national goals, to formulate transport policies and programs on the basis of these goals, and to look at the transport network as an integrated system. National objectives will not be achieved if transport is overemphasized or underemphasized, to the detriment of education, housing, urban renewal, and other economic and social goals.

The task of overcoming poverty is global and the scientific and technological means of achieving abundance are at hand to meet the challenge. One of the preconditions for success is a well-conceived attack on the transport aspects of the problem. What is required is a combined strategy by rich countries and poor that will create the standards of mobility on which the rest of the development effort depends.

APPENDIXES

Tables

TABLE A.1. *World Highway Expenditures in 1960*

(In U.S. dollars)

	Total (In millions)	Per Capita	Per Square Mile	Per Motor Vehicle[a]
Continent				
Africa	389[b]	1.58	33	162
Asia	1,108	1.18	195	309
Europe	3,813	9.85	1,992	139
(EEC Countries)	(2,048)	(11.85)	(4,546)	(130)
North America[c]	12,524	63.25	1,677	159
Latin America	813	3.93	102	184
Oceania	424	32.61	137	122
World Total[d]	19,071	9.57	503	159
Selected Less Developed Countries				
Brazil	286.5[e]	4.4	87.1	254.7
Argentina	75.0[f]	3.6	69.9	76.5
Mexico	60.0[e]	1.7	78.9	76.4
Colombia	39.5	2.8	89.8	236.5
Nigeria	34.9	1.0	93.5	742.2
Iran	16.7[f]	0.8	26.6	132.5
Peru	8.5	0.8	16.5	96.6
Tanganyika	7.1	0.8	19.6	181.8
U. A. R. (Egypt)	17.2	0.7	44.5	153.4
Indonesia	52.5	0.6	71.4	191.0
India	190.5	0.5	155.9	342.0
Pakistan	30.0	0.3	82.2	389.6
Afghanistan	3.7	0.3	14.8	369.5
Nyasaland	2.5	0.1	51.9	212.0
Selected Developed Countries				
United States	11,178.0	61.9	3,092.1	151.3
Canada	1,346.0	75.6	349.4	268.3
Sweden	215.1	28.9	1,243.5	150.6
West Germany	1,201.6	21.6	12,516.7	154.1
Denmark	65.6	14.4	3,333.3	105.3
France	450.5	10.0	2,115.0	36.0
United Kingdom	518.9	9.9	5,520.5	65.2
Italy	296.0	6.0	2,666.7	51.6

Sources: Highway expenditures from the International Road Federation, "World Highway Statistics—1960," *Staff Report* (1960); estimates of population, area, and motor vehicles from the United Nations, *Statistical Yearbook, 1961* (1961).

[a] Motor vehicles include automobiles, trucks, buses, motorcycles, and bicycles, except for the United States and Colombia which exclude motorcycles and motor bicycles.

[b] Algeria, Tunisia, Morocco, and the Union of South Africa comprise one-third of the entire expenditures.

[c] Composed of Canada and the United States. Of $12,524 million, $11,178 million is U. S. expenditures.

[d] Excludes Albania, Bechuanaland, British Guiana, Communist China, Czechoslovakia, East Germany, Hungary, North Korea, Rumania, U.S.S.R., and the West Indies.

[e] Does not include urban roads. [f] National system only.

TABLE A.2. *World Motor Vehicles, 1960*

Country	Total Motor Vehicles (In thousands)	Motor Vehicles Per 10,000 Persons	Commercial Vehicles Per 10,000 Persons	*Percent Increase in Motor Vehicles 1950–60*
Africa	2,572.9			
Algeria	245.0	222	68	*205*
Angola	41.7	91	26	*334*
Cameroon	29.8	73	49	*214*
Central African Republic	4.5	37	19	—
Chad	6.5	25	18	—
Congo (Leopoldville)[a]	60.5	43	16	*129*
Dahomey[a]	6.7	35	20	—
Ethiopia	24.0	12	4	*196*
French Somaliland	2.3	343	60	*360*
Gabon	5.6	127	86	—
Gambia	2.1	74	46	*163*
Ghana	38.4	57	27	*146*
Guinea[b]	9.5	32	19	—
Ivory Coast	22.7	70	35	—
Kenya	77.7	109	18	*140*
Libya	26.9	225	79	*541*
Madagascar	41.8	78	37	*156*
Mali[a]	6.2	15	9	—
Mauritania	2.0	28	22	—
Mauritius	12.8	200	60	*172*
Morocco	171.9	148	40	*106*
Mozambique	42.8	67	15	*272*
Niger	3.8	13	9	*328*
Nigeria	60.7	17	7	*328*
Nyasaland	11.7	41	19	*225*
Reunion	10.6	316	116	*231*
Northern Rhodesia	47.0	193	54	*226*
Southern Rhodesia	123.4	402	113	*152*
Ruanda-Urundi	5.8	12	5	—
Senegal	35.2	118	51	—
Sierra Leone	8.2	34	13	*646*
Somalia[a]	5.9	30	18	*74*
South Africa	1,122.0	711	144	*87*
Sudan	28.9	25	12	*211*
Tanganyika	33.5	36	9	*156*
Tunisia	67.5	162	56	*153*
Uganda	30.9	46	8	*259*
UAR	90.8	35	8	17
Upper Volta	5.6	15	11	—

Source: United Nations, *Statistical Yearbook, 1957*, and *Statistical Yearbook, 1962*.
[a] 1959.
[b] 1957.
[c] 1958.

TABLE A.2. *Continued*

Country	Total Motor Vehicles (In thousands)	Motor Vehicles Per 10,000 Persons	Commercial Vehicles Per 10,000 Persons	*Percent Increase in Motor Vehicles 1950–60*
Latin America	4,174.5			
Argentina	862.2	431	194	*55*
Bolivia[a]	38.6	112	70	*197*
Brazil[a]	938.0	143	56	*136*
British Guiana	13.1	231	58	*236*
Chile	126.4	172	94	*76*
Colombia	172.5	122	59	*196*
Costa Rica	32.5	278	97	*322*
Cuba[c]	210.5	310	76	*101*
Dominican Republic	17.3	58	21	*125*
Ecuador	28.3	66	44	*130*
El Salvador	29.2	112	35	*244*
Guadeloupe	12.9	478	196	*135*
Guatemala	33.4	89	32	*161*
Haiti[a]	9.5	27	10	*150*
Honduras	10.7	57	28	*234*
Jamaica	42.2	—	—	*157*
Martinique	14.0	505	191	—
Mexico	802.6	230	92	*165*
Nicaragua	14.1	96	37	*422*
Panama	23.9	227	74	—
Paraguay[a]	6.4	36	9	*94*
Peru	143.8	132	59	*142*
Puerto Rico	169.6	718	156	*210*
Surinam	5.4	200	44	*218*
Trinidad, Tobago	48.0	569	133	*146*
Venezuela	369.4	490	134	*173*
North America	79,163.3			
Canada	5,221.8	2,931	627	*104*
United States	73,941.5	4,093	676	*50*
Asia	3,771.1			
Aden	11.4	99	17	*613*
Brunei	3.8	453	155	*850*
Burma	36.9	18	9	*88*
Cambodia	15.6	32	12	—
Ceylon	120.2	122	38	*148*
China (Taiwan)	19.0	18	10	*144*
Cyprus	33.1	588	103	*373*
Federation of Malaya	128.2	186	46	*215*
India	529.1	12	6	*98*
Indonesia	195.1	21	10	*225*

TABLE A.2. *Continued*

Country	Total Motor Vehicles (In thousands)	Motor Vehicles Per 10,000 Persons	Commercial Vehicles Per 10,000 Persons	*Percent Increase in Motor Vehicles 1950–60*
Iran	136.0	67	22	*312*
Iraq	60.1	85	28	*215*
Israel	50.3	238	113	*99*
Japan	1,765.0	189	144	*658*
Jordan	10.9	64	27	*142*
Korea, Republic of	30.4	12	7	*275*
Laos	5.0	28	10	*614*
Lebanon	54.2	329	49	*276*
North Borneo	5.4	119	31	*391*
Pakistan	83.8	9	3	*98*
Philippines[a]	140.3	51	24	*40*
Singapore	75.4	461	91	*196*
Syria	26.7	59	27	*178*
Thailand	87.7	34	20	*481*
Turkey	94.6	34	25	*257*
Viet Nam, Republic of	52.9	38	14	*289*
Europe	28,389.5			
Austria	483.2	682	112	*391*
Belgium	929.8	1,016	193	*122*
Denmark	578.0	1,262	371	*224*
Finland	255.9	575	163	*318*
France	7,180.3	1,577	359	*180*
Germany, Federal Republic of	5,066.0	912	131	*333*
Greece	80.1	96	44	*173*
Iceland	21.6	1,227	358	*102*
Ireland	219.5	775	161	*86*
Italy	2,451.1	497	93	*329*
Luxembourg	45.6	1,452	274	*228*
Netherlands	679.5	592	146	*206*
Norway	368.5	1,028	316	*215*
Poland	237.5	80	40	—
Portugal	208.0	233	57	*133*
Spain	430.7	143	50	*159*
Sweden	1,309.2	1,750	154	*279*
Switzerland	569.9	1,065	113	*204*
United Kingdom	7,182.1	1,367	288	*118*
Yugoslavia	93.0	50	21	*292*
Oceania	3,372.9			
Australia	2,731.5	2,658	786	*116*
New Zealand	641.4	2,704	528	*100*
World Total	121,444.2			

TABLE A.3. *Intercity Freight and Passenger Traffic in the United States, 1940, 1950, and 1960*

Type of Transport	Freight Traffic (In billions of ton-miles)			Passenger Traffic (In billions of passenger miles)		
	1940	1950	1960	1940	1950	1960
Railways[a]	379.2	596.9	579.1	24.8	32.5	21.6
Motor Trucks	62.0	172.9	299.4	—	—	—
Intercity Buses	—	—	—	11.5	26.4	19.9
Inland Waterways	118.1	163.3	223.0	1.3	1.2	2.1
Pipelines	59.3	129.2	228.6	—	—	—
Domestic Airways	—	0.3	0.8	1.0	10.1	34.0
Total	618.6	1,062.6	1,330.9	38.6	70.2	77.6
PERCENTAGE DISTRIBUTION[b]						
Railways[a]	*61*	*56*	*44*	*64*	*46*	*28*
Motor Trucks	*10*	*16*	*23*	—	—	—
Intercity Buses	—	—	—	*30*	*38*	*26*
Inland Waterways	*19*	*15*	*17*	*3*	*2*	*3*
Pipelines	*10*	*12*	*17*	—	—	—
Domestic Airways	—	—	—	*3*	*14*	*44*
Total	*100*	*100*	*100*	*100*	*100*	*100*

Sources: 1940 and 1950 data on freight traffic from Interstate Commerce Commission, Bureau of Transport Economics and Statistics, "Intercity Ton-Miles 1939–1959," Statement No. 6103 (1961); 1960 data from Interstate Commerce Commission, *Annual Report, 1960*. For passenger traffic: Interstate Commerce Commission, *Annual Report, 1940, 1950, 1960*.

[a] Revenue ton-miles including electric railways, express, and mail for freight traffic.

[b] Totals do not always add to 100 due to rounding.

TABLE A.4. *Freight and Passenger Traffic in the Union of Soviet Socialist Republics, 1940 and 1962*

Type of Transport	Freight Traffic (In billions of ton-kms.)		Passenger Traffic (In billions of passenger kms.)	
	1940	1962	1940	1962
Railways	415.0	1,646.3	98.0	189.3
Rivers	36.1	109.8	3.8	4.6
Marine	23.8	173.1	0.9	1.3
Pipelines	3.8	74.5	—	—
Highways	8.9	113.0	3.4	81.5
Airways	0.02	0.89	0.2	20.3
Total	487.6	2,117.6	106.3	297.0
		PERCENTAGE DISTRIBUTION[a]		
Railways	*85.1*	*77.7*	*92.2*	*63.7*
Rivers	*7.4*	*5.2*	*3.6*	*1.6*
Marine	*4.9*	*8.2*	*0.9*	*0.4*
Pipelines	*0.8*	*3.5*	—	—
Highways	*1.8*	*5.3*	*3.2*	*27.4*
Airways	*0.01*	*0.04*	*0.2*	*6.8*
Total	*100.0*	*100.0*	*100.0*	*100.0*

Source: Central Statistical Board, the Council of Ministers of the USSR, Moscow, 1963.
[a] Totals do not always add to 100 due to rounding.

TABLE A.5. *Proposed or Planned Transport Investment Programs, Selected Countries*[a]

(Currency items in millions)

Country	Total	Railways	Highways	Trucks and Buses	Water Transport	Ports	Air Transport
Argentina (in pesos)	182,427.0	100,204.0	69,874.0	—	12,349.0	—	—[b]
Chile (in escudos)	1,389.0	300.2	498.0	399.2	95.2[c]	44.8	51.6
Colombia (in pesos)	2,467.6	326.3	1,822.5	—	7.5	129.3	182.0[d]
Iran (in rials)	34,900.0	4,300.0	23,700.0	—	—	2,900	4,000.0[d]
East Pakistan (in U.S. dollars)	269.4	104.7	54.8	29.9	77.3		2.7
West Pakistan (in U.S. dollars)	529.2	186.0	128.7	162.0	44.3		8.2
Philippines (in pesos)[e]	632.5	186.0	295.0	—	—	73.5	78.0
Senegal (in francs)	15,720.0	2,172.0	11,235.0	—	1,225.0		1,088.0[d]
			PERCENTAGE DISTRIBUTION				
Argentina	*100.0*	*54.9*	*38.3*	—	*6.8*	—	—
Chile	*100.0*	*21.6*	*35.9*	*28.7*	*6.9*	*3.2*	*3.7*
Colombia	*100.0*	*13.2*	*73.9*	—	*0.3*	*5.2*	*7.4*
Iran[f]	*100.0*	*12.3*	*67.9*	—	—	*8.3*	*11.5*
East Pakistan	*100.0*	*38.9*	*20.3*	*11.1*	*28.7*		*1.0*
West Pakistan	*100.0*	*35.1*	*24.3*	*30.6*	*8.4*		*1.6*
Philippines	*100.0*	*29.4*	*46.6*	—	—	*11.6*	*12.3*
Senegal	*100.0*	*13.8*	*71.5*	—	*7.8*		*6.9*

Sources: Argentina data from *A Long Range Transportation Plan for Argentina*, Transportation Planning Group, Republic of Argentina, Buenos Aires, 1962, Main Report, p. 75. Chile: *National Economic Development Program for Chile, 1961–70*, Government of Chile, 1961. Colombia: Ministry of Public Works, Republic of Colombia, *Plan for Improvements in National Transportation* (Report prepared by Parsons, Brinckerhoff, Quade, and Douglas, December 1961); 1962–71 expenditures based on the table, "Summary of Recommended Investments—All Modes of Transportation." Iran: The Plan Organization, *Transport and Communication—Third Plan Frame*, Teheran, 1961, based on Table I, p. 11. East and West Pakistan: Corps of Engineers, Department of the Army, *Transport Survey of East Pakistan*, Washington, 1961, Vol. I, p. 23, and *Transport Survey of West Pakistan*, Washington, 1960, Vol. I, p. 29. Philippines: The Republic of the Philippines, *Five-Year Integrated Socio-Economic Program for the Philippines, 1963–67*, based on the table on p. 88. Senegal: *Le Plan Quadriennal de Developpement, 1961–64*, Dakar, 1961.

[a] Proposed expenditures are for the following periods: Argentina, 1962–67; Chile, 1961–70; Colombia, 1962–71; Iran, 1962–68; East and West Pakistan, 1960–65; Philippines, 1963–67; Senegal, 1961–64.

[b] Air transport was not included in the Argentina transport survey.

[c] Includes shipping only.

[d] Includes airports only.

[e] When the private sector is added, the transport expenditures are as follows:

Purpose	Millions of Pesos	*Percent*
Railways	186.0	*5.5*
Highways	295.0	*8.7*
Ports	73.5	*2.2*
Airports	78.0	*2.3*
Airplanes	157.4	*4.7*
Trucks and Buses	1,953.3	*57.7*
Shipping	642.6	*19.0*
Total	3,385.8	*100.0*

[f] When oil pipeline expenditures are included, the percentage distribution is as follows:

	Percent
Highways	59.4
Railways	10.8
Ports	7.3
Airports	10.0
Oil pipelines	12.5
Total	100.0

TABLE A.6. *Railways of the World, 1960*[a]

Country	Number of Miles	Per 1,000 Square Miles	Per 10,000 Population
Africa	38,577		
South Africa	13,564	28.7	8.6
East Africa (British)[b]	3,446	5.1	1.5
Congo (Leopoldville)	3,108	3.4	2.2
Sudan	2,645	2.7	2.6
Rhodesia[c]	2,599	3.6	3.9
Algeria	2,532	3.0	2.5
Angola	1,792	3.7	3.9
Nigeria	1,780	5.2	2.7
Mozambique	1,662	5.6	2.6
Tunisia	1,213	20.9	3.0
Morocco	1,090	6.2	0.9
Ethiopia	620	1.6	0.3
Ghana	591	6.4	0.9
Madagascar	533	2.3	1.0
Cameroon	313	1.9	1.0
Sierra Leone	311	11.1	1.2
Nyasaland	289	5.9	1.0
Togoland	274	12.5	1.9
Latin America	85,340		
Argentina	27,280	25.4	13.0
Brazil	23,253	7.1	3.4
Mexico	14,577	19.2	4.2
Chile	4,812	16.8	6.3
Cuba	3,562	80.6	5.3
Colombia	2,150	4.9	1.5
Uruguay	1,883	26.1	7.0
Bolivia	1,734	4.2	5.0
Peru (est.)	1,617	3.1	1.5
Honduras	767	17.8	3.9
Venezuela	666	1.9	1.0
Guatemala	509	12.1	1.4
Ecuador	615	5.3	1.4
Costa Rica	407	17.4	3.5
El Salvador	375	45.4	1.4
Paraguay	309	2.0	1.8
Asia	101,047		
India	35,213	28.8	0.8
China-Mainland (est.)	19,500	8.6	0.3
Japan	12,678	88.9	1.4
Pakistan	7,042	19.3	0.8

Sources: Development of World's Railway Mileage, *Directory of Railway Officials and Yearbook, 1961–62* pp. 542–44 and *1960–61*, pp. 506–08. London; population and land area estimates from United Nations, *Statistical Yearbook 1961*.

[a] Length of rail lines does not include light railways, steam tramways, and interurban electric lines but refers to the total mileage open in 1950 and 1960. Countries with less than 250 miles not included.

[b] Tanganyika, Uganda, and Kenya.

[c] Includes Bechuanaland, with 399 miles.

TABLE A.6. *Continued*

Country	Number of Miles	Per 1,000 Square Miles	Per 10,000 Population
Turkey	4,850	16.4	1.7
Indonesia	3,788	5.2	0.4
Egypt[d]	2,945	7.6	1.1
Iran	2,178	3.5	1.1
Thailand	2,171	10.9	0.9
Burma	1,858	7.1	0.9
Republic of Korea	1,850	49.4	0.7
Iraq	1,038	6.0	1.5
Malaya	1,028	20.3	1.5
Ceylon	898	35.5	0.9
Viet Nam	837	12.9	0.6
Philippines	633	5.5	0.2
China—Taiwan	590	42.5	0.6
Syria	526	7.3	1.2
Saudi Arabia[e]	356	0.4	0.6
Israel	261	32.7	1.2
Lebanon	254	63.5	1.5
Europe, North America, Oceania	**539,815**		
United States[f]	218,089	60.3	12.1
USSR	76,767	8.9	3.6
Canada	43,870	11.4	24.3
France	24,145	113.5	5.3
West Germany	22,738	237.1	4.1
United Kingdom[g]	19,068	202.3	3.6
Poland (est.)	16,711	138.9	5.6
Italy	10,190	87.6	2.0
East Germany	10,028	240.8	5.8
Sweden	9,197	53.2	12.3
Spain[h]	8,335	42.6	2.8
Czechoslovakia	8,164	165.3	6.0
Yugoslavia	7,374	74.7	4.0
Rumania	6,260	68.4	3.4
Hungary	5,447	151.7	5.5
Austria	4,093	126.4	5.8
Finland	3,320	25.5	7.4
Switzerland	3,180	196.0	5.9
Belgium	2,869	245.2	3.2
Norway	2,792	22.3	7.8
Bulgaria	2,072	48.4	2.7
Netherlands	1,928	150.6	1.7
Republic of Ireland	1,809	66.7	6.4
Greece	1,596	30.8	1.9
Australia[i]	26,127	8.8	25.1
New Zealand	3,336	32.3	13.9

[d] State railways only.
[e] Diesel operated from the beginning in 1949.
[f] Includes Alaska.
[g] Includes Northern Ireland.
[h] Spanish totals show broad gauge lines only.
[i] State mileages only. The only lengthy private line is the Midland Railway of Western Australia, which adds 277 miles.

TABLE A.7. *World Rail Freight and Passenger Traffic, 1960*

Country	Freight Traffic (Ton-Kms.) Total (In millions)	Freight Per Capita	Freight *Percent Increase 1950–60*	Passenger Traffic (Passenger-Kms.) Total (In millions)	Passenger Per Capita	Passenger *Percent Increase 1950–60*
Africa						
Algeria[a]	1,728	157	*44*	626	57	*(−32)*
East Africa (British)[b]	2,666	116	*35*	—	—	—
Cameroon	122	30	*76*	90	22	*7*
Congo (Brazzaville)	209	263	—	62	78	—
Congo (Leopoldville)[c]	2,213	158	*42*	378	27	*144*
Dahomey	46	24	—	71	37	—
Ethiopia[d]	162	81	*86*	53	3	*15*
Ghana	357	53	*43*	276	41	*13*
Guinea[c]	41	14	—	47	16	—
Ivory Coast	213	67	—	220	69	—
Madagascar	131	24	*49*	136	25	*66*
Mauritius	20	29	—	—	—	—
Morocco	1,757	152	*44*	477	41	*(−24)*
Mozambique[c]	1,854	290	*125*	188	29	*56*
Nigeria	1,931	55	*76*	699	20	*22*
Nyasaland	116	41	*49*[e]	—	—	—
Rhodesia (S. and N.)[f]	6,890	1,253	*87*	—	—	—
Senegal[g]	270	90	—	278	94	—
Sierra Leone	25	10	*6*	89	36	*124*
South Africa	30,864	1,953	*58*	—	—	—
Sudan	1,608	136	*118*	—	—	—
Tunisia	971	231	*24*	351	84	*31*
UAR (Egypt)[h,i]	1,658	64	*8*	4,165	160	*68*
Latin America						
Argentina	15,134	757	*(−14)*	13,421	671	*2*
Bolivia[i]	300	86	*21*	236	67	*49*
Brazil[c]	12,689	192	*58*	14,639	222	*45*
Chile	2,220[c,j]	268[c,j]	*6*[c,j]	1,906	261	*20*
Costa Rica[k]	59	49	*33*	37	31	*(−41)*
Colombia	746	53	*34*	598	43	*(−24)*
Cuba[i]	1,101	162	*0*	—	—	—
Ecuador[l]	106	25	*5*	113	26	*(−7)*
Guatemala	270	72	*13*	—	—	—
Jamaica[m]	70	44	*245*	46	29	*17*
Mexico	13,931	398	*48*	4,148	119	*37*
Nicaragua	23	15	*12*	60	40	*(−67)*
Paraguay[c]	18	10	*(−92)*	31	17	*(−100)*
Peru[c]	420	39	*4*	259	24	*8*
Trinidad, Tobago	12	14	*3*	—	—	—
Venezuela	20	3	*18*	25	3	*56*

Source: United Nations, *Statistical Yearbook, 1961.*
[a] Chemins de fer algériens only.
[b] Kenya, Uganda, and Tanganyika. Including road and lake services.
[c] 1959 data. Percent increase, 1950–59.
[d] Including traffic of French Somaliland portion of Djibouti-Addis Ababa line.
[e] 1954–60 increase.
[f] Beginning 1959, excluding Bechuanaland-Mahalapye line.
[g] Including Kidira-Bamako-Koulikoro line which lies in Mali.
[h] Government railways only.
[i] 1957 data. Percent increase, 1950–57.
[j] Gross ton-kms. of principal railways.
[k] Beginning 1957 for freight traffic and 1956 for passenger traffic, Ferro-carril del Norte only, which accounted for approximately half of the total traffic.
[l] 1956 data. Percent increase, 1950–56.
[m] 1959 data. Percent increase, 1952–59.

TABLE A.7. *Continued*

Country	Freight Traffic (Ton-Kms.) Total (In millions)	Freight Per Capita	Freight *Percent Increase 1950–60*	Passenger Traffic (Passenger-Kms.) Total (In millions)	Passenger Per Capita	Passenger *Percent Increase 1950–60*
Asia						
Burma	776	38	*782*	1,528	74	*754*
Cambodia	74	15	*37*	83	17	*152*
China-Mainland[c]	265,260	410	*574*	45,670	142	—
China-Taiwan	2,053	194	*111*	3,609	340	*57*
Federation of Malaya	706	102	*78*	612	89	*16*
Hong Kong	12	4	*0*	144	48	*(−6)*
India[c]	69,120	160	*57*	74,519	172	*11*
Indonesia[c]	1,046	11	*45*	6,627	72	*75*
Iran[c]	2,150	107	*179*	1,997	99	*572*
Iraq	768	108	*19*	656	92	*24*
Israel	220	105	*210*	350	167	*422*
Japan	53,859	578	*64*	159,620	1,713	*131*
Republic of Korea	3,044	93	*194*	4,935	150	*329*
Lebanon	36	23	*(−21)*	5	3	*2*
Pakistan	8,215	89	*85*	11,035	119	*20*
Philippines	216	8	*27*	824[c]	30[e]	*106[c]*
Syria	107	24	*(−8)*	42	9	*92*
Thailand	1,138	45	*137*	2,353	92	*64*
Turkey	4,322	157	*74*	4,396	159	*76*
Republic of Viet Nam	141	10	*187*	542	39	*2,130*
Europe, Oceania, North America						
Australia[h]	13,020	1,264	*28*	—	—	
Austria[h]	7,879	1,113	*39*	6,614	934	*54*
Belgium[n]	6,359	695	*16*	8,577	937	*22*
Bulgaria	6,981	888	*171*	3,617	460	*58*
Canada	95,548	—	*18*	3,643	—	*(−24)*
Czechoslovakia	47,407	3,486	*154*	19,335	1,422	—
Denmark	1,407[c]	307[c]	*7[c]*	3,359	733	*2*
Finland	4,873	1,083	*41*	2,343	521	*7*
France[o]	56,886	1,250	*46*	32,040	704	*21*
Germany-East	32,860	2,054[p]	*118*	21,288	1,331[p]	*15*
Germany-West[h]	56,437	1,057[p]	*17*	38,583	723[p]	*28*
Greece	363	44	*86*	1,030	124	*67*
Hungary	13,337	1,334	*146*	14,324	1,432	*36[q]*
Ireland	345	123	*(−49)*	—		
Italy[h]	15,765	3,191	*53*	27,429	5,552	*35*
Luxembourg	641	2,041	*48*	230	733	*1*
Netherlands	3,410	297	*13*	7,670	667	*23*
Norway	1,514	422	*10*	1,733	483	*13*
Poland	66,547	2,241	*90*	30,942	1,042	*17*
Portugal	762	86	*46*	2,147	241	*55*
Rumania	19,821	1,077	*161*	10,737	584	*32*
Spain[r]	6,059	202	*(−6)*	7,341	245	*4*
Sweden	10,930	1,461	*27*	5,187	694	*(−28)*
Switzerland	4,346	805	*95*	7,843	1,452	*22*
United Kingdom[s]	30,496	581	*(−19)*	34,677	661	*8*
United States[t]	835,421	4,624	*(−3)*	34,216	189	*(−50)*
U.S.S.R.	1,504,400	7,017	*150*	170,800	797	*94*
Yugoslavia	13,895	751	*40*	10,448	565	*26*
New Zealand[h]	1,970	821	*17*	—	—	—

[n] Societe Nationale des Chemins de fer belges only.
[o] Societe Nationale des Chemins de fer francais only.
[p] Excludes East and West Berlin. [q] 1952–60 increase. [r] Spanish National Railways (RENFE) only.
[s] British Railways only. [t] Excludes Hawaii and Alaska.

TABLE A.8. *Transport Loans by the World Bank, Fiscal Years 1961–63*

(In millions of U.S. dollars)

Countries	Total Loans	Railways	Roads	Ports
Countries Aided in 1961				
Argentina	48.5	—	48.5	—
Burma	14.0	14.0	—	—
Chile	6.0	—	6.0	—
Colombia	5.4	5.4	—	—
India	70.0	70.0	—	—
Israel	27.5	—	—	27.5
Japan	80.0	80.0	—	—
Mexico	25.0	—	25.0	—
Panama	7.2	—	7.2	—
Peru	5.5	—	5.5	—
Thailand	22.0	22.0	—	—
Total	311.1	191.4	92.2	27.5
Percent of Total Transport	*100.0*	*61.5*	*29.6*	*8.8*
Transport as Percent of Total IBRD Loans	*51.0*			
Countries Aided in 1962				
Colombia	19.5	—	19.5	—
Costa Rica	5.5	—	5.5	—
India	71.0	50.0	—	21.0
Japan	40.0	—	40.0	—
Mexico	30.5	—	30.5	—
Peru	10.0	—	10.0	—
Philippines	8.5	—	—	8.5
South Africa	11.0	11.0	—	—
Venezuela	45.0	—	45.0	—
Total	241.0	61.0	150.0	29.5
Percent of Total Transport	*100.0*	*25.3*	*62.5*	*12.2*
Transport as Percent of Total IBRD Loans	*27.3*			
Countries Aided in 1963				
Colombia	30.0	30.0	—	—
Israel	22.0	—	22.0	—
Nigeria	13.5	—	—	13.5
Pakistan	23.0	23.0	—	—
Peru	13.25	13.25	—	—
Thailand	35.0	—	35.0	—
Uruguay	18.5	—	18.5	—
Yugoslavia	35.0	—	35.0	—
Total	190.25	66.25	110.5	13.5
Percent of Total Transport	*100.0*	*34.8*	*58.1*	*7.1*
Transport as Percent of Total IBRD Loans	*42.4*			

Sources: International Bank for Reconstruction and Development, *Sixteenth Annual Report, 1960–1961; Seventeenth Annual Report, 1961–1962;* and *Eighteenth Annual Report, 1962–1963.*

TABLE A.9. *Transport Loans by the International Development Association, June 1961–June 1963*

(In millions of U.S. dollars)

Country	Total Loans	Roads	Railways	Ports and Inland Waterways	Telecommunications	Others[a]
Chile	19.0	19.0	—	—	—	—
China	15.3	—	—	2.2	—	13.1
Colombia	19.5	19.5	—	—	—	—
Costa Rica	5.5	5.5	—	—	—	—
El Salvador	8.0	8.0	—	—	—	—
Ethiopia	13.5	13.5	—	—	—	—
Haiti	0.35	0.35	—	—	—	—
Honduras	9.0	9.0	—	—	—	—
India	300.0	60.0	67.5	18.0	42.0	112.5
Jordan	2.0	—	—	—	—	2.0
Korea	14.0	—	14.0	—	—	—
Nicaragua	3.0	—	—	—	—	3.0
Pakistan	32.5	—	—	2.0	—	30.5
Paraguay	6.0	—	6.0	—	—	—
Sudan	13.0	—	—	—	—	13.0
Swaziland	2.8	2.8	—	—	—	—
Tunisia	5.0	—	—	—	—	5.0
Turkey	26.7	—	—	—	—	26.7
Total	495.15	137.6	87.5	22.2	42.0	205.8
Percent of Total	*100.0*	*27.8*	*17.7*	*4.5*	*8.5*	*41.6*

Source: International Development Association, *Annual Report, 1962–63*, pp. 30–33.
[a] Others include loans made for irrigation, water development, power, industry, and flood control projects.

TABLE A.10. *Transport Loans, Export-Import Bank*[a]

(In thousands of dollars)

Type of Transport	Total Loans[b]	Africa	Asia	Europe	Latin America	Oceania
Railways	853,234	56,686	127,295	59,353	609,325	575
Aircraft and airports	428,751	41,700	102,218	166,147	92,878	25,808
Highways	414,068	21,931	19,337	55,377	317,423	—
Harbor development	116,965	1,167	45,325	25,000	45,473	—
Vessels	76,071	495	18,118	7,091	50,367	—
Automotive equipment	97,844	217	60,132	6,468	30,962	65
Automobile industry equipment	113,967	—	43,713	60,200	10,054	—
Construction equipment	35,262	388	1,826	2,178	29,977	893
Transport Total	2,136,162	122,584	417,964	381,814	1,186,459	27,341
Total Eximbank Credits	13,742,387[c]	497,081	2,988,830	4,376,584	5,036,798	54,224
PERCENTAGE DISTRIBUTION						
Railways	39.9	46.2	30.5	15.5	51.4	2.1
Aircraft and airports	20.1	34.0	24.5	43.5	7.8	94.4
Highways	19.4	17.9	4.6	14.5	26.8	—
Harbor development	5.5	1.0	10.8	6.6	3.8	—
Vessels	3.6	0.4	4.3	1.9	4.2	—
Automotive equipment	4.6	0.2	14.4	1.7	2.6	0.2
Automobile industry equipment	5.3	—	10.5	15.8	0.9	—
Construction equipment	1.7	0.3	0.4	0.6	2.5	3.3
Total	100.0	100.0	100.0	100.0	100.0	100.0
Transport as Percent of Total Eximbank Credits	15.5	24.7	14.0	8.7	23.6	50.4

Source: Derived from the table compiled by the office of the controller, the Export-Import Bank of Washington, August 1963.

[a] Credits authorized from 1934 through June 1963. Total number of credits extended by the Eximbank amounted to 2,955 and 89 countries received the credits over the period of its existence.

[b] Totals differ slightly from the source due to rounding.

[c] Includes $788,870,000 "other" loans.

TABLE A.11. *Funds Obligated for Transport by the International Cooperation Administration, 1956–58*

(In thousands of dollars)

Country[a]	Total Project Aid	Funds for Transport	*Transport as Percent of Total Project Aid*
Afghanistan	39,891	20,716	*51.9*
Argentina	245	85	*34.7*
Bolivia	11,179	2,990	*26.7*
Brazil	12,081	941	*7.8*
Cambodia	32,403	24,324	*75.1*
Ceylon	9,760	3,080	*31.2*
Chile	8,305	713	*8.6*
Colombia	3,734	212	*5.7*
Cuba	1,492	222	*14.9*
Ecuador	9,603	232	*2.4*
Ethiopia	16,811	905	*5.4*
Greece	2,085	66	*3.2*
India	51,583	15,451	*30.0*
Indonesia	44,074	8,661	*19.7*
Iran	24,908	3,465	*13.9*
Iraq	8,633	1,284	*14.9*
Israel	4,841	194	*4.0*
Laos	16,722	6,362	*38.1*
Liberia	5,935	598	*10.1*
Mexico	2,236	149	*6.7*
Nepal	10,375	3,487	*33.6*
Pakistan	79,232	20,999	*26.5*
Paraguay	5,533	691	*12.5*
Peru	10,096	91	*0.9*
Philippines	39,823	12,325	*30.9*
Thailand	52,073	31,057	*59.6*
Turkey	19,391	1,534	*7.9*
Uruguay	573	3	*0.5*
Total ICA Project Aid	1,396,424	410,676	*29.4*

Sources: International Cooperation Administration, *Operations Report, 1956, 1957*, and *1958*.
[a] Omits Japan and Austria, which received approximately $6.6 million.

TABLE A.12. *Transport Financing by the International Cooperation Administration with U.S. Dollars and U.S. Owned Local Currency, 1955–61*[a]

Purpose	Total	Far East	Near East and South Asia	Europe	Latin America	Africa
	IN THOUSANDS OF DOLLARS					
Highways	400,252	180,901	112,221[b]	39,023	50,339	17,768
Railways	257,717	125,624	90,191	33,331	451	8,120
Air Transport	132,723	32,280	83,636	3,611	9,305	3,891
Marine Transport	68,259	35,170	28,206	653	2,697	1,533
Miscellaneous[c]	120,853	3,903	26,122[d]	88,955[e]	1,754	119
Total	979,804[f]	377,878	340,376	165,573	64,546	31,431
Total Loan Obligation	$4.9 billion					
	PERCENTAGE DISTRIBUTION					
Highways	*40.0*	*47.9*	*33.0*	*23.6*	*78.0*	*56.5*
Railways	*26.3*	*33.3*	*26.5*	*20.1*	*0.7*	*25.8*
Air Transport	*13.5*	*8.5*	*24.6*	*2.2*	*14.4*	*12.4*
Marine Transport	*7.0*	*9.3*	*8.3*	*0.4*	*4.2*	*4.9*
Miscellaneous	*12.3*	*1.0*	*7.7*	*53.7*	*2.7*	*0.4*
Total	*100.0*	*100.0*	*100.0*	*100.0*	*100.0*	*100.0*
Transport as Percent of Total Loans	*20.0*					

Source: International Cooperation Administration, Office of Statistics and Reports, *Projects by Field of Activity and Country,* annual reports for fiscal years 1955–61.

[a] Project funding by field of activity instituted by ICA from fiscal year 1955 on. Figures for fiscal years 1955–57 include reallotments of deobligated prior years' funds.

[b] Includes motor vehicle transportation, and regional transit of Afghanistan and Pakistan.

[c] Includes transport equipment, machinery, surveys, planning, training and others.

[d] Includes Nepal's ropeway project.

[e] Includes over $88 million allocated for transportation in Yugoslavia from the U.S. owned local currency. Classification of transport field is not available.

[f] Includes dollar-financed projects plus projects with obligations in Sec. 402 and P.L. 480, Title I currencies.

TABLE A.13. *Transport Financing by U.S. Development Loan Fund 1958–61*[a]

Purpose	Total	Africa	Europe	Far East	Latin America[b]	Near East	South Asia[c]
				IN MILLIONS OF DOLLARS			
Highways	246.7	5.5	—	28.8	100.2	63.2	49.0
Railways	226.9	5.9	39.9	21.8	—	6.0	153.4
Air Transport	53.3	28.5	—	—	17.1	—	7.7
Ports and Inland Waterways	25.2	—	—	19.2	—	—	6.1
Automotive Plants	9.8	—	—	2.6	—	—	7.2
Total	561.9	39.9	39.9	72.4	117.3	69.2	223.4
Total Development Loan Fund Loans	1,954.4	120.8	137.0	274.1	219.9	417.7	784.8
				PERCENTAGE DISTRIBUTION			
Highways	*44*	*14*	—	*40*	*85*	*91*	*22*
Railways	*40*	*15*	*100*	*30*	—	*9*	*69*
Air Transport	*10*	*71*	—	—	*15*	—	*4*
Ports and Inland Waterways	*5*	—	—	*26*	—	—	*3*
Automotive Plants	*2*	—	—	*4*	—	—	*3*
Total	*100*	*100*	*100*	*100*	*100*	*100*	*100*
Transport as Percent of Total	*28.7*	*32.9*	*29.1*	*26.4*	*53.4*	*16.6*	*28.5*

Sources: Development Loan Fund, *Report of Activities During Calendar Year 1960* (May 1961), Table I, pp. 1–5; International Cooperation Administration, *Operations Report, Data as of June 30, 1961*, pp. 56–58.

[a] Loans obligated or approved as of June 30, 1961.

[b] This amount includes $25 million loans to Colombia and Peru respectively. These loans were for roads as well as for housing and resettlement. A breakdown of the figure on roads is not available.

[c] The figure includes a loan of $35 million to India made available for the financing of roads, cement, jute, and refractories. A breakdown of this figure on roads is not available.

TABLE A.14. *Development Grants and Technical Assistance, Agency for International Development, 1962*[a]

Field of Activity	Total	Far East	Near East	South Asia	Africa	Latin America	Europe	Non-Regional
				IN THOUSANDS OF DOLLARS				
Food and Agriculture	54,165	5,401	6,332	4,801	23,950	13,648	33	—
Industry and Mining	27,172	10,805	2,794	5,065	3,982	4,331	195	—
Transportation	24,411	4,158	1,900	1,217	13,214	3,906	16	—
Labor	2,984	487	420	244	472	1,361	—	—
Health and Sanitation	44,100	16,628	1,324	13,539	2,459	8,563	1,435	152
Education	80,374	10,269	2,925	8,414	31,442	21,166	—	6,158
Public Safety	7,102	2,457	449	133	1,752	2,311	—	—
Public Administration	19,115	2,821	2,021	1,837	6,264	6,172	—	—
Community Development and Social Welfare	3,934	545	247	67	1,165	1,910	—	—
Housing	1,274	16	—	—	191	1,067	—	—
General and Miscellaneous	55,215	1,813	643	3,409	10,472	5,127	310	33,441
Technical Support	32,871	7,391	3,953	7,444	7,904	5,153	742	284
Total	352,718	62,793	23,008	46,169	103,268	74,716	2,731	40,034
				PERCENTAGE DISTRIBUTION				
Food and Agriculture	*15*	*9*	*28*	*10*	*23*	*18*	*1*	—
Industry and Mining	*8*	*17*	*12*	*11*	*4*	*6*	*7*	—
Transportation	*7*	*7*	*8*	*3*	*13*	*5*	*1*	—
Labor	*1*	*1*	*2*	*1*	*1*	*2*	—	—
Health and Sanitation	*13*	*26*	*6*	*29*	*2*	*12*	*53*	—[b]
Education	*23*	*16*	*13*	*18*	*30*	*28*	—	*15*
Public Safety	*2*	*4*	*2*	—[b]	*2*	*3*	—	—
Public Administration	*5*	*5*	*9*	*4*	*6*	*8*	—	—
Community Development and Social Welfare	*1*	*1*	*1*	—[b]	*1*	*3*	—	—
Housing	—[b]	—[b]	—	—	—[b]	*1*	—	—
General and Miscellaneous	*16*	*3*	*3*	*7*	*10*	*7*	*11*	*84*
Technical Support	*9*	*12*	*17*	*16*	*8*	*7*	*27*	*1*
Total	*100*	*100*	*100*	*100*	*100*	*100*	*100*	*100*

Source: Agency for International Development, *Operations Report: Data as of June 30, 1962* (1962).
[a] Includes project re-obligations in fiscal year 1962.
[b] Less than 1 percent.

TABLE A.15. *Development Loan Fund Projects, Agency for International Development, 1962*[a]

Field of Activity	Total	Far East	Near East	South Asia	Africa	Latin America
	IN THOUSANDS OF DOLLARS					
Food and Agriculture	73,800	11,100	31,700	—	1,000	30,000
Industry and Mining	315,750	30,450	3,000	220,300	62,000	—
Transportation	95,700	—	10,000	74,000	9,200	2,500
Health and Sanitation	10,000	—	—	—	1,400	8,600
General and Miscellaneous	47,500	—	10,000	27,500	2,000	8,000
Total	542,750	41,550	54,700	321,800	75,600	49,100
	PERCENTAGE DISTRIBUTION					
Food and Agriculture	*14*	*27*	*58*	—	*1*	*61*
Industry and Mining	*58*	*73*	*6*	*69*	*82*	—
Transportation	*18*	—	*18*	*23*	*12*	*5*
Health and Sanitation	*2*	—	—	—	*2*	*18*
General and Miscellaneous	*9*	—	*18*	*9*	*3*	*16*
Total	*100*[b]	*100*	*100*	*100*[b]	*100*	*100*

Source: Agency for International Development, *Operations Report: Data as of June 30, 1962* (1962), p.26.
[a] Project obligations in fiscal year 1962.
[b] Does not add to 100 due to rounding.

TABLE A.16. *Supporting Assistance—Agency for International Development, 1962*[a]

Field of Activity	Total	Far East	Near East	South Asia	Africa	Latin America	Others
			IN THOUSANDS OF DOLLARS				
Food and Agriculture	5,975	—	250	—	260	5,326	139
Industry and Mining	4,388	2,980	—	56	—	874	478
Transportation	53,816	12,672	7,112	28,343	3,051	2,278	360
Health and Sanitation	4,733	313	700	—	90	2,498	1,132
Education	10,078	1,361	115	—	1,369	7,233	—
Public Safety	5,728	5,148	—	—	—	580	—
Public Administration	402	—	—	—	—	309	93
Community Development and Social Welfare	5,366	4,551	—	—	65	750	—
Housing	42	—	—	—	42	—	—
General and Miscellaneous	7,815	2,202	15	1,488	261	3,107	742
Technical Support	3,874	1,952	875	—	390	242	415
Total	102,216	31,178	9,067	29,887	5,528	23,197	3,359
			PERCENTAGE DISTRIBUTION				
Food and Agriculture	*6*	—	*3*	—	*5*	*23*	*4*
Industry and Mining	*4*	*10*	—	*0*	—	*4*	*14*
Transportation	*53*	*41*	*78*	*95*	*55*	*10*	*11*
Health and Sanitation	*5*	*1*	*8*	—	*2*	*11*	*34*
Education	*10*	*4*	*1*	—	*25*	*31*	—
Public Saftey	*6*	*17*	—	—	—	*3*	—
Public Administration	—[b]	—	—	—	—	*1*	*3*
Community Development and Social Welfare	*5*	*15*	—	—	*1*	*3*	—
Housing	*0*	—	—	—	*1*	—	—
General and Miscellaneous	*8*	*7*	*0*	*5*	*5*	*13*	*22*
Technical Support	*4*	*6*	*10*	—	*7*	*1*	*12*
Total	*100*[c]	*100*[c]	*100*	*100*	*100*[c]	*100*	*100*

Source: Agency for International Development, *Operations Report: Data as of June 30, 1962* (1962), p. 27.
[a] Includes project re-obligations during the fiscal year 1962.
[b] Less than 1 percent.
[c] Exceeds 100 because of rounding.

Bibliography

Aitken, Hugh G. J., ed. *The State and Economic Growth.* Papers of a conference held on October 11–13, 1956, under the auspices of the Committee on Economic Growth. New York: Social Science Research Council, 1959. 389 pp.

Argentina, Republic of, Transportation Planning Group. *A Long Range Transportation Plan for Argentina.* Buenos Aires, 1962.

Arnold, H. J. P. *Aid for Developing Countries.* London: Bodley Head, 1962. 159 pp.

Asher, Robert E. *Grants, Loans, and Local Currencies: Their Role in Foreign Aid.* Washington: Brookings Institution, 1961. 142 pp.

———. "Multilateral Versus Bilateral Aid: An Old Controversy Revisited," *International Organization,* Vol. XVI, Autumn 1962. (Brookings Reprint No. 66, January 1963. 23 pp.)

Ashton, Thomas S. *An Economic History of England: The 18th Century.* London: Methuen & Co., 1955. 257 pp.

Baran, Paul A. *The Political Economy of Growth.* New York: Monthly Review Press, 1957. 308 pp.

Bauer, Peter T. *Economic Analysis and Policy in Underdeveloped Countries.* Durham, N. C.: Duke University Press, 1957. 145 pp.

Bauer, Peter T. and Basil Yamey. *The Economics of Under-Developed Countries.* Chicago: University of Chicago Press, 1957. 271 pp.

Beckmann, Martin, C. B. McGuire, Christopher B. Winsten. *Studies in the Economics of Transportation.* New Haven: Yale University Press, 1956. 232 pp.

Benham, Frederic Charles. *Economic Aid to Underdeveloped Countries.* London: Oxford University Press, 1961. 121 pp.

Berle, Adolf A. *Latin America: Diplomacy and Reality.* New York and Evanston, Ill.: Harper & Row, 1962. 144 pp.

Bidwell, Percy Wells, and John I. Falconer. *History of Agriculture in the Northern United States, 1620–1860.* Washington: Carnegie Institution of Washington, May 1925. 512 pp.

Black, Eugene Robert. *The Diplomacy of Economic Development.* Cambridge: Harvard University Press, 1960. 74 pp.

Blanchard, Wendell, and others. *Thailand: Its People, Its Society, Its Culture* (Country Survey Series). New Haven: Human Relations Area Files, 1958. 528 pp.

Clark, Colin. *The Conditions of Economic Progress.* New York: Macmillan Co., 1957. 720 pp.

———. *National Income and Outlay.* New York: Macmillan Co., 1937. 303 pp.

Committee to Strengthen the Security of the Free World. "The Scope and Distribution of United States Military and Economic Assistance Programs," (Clay Report). U. S. Department of State, March 20, 1963. 25 pp.

Conference of the Universities-National Bureau Committee for Economic Research. *Capital Formation and Economic Growth.* Report of the National Bureau of Economic Research. Princeton: Princeton University Press, 1955. 677 pp.

Denison, Edward F. *The Sources of Economic Growth in the United States and the Alternatives Before Us.* Supplementary Paper No. 13, published by the Committee for Economic Development, 1962. 297 pp.

Domar, Evsey D. *Essays in the Theory of Economic Growth.* New York: Oxford University Press, 1957. 272 pp.

Foster, George M. *Traditional Cultures, and the Impact of Technological Change.* New York: Harper & Brothers, 1962. 292 pp.

Furtado, Celso. *The Economic Growth of Brazil.* Berkeley and Los Angeles: University of California Press, 1963. 285 pp.

Galbraith, John Kenneth. *The Affluent Society.* Boston: Houghton Mifflin, 1958. 368 pp.

———. *Economic Development in Perspective.* Cambridge: Harvard University Press, 1962. 76 pp.

Garrison, William Louis, and others. *Studies of Highway Development and Geographic Change.* Seattle: University of Washington Press, 1959. 291 pp.

Glick, Philip M. *The Administration of Technical Assistance.* Chicago: University of Chicago Press, 1957. 390 pp.

Golay, Frank H. *The Philippines: Public Policy and National Economic Development.* Ithaca: Cornell University Press, 1961. 455 pp.

Gold, Norman L. *Productive Uses of Nuclear Energy.* Report on Regional Economic Development and Nuclear Power in India. Washington: National Planning Association, 1957. 132 pp.

Goodrich, Carter. *Government Promotion of American Canals and Railroads 1800–1890.* New York: Columbia University Press, 1960. 382 pp.

Gruber, Ruth, ed. *Science and the New Nations: The Proceedings of the Conference.* New York: Basic Books, 1961. 314 pp.

Hagen, Everett E. *The Economic Development of Burma.* Washington: National Planning Association, 1956. 88 pp.

———. *On the Theory of Social Change: How Economic Growth Begins.* A Study from the Center for International Studies, Homewood, Ill.: Dorsey Press, 1962. 557 pp.

Hance, William A. *African Economic Development.* New York: Harper &Brothers, 1958. 307 pp. (Council on Foreign Relations Publications)

Hanser, Philip H. "Implications of Population Trends for Regional and Urban

Planning in Asia," ECAFE Working Paper No. 2, Seminar on Regional Planning, Tokyo, July-August 1958.

Harris, George L. and others, eds. *Egypt* (Country Survey Series) New Haven: Human Relations Area Files, 1957. 370 pp.

Harris, Seymour E. *Economic Planning: The Plans of Fourteen Countries with Analyses on the Plans.* New York: Alfred A. Knopf, 1949. 577 pp.

Hayes, Samuel P., Jr. *Measuring the Results of Development Projects, A Manual for the Use of Field Workers*, prepared for UNESCO, Paris, 1959. 100 pp.

Heilbroner, Robert L. *The Great Ascent: The Struggle for Economic Development in Our Time.* New York and Evanston, Ill.: Harper & Row, 1963. 189 pp.

Higgins, Benjamin H. *Economic Development: Principles, Problems, and Policies.* New York: W. W. Norton & Co., 1959. 803 pp.

———. *United Nations and U.S. Foreign Economic Policy.* Homewood, Ill.: Richard D. Irwin, 1962. 235 pp.

Hirschman, Albert O., *The Strategy of Economic Development.* New Haven: Yale University Press, 1958. 217 pp.

Hogg, Vincent W. "Nigeria," *Road International.* Winter 1959–60. pp. 24–30.

Hunter, Holland. *Soviet Transportation Policy.* Cambridge: Harvard University Press, 1957. 416 pp.

India, Government of, Planning Commission, *The New India.* New York: Macmillan Co., 1958. 412 pp.

International Bank for Reconstruction and Development, *The Economic Development of Libya.* Report of a Mission organized at the request of the Government of Libya. Baltimore: Johns Hopkins Press, 1960. 524 pp.

———. *The Economic Development of Mexico.* Combined Mexican Working Party. Baltimore: Johns Hopkins Press, 1953. 392 pp.

———. *The Economic Development of Nigeria.* Report of a Mission organized by IBRD at the request of the Governments of Nigeria and the United Kingdom. Baltimore: Johns Hopkins Press, 1955. 686 pp.

———. *The Economic Development of Tanganyika.* Economic Survey Mission to Tanganyika. Baltimore: Johns Hopkins Press, 1961. 548 pp.

———. *The Economic Development of Uganda.* Report of a Mission organized by IBRD at the request of the Government of Uganda. Baltimore: Johns Hopkins Press, 1962. 475 pp.

———. *A Public Development Program for Thailand.* Baltimore: Johns Hopkins Press, 1959. 301 pp.

———. *The World Bank in Africa.* Washington, D. C., July 1961.

———. *The World Bank in Asia.* Washington, D. C., October 1960.

International Bank for Reconstruction and Development and International Development Association, *The World Bank and IDA in the Americas.* Washington, D. C., January 1962.

International Road Federation, "World Highway Statistics," *IRF Staff Reports*, 1957–61. Washington, D. C.

International Union of Railways. *International Railway Statistics, Year 1961.* Paris: General Secretariat of the U.I.C., 1962.

Kindleberger, Charles. *Economic Development.* New York: McGraw-Hill, 1958. 325 pp.

Kuhn, Tillo E. *Public Enterprise Economics and Transport Problems.* Los Angeles and Berkeley: University of California Press, 1962. 243 pp.

Kuznets, Simon, Wilbert E. Moore, and Joseph J. Spangler, eds. *Economic Growth: Brazil, India, Japan.* Durham: Duke University Press, 1954. 613 pp.

Leibenstein, Harvey. *Economic Backwardness and Economic Growth.* Studies in the Theory of Economic Development. One of a series of books from the research program of the Institute of Industrial Relations, University of California. New York: John Wiley & Sons, 1957. 295 pp.

Loeb, Gustaaf Frits. *Industrialization and Balanced Growth: With Special Reference to Brazil.* New York: Gregory Lounz, 1958. 159 pp.

Mason, Edward S. *Economic Planning in Underdeveloped Areas.* New York: Fordham University Press, 1958. 87 pp.

Meade, James Edward. *A Neo-Classical Theory of Economic Growth.* London: Allen & Unwin, 1961. 146 pp.

Meier, Gerald M. and Robert Baldwin. *Economic Development: Theory, History, Policy.* New York: John Wiley & Sons, 1957. 588 pp.

Melton, Lee J. "The Transportation Company: An Economic Inevitability," *Highway Research Board Proceedings,* Vol. 39, Washington, 1960. pp. 39–45.

Meyer, John R., and others. *The Economics of Competition in the Transportation Industries.* Cambridge: Harvard University Press, 1959. 359 pp.

Milne, Alastair Murray, *The Economics of Inland Transport.* London: Sir Isaac Pitman & Sons, 1955. 292 pp.

Ministry of Public Works, Republic of Colombia. *Plan for Improvements in National Transportation* (Report prepared by Parsons, Brinckerhoff, Quade, and Douglas). Bogota: 1961.

Moulton, Harold G. and Junichi Ko. *Japan: An Economic and Financial Appraisal.* Washington: Brookings Institution, 1931. 645 pp.

Myrdal, Gunnar. *Economic Theory and Underdeveloped Regions.* London: Jerold Duckworth & Co., 1957. 169 pp.

———. *Rich Lands and Poor: The Road to World Prosperity.* New York: Harper & Row, 1957. 168 pp.

Nelson, James C. *Railroad Transportation and Public Policy.* Washington: Brookings Institution, 1959. 512 pp.

Nelson, Robert S. and Edward M. Johnson, eds. *Technological Change and the Future of the Railways.* Selected papers from a three-day conference conducted by the Transportation Center at Northwestern University, Evanston, Illinois, 1961. 239 pp.

Netschert, Bruce C. and Sam H. Schurr. *Atomic Energy Applications, With Reference to Underdeveloped Countries.* Baltimore: Johns Hopkins Press, 1957. 129 pp.

Nurske, Ragnar. *Problems of Capital Formation in the Underdeveloped Countries.* New York: Oxford University Press, 1953. 163 pp.

Oshima, Harry T. "A Strategy for Asian Development," *Economic Development and Cultural Change,* Vol. X, No. 3, April 1962. Chicago: University of Chicago Press. pp. 294–316.

Owen, Wilfred. *Automotive Transportation: Trends and Problems.* Washington: Brookings Institution, 1949. 154 pp.

———. *Cities in the Motor Age.* New York: Viking Press, 1959. 176 pp.

———. *The Metropolitan Transportation Problem.* Washington: Brookings Institution, 1956. 301 pp.

———. *Transport in Pakistan.* Notes prepared for the Planning Commission. Karachi: Government of Pakistan Press, 1959. 39 pp.

———. *Transport Survey of West Pakistan.* A paper prepared for the Planning Commission. Karachi: Government of Pakistan Press, 1960. 31 pp.

———. "Transportation and Economic Development," *American Economic Review,* May 1959. (Brookings Reprint No. 33, August 1959, 9 pp.)

———. "Transportation and Technology," *American Economic Review,* May 1962. (Brookings Reprint No. 59, July 1962, 9 pp.)

———. "The Transport Revolution in Europe," *Europe's Needs and Resources: Trends and Prospects in Eighteen Countries.* New York: Twentieth Century Fund, 1961. (Brookings Reprint No. 53, December 1961, 33 pp.)

Owen, Wilfred and Charles L. Dearing. *Toll Roads and the Problem of Highway Modernization.* Washington: Brookings Institution, 1951. 204 pp.

Papenek, Gustav F. "Framing a Development Program," *International Conciliation,* No. 527, Carnegie Endowment for International Peace, March 1960. pp. 307–72.

Patch, Richard W. "Bolivia's Developing Interior," *American Universities Field Staff Reports Service,* West Coast South America Series, Vol. IX, No. 3 (Bolivia), 1962. 13 pp.

The President's Task Force on Foreign Economic Assistance. *An Act for International Development: A Summary Presentation, Fiscal Year 1962.* June 1961. 189 pp.

Rangnekar, D. K. *Poverty and Capital Development in India: Contemporary Investment Patterns, Problems, and Planning.* Issued under the auspices of the Royal Institute of International Affairs. New York: Oxford University Press, 1958. 316 pp.

Rosenstein-Rodan, P. N. "International Aid for Underdeveloped Countries," *The Review of Economics and Statistics,* Vol. XLIII, 1961. pp. 107–38.

Roberts, Merrill J. "Transport Dynamics and Distribution Management," *Business Horizons,* Vol. 4, No. 3, Fall 1961. pp. 37–48.

Rostow, Walt Whitman. *The Stages of Economic Growth: A Non-Communist Manifesto.* Cambridge (England): University Press, 1960. 178 pp.

Sampson, Henry, ed. *World Railways 1961–62.* Seventh Edition. London, 1962.

Savage, Christopher Ivor. *An Economic History of Transport*. London: Hutchinson, 1959. 216 pp.

Saxena, K. K. *Indian Railways: Problems and Prospects*. Bombay: Vora & Co., 1962. 268 pp.

Schumacker, E. F. *Roots of Economic Growth*. Gandhian Institute of Studies, Varanasi, India, 1962. 56 pp.

Science, Technology, and Development. United States papers prepared for the United Nations Conference on the Application of Science and Technology for the Benefit of the Less Developed Areas, Vols. I–XII. Washington: Government Printing Office, 1963.

Staley, Eugene. *The Future of Underdeveloped Countries*, Council on Foreign Relations. New York: Harper and Brothers, 1954. 410 pp.

Stanford Research Institute, *The Economic Coordination of Transport Development in Nigeria*. Menlo Park, California, 1961.

Teilhard de Chardin, Pierre. *The Phenomenon of Man*. New York: Harper & Brothers, 1959. 318 pp.

Thomas, Benjamin Earl. *Transportation and Physical Geography in West Africa*. University of California, 1960. 54 pp.

Tinbergen, Jan. *The Design of Development*. Baltimore: Johns Hopkins Press, 1958. 99 pp.

———. "The Appraisal of Road Construction: Two Calculation Schemes," *The Review of Economics and Statistics*, Vol. XXXIX, No. 3, August 1957. pp. 241–49.

———. *Shaping the World Economy: Suggestions for an International Economic Policy*. New York: Twentieth Century Fund, 1962. 330 pp.

Thornburg, Max W., Graham Spry, and George Soule. *Turkey: An Economic Appraisal*. New York: Twentieth Century Fund, 1949. 324 pp.

Toynbee, Arnold Joseph. *America and the World Revolution, and Other Lectures*. New York: Oxford University Press, 1962. 231 pp.

Transportation Consultants, Inc. *A Comprehensive Evaluation of Thailand's Transportation System Requirements*. Washington, D. C., June 1959.

Troxel, Charles Emery. *Economics of Transport*. New York: Rinehart & Co., 1955. 837 pp.

Ulmer, Melville J. *Capital in Transportation, Communications, and Public Utilities: Its Formation and Financing*. National Bureau of Economic Research. Studies in Capital Formation and Financing, 4. Princeton: Princeton University Press, 1960. 548 pp.

United Nations. Economic Commission for Asia and the Far East. *Economic Bulletin for Asia and the Far East*, Vol. XII, No. 1. Bangkok, June 1961. 73 pp.

———. ———. *Economic Development and Planning in Asia and the Far East:* VI. Transport Development, Vol. XI, No. 3, December 1960. 86 pp.

———. ———. *Economic Development and Planning in Asia and the Far East*, Vol. XII, No. 3, December 1961.

———. ———. *Economic Survey of Asia and the Far East.* Annual survey issued as United Nations Document E/CN11/191.

———. ———. *Programming Techniques for Economic Development, with Special Reference to Asia and the Far East.* Bangkok, 1960. 130 pp. (Development Programming Techniques Series, No. 1).

———. Economic Commission for Europe. *Annual Bulletin of Transport Statistics for Europe—1960.* Geneva, 1961. 82 pp.

———. ———. *Economic Survey of Europe,* 1956–61.

———. Economic Commission for Latin America. *Economic Survey of Latin America,* annually issued.

———. Economic and Social Affairs Department. *Multilateral Economic Cooperation in Latin America.* Vol. I: Text and Documents. Paris, 1962. 165 pp.

———. Secretariat, Statistical Office, *Statistical Yearbook,* 1956–1961.

U. S. Department of the Army, Corps of Engineers. *Transportation Survey of East Pakistan,* Vols. I–III, Washington, D. C., 1961.

U. S. Department of the Army, Office of the Chief of Engineers. *Transportation Survey of West Pakistan,* Vols. I and II. Washington, D. C., 1962.

U. S. Congress. House. Committee on Foreign Affairs. *The International Development and Security Act.* Hearings, 87 Cong. 1 sess. Washington: Government Printing Office, 1961.

———. ———. Committee on Government Operations. *Cambodian Port Highway. Afghanistan Highway Contracts.* Hearings, 87 Cong. 1 sess. Washington: Government Printing Office, 1961. 123 pp.

———. Joint Economic Committee, Subcommittee on Foreign Economic Policy. *Economic Policies Toward Less Developed Countries.* (Study by Raymond F. Mikesell and Robert L. Allen.) Washington: Government Printing Office, 1961. 96 pp.

———. Senate. Committee on Foreign Relations. *Foreign Assistance Act of 1962.* Hearings, 87 Cong. 2 sess. Washington: Government Printing Office, 1962. 643 pp.

———. ———. *The Peace Corps.* Hearings, 87 Cong. 1 sess. Washington: Government Printing Office, 1961. 254 pp.

———. ———. Special Committee, Study No. 1 on U. S. Foreign Aid Program. *The Objectives of United States Economic Assistance Programs.* Prepared by Center for International Studies, Massachusetts Institute of Technology. Washington: Government Printing Office, 1957. 73 pp.

———. ———. Special Committee, Study No. 5 on U. S. Foreign Aid Program. *Agricultural Surplus Disposal and Foreign Aid.* Prepared by National Planning Association. Washington: Government Printing Office, 1957. 41 pp.

———. ———. Special Committee, Study No. 6 on U. S. Foreign Aid Program. *Administrative Aspects of United States Foreign Assistance Programs.* Prepared by the Brookings Institution. Washington: Government Printing Office, 1957. 124 pp.

Walinsky, Louis J. *Economic Development of Burma, 1951–60*. New York: Twentieth Century Fund, 1962. 680 pp.

Ward, Barbara. *Five Ideas that Changed the World*. New York: W. W. Norton & Co., 1959. 188 pp.

———. *The Rich Nations and the Poor Nations*. New York: W. W. Norton & Co., 1962. 159 pp.

White, Gilbert F. "The Mekong River Plan, " *Scientific American*, Vol. 208, No. 4. April 1963.

Index*

* References to tables are in italics.

ASIA
Barren Areas Above Timber
Evergreen Trees
Deciduous Trees
Shrub
Grass
Tundra
Barren Arid Areas
Ice Pack
Below Sea Level No Vegetation Shown
Cities
Boundary of Asia
1 inch = 925 Statute Miles
Miles 0 200 400 600 800 1000
Lambert Azimuthal Equal Area Projection
EUROPE
AFRICA
ASIA
(U. S. S. R.)
Pacific Ocean
Indian Ocean
Arabian Sea
Bay of Bengal
South China Sea
East China Sea
Yellow Sea
Sea of Japan
Sea of Okhotsk
Mediterranean Sea
Black Sea
Caspian Sea
Aral Sea
Baltic Sea
Red Sea
Persian Gulf
Lake Baykal
Lake Balkhash
Koko Nor
URAL MOUNTAINS
CAUCASUS MTS
ZAGROS MTS
ELBURZ MTS
HINDU KUSH
PAMIR
KARAKORAM RA.
HIMALAYA MOUNTAINS
MT. EVEREST 29,028 FT
KUNLUN MTS
ASTIN TAGH
NAN SHAN
TIEN SHAN
ALTAI MOUNTAINS
SAYAN MTS
YABLONOVYY MTS
STANOVOI MTS
GREATER KHINGAN MTS
SIKHOTE ALIN MTS
VERKHOYANSK MTS
CHERSKIY MTS
TSINLING SHAN
WESTERN GHATS
EASTERN GHATS
WEST SIBERIAN LOWLAND
CENTRAL SIBERIAN UPLANDS
KIRGHIZ STEPPE
PLATEAU OF ANATOLIA
PLATEAU OF IRAN
PLATEAU OF TIBET
PLATEAU OF MONGOLIA
TAKLA MAKAN (DESERT)
GOBI DESERT
RUB AL KHALI (DESERT)
INDIAN DES. (THAR)
ARABIA
SAUDI
TRUCIAL COAST
MUSCAT AND OMAN
ADEN
YEMEN
ETHIOPIA
SOMALIA
SUDAN
EGYPT (U.A.R.)
ISRAEL
JORDAN
LEB.
SYRIA
CYPRUS
TURKEY
IRAQ
KUWAIT
IRAN
AFGHANISTAN
PAKISTAN
INDIA
NEPAL
BHUTAN
CEYLON
BURMA
THAILAND
LAOS
CAMBODIA
NORTH VIETNAM
SOUTH VIETNAM
MALAYSIA
MALAY PENINSULA
BRUNEI
BORNEO
INDONESIA
CELEBES
SUMATRA
NEW GUINEA
PHILIPPINES
LUZON
MINDANAO
FORMOSA (TAIWAN)
CHINA
MONGOLIA
N. KOREA
S. KOREA
JAPAN
HONSHU
HOKKAIDO
SAKHALIN
Gibraltar
Algiers
Tripoli
Rome
Berlin
Moscow
Arkhangelsk
Volgograd
Istanbul
Chelyabinsk
Novosibirsk
Irkutsk
Yakutsk
Okhotsk
Petropavlovsk
Ulan Bator
Tashkent
Urumchi
Cairo
Jerusalem
Baghdad
Tehran
Mecca
Riyadh
Khartoum
Aden
Muscat
Karachi
Kabul
Rawalpindi
Delhi
New Delhi
Bombay
Madras
Colombo
Calcutta
Lhasa
Rangoon
Bangkok
Saigon
Hanoi
Kunming
Chungking
Wuhan
Nanking
Shanghai
Canton
Victoria
Taipei
Peking
Mukden
Pyongyang
Seoul
Tokyo
Manila
Kotabaru
Volga R.
Dnepr R.
Ob R.
Irtysh R.
Yenisey R.
Lena R.
Amur R.
Sungari
Syr Darya R.
Amu Darya R.
Tigris
Euphrates
Nile R.
Indus R.
Ganges R.
Godavari R.
Irrawaddy R.
Salween R.
Mekong R.
Yangtze R.
Hwang Ho
Si R.
G. of Mannar
Tropic of Cancer
Equator
40°E
60°E
80°E
100°E
120°E
140°E
40°N
20°N
0°
20°S
40°S
©RAND McNALLY & CO.